# No Other Gods before Me?

# No Other Gods before Me?

## *Evangelicals and the Challenge of World Religions*

**John G. Stackhouse, Jr., editor**

**Baker Academic**
A Division of Baker Book House Co

R

Regent College Publishing

© 2001 by John G. Stackhouse, Jr.

Published by Baker Academic
a division of Baker Book House Company
P.O. Box 6287, Grand Rapids, MI 49516-6287

Printed in the United States of America

### Library of Congress Cataloging-in-Publication Data

No other gods before me? : evangelicals and the challenge of world religions / John G. Stackhouse, Jr. editor.
    p. cm.
    Includes bibliographical references and indexes.
    ISBN 0-8010-2291-6 (pbk.)
    1. Theology of religions (Christian theology)—Congresses. 2. Evangelicalism—Congresses. I. Stackhouse, John Gordon.
BT83.85.N6  2001
261.2—dc21                                                                              2001035205

For  information about Baker Academic, visit our web site:
www.bakerbooks.com/academic

To
SIR NORMAN ANDERSON

# Contents

# Contributors

Miriam Adeney (Ph.D., Washington State University) is an anthropologist who holds two academic appointments: Associate Professor of Global and Urban Ministries at Seattle Pacific University and Teaching Fellow at Regent College.

Ken R. Gnanakan (Ph.D., King's College, University of London) is a scholar and environmentalist based in Bangalore, India. He is the founder of ACTS Ministries, a holistic mission program, and General Secretary of the Asian Theological Association.

Stanley J. Grenz (D.Theol., University of Munich) is the Pioneer McDonald Professor of Baptist Heritage, Theology, and Ethics at Carey Theological College, Vancouver, and Professor of Theology at Regent College.

Paul J. Griffiths (Ph.D., University of Wisconsin-Madison) is a Buddhologist and philosopher of religion who serves as the Schmitt Professor of Catholic Studies at the University of Illinois at Chicago.

Irving Hexham (Ph.D., University of Bristol) is an expert on new religious movements in the West and serves as Professor of Religious Studies at the University of Calgary, Alberta.

Gerald R. McDermott (Ph.D., University of Iowa) is Associate Professor of Religion and Philosophy at Roanoke College, Salem, Virginia.

Richard J. Mouw (Ph.D., University of Chicago) is President and Professor of Christian Philosophy at Fuller Theological Seminary, Pasadena, California.

Gerald J. Pillay (Ph.D., Rhodes University; D.Th., University of Durban–Westville) serves as Professor of Theology and as Dean of the School of Liberal Arts at the University of Otago, Dunedin, New Zealand.

John G. Stackhouse, Jr. (Ph.D., University of Chicago) is the Sang-woo Youtong Chee Professor of Theology and Culture at Regent College.

Amos Yong (Ph.D., Boston University) is Assistant Professor of Theology at Bethel College, St. Paul, Minnesota.

# Preface

JOHN G. STACKHOUSE, JR.

Evangelical academic theology has enjoyed the splendid isolation of so much Western thought in the modern era as it has comfortably worked within the familiar range of categories inherited from our European, Greco-Roman, and Judeo-Christian cultural forebears. The reality of the world's great religions, however, has now become inescapable for all Westerners, and thus for evangelical theologians, as devotees of these religions reside among us as neighbors, not merely as figures in textbooks or missionary photographs.

The pressure of our increasing acquaintance with other religions has prompted evangelical theologians to wonder about the destiny of those who have never heard the gospel. This issue, a question that cuts to the heart of both evangelical theology and evangelical mission, certainly deserves the attention it has received. But it is hardly the only question that needs to be asked about the world's religions. Furthermore, it cannot itself be answered fully outside the context of a comprehensive theology of religions. This volume seeks, therefore, to provoke evangelical theologians to undertake that larger project.

Because the state of the evangelical art of a theology of religions is still so rudimentary and fragmented, this volume manifests those characteristics. Each essay stands alone as an exploration, venturing to criticize some things and offer others in exchange, taking up some issues and leaving others aside. None of them purports to offer a comprehensive scheme for understanding the world's religions under divine providence, although some are more wide-ranging than others. In each case, however, the author outlines key concerns that should be taken seriously by everyone working in this theological zone.

11

The essays originally were presented at the Regent College Theology Conference held in October 2000. The invitation to each presenter was quite simple: What is the one thing you want to say to evangelical theologians about an evangelical theology of religions? Regent College deliberately sought a mix of perspectives—in academic discipline, geographical and ethnic background, type of academic institution, and more. The presenters listened to each other's papers, responded to them, and then revised their essays. These are the six major contributions to this volume.

I then asked three well-qualified scholars, from quite different vantage points, to read these papers and offer responses that would move the conversation along some more. I am delighted that Messrs. Gnanakan, Griffiths, and Mouw have done so in their distinctive voices. My afterword concludes this volume—but not the discussion, I trust—as it offers a guide to the theological task before us, a daunting task indeed.

It is, however, a crucial task. It is crucial apologetically and evangelistically, of course. We must know what to think of our neighbors' religions if we are to represent the gospel helpfully to them. It is crucial also in broader missional terms. We must know what to think of our neighbors' religions if we are to love and serve them best in Christ's name.

The theology of religions is highly stimulating, however, even in academic theological terms. I have found that my own classes in systematic theology become much more lively when I point out, from my background in teaching world religions, how very different are the conceptions of God, the world, the nature of the human predicament, the goal of human well-being, and the solution to global troubles among the various faiths. I find that these alternatives stretch my own theological categories, expand my theological possibilities, and challenge my theological assumptions. And they do so in ways by no means inimical to evangelical conviction, but rather in a way quite evangelical indeed: They drive me to search the Scriptures again to find out what really is there, rather than what this or that Christian tradition has affirmed is there. Such provocations also encourage me to consider again just how evangelical theology has been, and ought to be, constructed to answer questions to which the Bible itself only occasionally and suggestively speaks.

Let me say that I don't agree with much of what I have read in the essays that follow. For that matter, the contributors don't all agree with each other either! And that's as one would expect things to be on a growing edge of a relatively new theological endeavor—again, relatively new for us evangelicals. (Our Roman Catholic and liberal Protestant friends have been at this task much longer.)

So I invite you to read these essays not as offering some comprehensive and coherent view of a theology of religions. Instead, I hope they will be to you what they have been to me: stimuli to continue in this worthy work so as to arrive—before too long, one may hope!—at an evangelical theology of religions that can help us better understand our own faith, yes, but especially to understand and to love our neighbors in the name of the one true God.

I am delighted to underscore my gratitude for the work of the contributors themselves. I also am glad for the ongoing support for the Regent College Theology Conference offered by Baker Book House and particularly editor Robert Hosack. Bill Reimer, Peter Quek, Renée Swanson, and Stan Grenz cheerfully and generously worked with me to run this particular conference. Editor Melinda Van Engen, with her blend of efficiency, realism, and grace, helped me shepherd these contributions into print. Keith Grant compiled the index, reliably as always. And I thankfully acknowledge as well the financial assistance of the Social Sciences and Humanities Research Council of Canada.

This volume is dedicated to the memory of Sir Norman Anderson, who not only thought theologically about the world's religions but also actually studied and taught them with respect.

# Part 1
# Programmatic Proposals

# 1

# What If Paul Had Been from China?

## *Reflections on the Possibility of Revelation in Non-Christian Religions*

### GERALD R. MCDERMOTT

Since Adolf von Harnack's initial claim that Greek philosophy distorted the early Christian gospel,[1] historians and theologians have debated how much Greek thinking permeated Christian thinking, and whether this permeation was good or bad. While these questions will probably never be finally resolved, no serious scholar denies that such infiltration occurred, or that it took place even within the first generation of the church. The general consensus of Pauline scholars, for example, is

---

1. Adolf von Harnack, *What Is Christianity?* (New York: Harper & Brothers, 1957). The most accessible introduction to Harnack is the English translation of the third German edition by Neil Buchanan, *History of Dogma*, 7 vols. (London: Williams and Norgate, 1897).

Of course, Harnack was not the first to make this claim; one recalls Tertullian's trenchant question, "What does Athens have to do with Jerusalem?" But Harnack's charge has headlined the debate in this recent era that has renewed the early church's engagement with non-Christian religions.

that Paul was influenced by the Hellenistic milieu and so both under-stood and proclaimed his vision of Christ in ways that reflect, at least in small part, a Hellenistic outlook.[2]

But what if Paul had been raised and educated in China rather than the Hellenistic world? Would his understanding of Christ have been different? Would the church, which reads Paul's writings as sacred Scripture, also see Christ differently?[3] This chapter seeks to answer this question, first, by exploring biblical suggestions that God's people learned from traditions outside Israel and the church. Then it argues that in the history of the unfolding of revelation, both in the Bible and church history, God has used other traditions to help the church inter-pret his redemption through Christ. I suggest that this history of reve-lation is the history of redemption and that God uses what I call "re-vealed types," even in non-Christian religions, in which Jesus Christ speaks and images the Triune God. Finally, I consider *why* God would choose to plant revealed types in non-Christian religions.

## Did God's People Learn from Traditions outside Israel and the Church?

The Bible suggests that there is knowledge of the true God outside the Hebrew and Christian traditions. The Book of Genesis, for exam-ple, relates the remarkable story of Melchizedek, a priest of the Canaan-ite deity El Elyon (roughly translated "God Most High"), whose identity is curiously merged with Abram's God (Gen. 14:17–24). When Abram calls Yahweh "El Elyon," he conjoins the two names, suggesting that they point to the same God, and gives Melchizedek's description of El Elyon (Maker of Heaven and Earth) to Yahweh.[4] Hence, Melchizedek

2. For example, see Troels Engberg-Pedersen, *Paul and the Stoics* (Louisville: West-minster, 2000); and Abraham J. Malherbe, *Paul and the Popular Philosophers* (Minneap-olis: Fortress Press, 1989).

3. In a sense, Paul did go to China in the person of Matthew Ricci, the Jesuit who settled in Chaoch'ing in 1583, and the countless missionaries who brought Paul to China in later centuries (I am indebted to John Stackhouse for this observation). But for a clue as to how a Chinese Paul might have seen Christ differently, one might look at the twentieth-century Chinese Bible teacher known in the West as Watchman Nee, whose *Normal Christian Life* (n.p.: Living Stream Ministry, 1980) portrays Christ in mystical terms colored by Nee's Asian perspective. For Ricci, see G. H. Dunne, *Generation of Giants: The First Jesuits in Chi-na* (London: Burns and Oates, 1962); Arnold Rowbotham, *Missionary and Mandarin: The Jesuits at the Court of China* (Berkeley: University of California Press, 1942); and Jonathan D. Spence, *The Memory Palace of Matteo Ricci* (New York: Viking Penguin, 1984).

4. While some scholars have claimed that it is anachronistic to refer to Abraham speaking of "Yahweh," John Sailhamer has argued convincingly that "already in Genesis 2:4b God (Elohim) is identified with the Lord (Yahweh), the God who called Abraham (Gen. 12:1) and delivered Israel from Egypt (Exod. 3:15). . . . From the perspective of the

is represented as worshiping the true God under the name of a Canaanite deity. Melchizedek has knowledge of the true God despite all appearances that he did not receive revelation[5] from the Hebrews.[6] Other people outside the Jewish tradition who "walked with" the true God were Abel, Enoch, Noah, Job, Abimelech, Jethro, Ruth, Naaman, and the Queen of Sheba. In the New Testament, Paul quotes approvingly the pagan poets Epimenides and Aratus in Acts 17:28. The story clearly suggests that they had religious knowledge of the true God.

Scripture also suggests that God's people learned from those outside the Jewish and Christian churches in ways that led to better understanding or presentation[7] of God. The author of Psalm 104, for instance, seems to have learned from the Egyptian hymn of Amenhotep IV (Akhenaten, early fourteenth century B.C.E.).[8] Both the psalm and hymn (which praises the deity manifested by Aten, the sun disk) contain remarkable parallels: God sending rain to water the earth and satisfy the beasts of the field and birds of the air, the earth returning to darkness and lions emerging when the sun retires, God's manifold works fulfilling the divine will, ships and fish sporting in the oceans be-

---

Pentateuch as a whole he is the God who has called the fathers into his good land, redeemed his people from Egypt, and led them again to the borders of the land." Hence, the author of Genesis identified Abraham's God with Yahweh. Sailhamer, *The Pentateuch as Narrative: A Biblical-Theological Commentary* (Grand Rapids: Zondervan, 1992), 82.

5. There is not room here to discuss precisely what I mean by revelation, but suffice it to say that revelation comprehends both events and propositions about those events, both ineffable at points and capable of rational description at others. It involves both an objective content of knowledge about God as well as a process or activity of the Spirit. In addition, there are many dimensions to revelation, as Avery Dulles has ably delineated: doctrine, history, inner experience, dialectical presence, and new awareness. Since revelation is poly-dimensional, its interpretation is always distorted when considered from only one dimension—like everything else about God. It is to be interpreted with humility, under the principle that Scripture is self-interpreting, and can be properly parsed only by the illumination of the Holy Spirit, which finally requires a vision of the beauty of God's holiness in Christ. For elucidation of these statements, see Gerald McDermott, *Can Evangelicals Learn from World Religions? Jesus, Revelation, and Religious Traditions* (Downers Grove, Ill.: InterVarsity Press, 2000), chap. 2.

6. This does not suggest that all of Melchizedek's beliefs were the same as Abraham's, or that all Canaanite beliefs about El Elyon were accurate. But the text does seem to imply that Melchizedek had important and commendable knowledge of the God who manifested himself as the Holy One of Israel. It means that true knowledge of God came to Melchizedek apart from revelation through the Abrahamic lineage.

7. "Presentation" if the biblical author did not increase understanding but simply used the pagan source to better express what he already understood.

8. For Akhenaten's hymn, see "The Hymn to the Aton," in James B. Pritchard, ed., *The Ancient Near East*, vol. 1, *An Anthology of Texts and Pictures* (Princeton: Princeton University Press, 1958), 226–30.

fore God, humans getting their food from God, and all creaturely life depending on the divine Spirit. To be sure, there are differences between the two accounts. For example, the elements are in different orders and especially vivid images are present only in the Egyptian poem. But two possibilities seem likely: These ideas were common to the ancient Near East and the psalmist used them, or the psalmist borrowed directly from the Egyptian source.[9] In either case, non-Hebrew sources influenced the Hebrew writer. Proverbs 22:17–24:22 is another example. According to James D. G. Dunn, it is well known that this text is "most probably drawn" from an earlier Egyptian wisdom tradition known as the Teaching of Amenemope.[10]

In the New Testament, Jesus praised the faith of pagans and urged Jews to learn from these pagan examples. He commended the widow at Zarephath and Naaman when visiting Nazareth (Luke 4:14–30). Both were pagans who had put their faith in the word of a Hebrew prophet. Jesus was "amazed" by the faith of the centurion who sought healing for his slave, observing that he had not seen such faith among Jews (Luke 7:9). Jesus also lauded the faith of the Canaanite woman in Matthew 15, recommended the ethical behavior of the Good Samaritan, and pointed out that a "foreigner" was the only leper among the ten to "return and give praise to God" (Luke 17:18 NIV). In all three cases, Jesus applauded the acts of faith of people who were not yet inside the Jewish or Christian circles of faith, and he recommended that his hearers learn from their examples.[11]

9. See A. Barucq, *L'expression de la louange divine et de la prière dans la Bible et en Égypte*, Bibliothèque d'Étude Tom. 33 (Cairo: Institut Français d'Archéologie Orientale, 1962); K.-H. Bernhardt, "Amenhophis IV and Psalm 104," *Mitteilungen des Instituts für Oreintforschung* 15 (1969): 193–206; P. C. Craigie, "The Comparison of Hebrew Poetry: Psalm 104 in the Light of Egyptian and Ugaritic Poetry," *Semitics* 4 (1974): 10–21; G. Nagel, "À propos des rapports du Psaume 104 avec les textes égyptiens," in *Festschrift A. Bertholet*, ed. W. Baumgartner et al. (Tubingen: J. C. B. Mohr, 1950); and Leslie C. Allen, *Psalms 101–150*, vol. 21 of *Word Biblical Commentary* (Waco: Word, 1983), 28–31.

10. James D. G. Dunn, "Biblical Concepts of Revelation," in *Divine Revelation*, ed. Paul Avis (Grand Rapids: Eerdmans, 1997), 7.

11. Naaman and the widow were putting their faith in prophets of Israel's God, but there is no sign that they became members of the Jewish community; interpreters debate, in fact, whether Naaman's faith was saving (see, for example, Jonathan Edwards, *Notes on Scripture*, ed. Stephen J. Stein, vol. 15 of *The Works of Jonathan Edwards* [New Haven: Yale University Press, 1998], 564–69). According to Craig Keener, Jesus' point was that "non-Jews [from Sidon and Syria, two particularly despised pagan areas] were the ones to accept two of the major signs prophets of the Old Testament," while Jews in Nazareth were not willing to accept Jesus. Hence, his hearers were to learn from the faith of those who were manifestly un-Jewish. Keener, *IVP Bible Background Commentary* (Downers Grove, Ill.: InterVarsity Press, 1993), 199–200.

Peter appears to have learned something new and profound about God from observing what God did in and for Cornelius before Cornelius had been introduced to the gospel. When Peter heard that an angel had directed Cornelius to go to his (Peter's) house, Peter's eyes were suddenly opened to God's ways with the Gentiles: "[Now] I truly understand that God shows no partiality, but in every nation anyone who fears him and does what is right is acceptable to him" (Acts 10:34–35 NRSV).

Paul told pagans in Lystra that the living God had revealed himself to their forefathers while at the same time permitting them to go their own ways; in the process God did not leave himself without a witness (Acts 14:17). In Athens Paul claimed a heathen altar as the property of the God he preached and enforced his doctrine not by miracles but by argument founded on the words of pagan poets.

Most of these examples and others[12] are connected in some way with Jewish communities of faith or Jesus. Therefore, they constitute hints and suggestions rather than proof of revelation among pagans. Nevertheless, they demonstrate that biblical authors believed knowledge of God existed outside the church and, indeed, that Jesus and Paul believed there was truth among those who knew little or nothing about the Christ.

## The Unfolding of Revelation

Andrew Walls has said that Christianity is in principle the most syncretistic religion in the world.[13] By this he means that the Christian God has chosen to unfold his truth gradually through time rather than in one blinding and all-encompassing flash of revelation and that he has used other religious and philosophical systems to help unfold and interpret his reality. As Cardinal Newman put it so elegantly:

As Adam gave names to the animals around him, so the Church from the first looked around the earth noting and visiting the doctrines she found. She began in Chaldea, and then sojourned among the Canaanites, and went down into Egypt, and then passed into Arabia, till she rested in her own land. Then to the merchants of Tyre, the wisdom of the East, luxury of Sheba, Babylon, the schools of Greece, sitting in the midst of the doctors, both listening and asking questions, claiming to herself what they said rightly, supplying their defects, completing their beginnings, expanding their surmises, and gradually by means of them enlarging the

12. McDermott, *Can Evangelicals Learn?* chap. 3.
13. Andrew F. Walls, *The Missionary Movement in Christian History* (Maryknoll, N.Y.: Orbis, 1996), 173.

range and refining the sense of her own teaching. In this way she has sucked the milk of the Gentiles and sucked the breasts of kings.[14]

Evidence abounds of this larger pattern in the history of the work of redemption: God redeems not only individuals and nations but the wisdom of the nations. Christianity has always borrowed from other faith traditions and baptized these borrowings into Christ by relating them to, and reconfiguring them in, the larger vision of God's revelation in Christ. In the Old Testament, for example, God used previously existing Mesopotamian religious rituals (sacred torches and censers in initiation and purification rites, and circumcision) to teach new religious concepts to Abraham and his progeny.[15] God also seems to have used Persian religious traditions to teach his people in Babylonian exile new understandings of cosmic warfare and life after death.

In the New Testament, we can see the influence of Hellenistic religion: The Hellenistic *theos* was often understood to be a single godhead behind many names and mythologies or an impersonal One behind all that is. New Testament authors used the word, already invested with the suggestion of the ground and force behind everything that exists, but added a new layer of meaning denoting the epitome and source of personhood. Such "translation" is always risky; while something may be gained by importing foreign connotations, something may also be lost when such connotations corrupt the original meaning. When unnamed believers from Cyprus and Cyrene used the new term "Lord" for Messiah (Christ) when speaking to Greeks in Antioch (Acts 11:20), they ran the risk of reducing Jesus to one more cult divinity alongside Lord Serapis or Lord Osiris. But because the new community was saturated in the Hebrew Scriptures, the Greco-Roman *kurios* was reshaped into a new kind of *kurios,* recognizably Jewish.[16]

This is the principle of "translation," as Andrew Walls calls it. The Christian faith takes the word of Christ into a new culture—which more often than not is animated by a religious vision. By using the language and indeed concepts of the new culture, the faith is reshaped and sometimes even expanded. Or to put it more precisely, knowledge of the original blinding revelation of God in Christ is expanded.[17]

14. John Henry Newman, *An Essay on the Development of Christian Doctrine* (Notre Dame: University of Notre Dame Press, 1989), 380.

15. McDermott, *Can Evangelicals Learn?* 80–82.

16. Walls, *Missionary Movement,* 34–35.

17. Ibid., xvii, 28–29. On translation as a cultural phenomenon in the missions context, see the important work of Lamin Sanneh, such as *Translating the Message: The Missionary Impact on Culture* (Maryknoll, N.Y.: Orbis, 1989); and idem, "Gospel and Culture: Ramifying Effects of Scriptural Translation," in *Bible Translation and the Spread of the Church: The Last 200 Years,* ed. P. C. Stine (Leiden: Brill, 1990), 1–23.

We see this pattern not only in the New Testament, where encounters with Hellenism helped to expand and develop the early
church's understanding of Christ and his redemption, but also in the
history of theology. Augustine, for example, was aided by Plotinus
and his Neoplatonic ontology to understand evil as lacking in sub-
stance, to break from Manicheism by seeing the biblical emphasis
on God's sovereignty and holiness, and to battle Donatism by seeing
that the church on earth will never be a company of the perfected.
Thanks to Aristotle's embrace of nature, Thomas Aquinas gained
confidence to articulate a biblical doctrine of the resurrection of the
body in an age that demeaned corporality. Aristotle also helped Thomas develop his concept of analogy, which ever since has helped
Christians understand how they can talk about an infinite God using
broken, finite language. Renaissance humanism's celebration of rhetoric helped John Calvin see the importance of preaching; its confidence in self-reformation through human effort may have stimulated Calvin's notable formulation of what we call sanctification;
and its conception of oratory as deliberately attuned to the ears of
an audience helped shape Calvin's classic presentation of God's ac-
commodation to human capacities.[18]

My suggestion that doctrine develops—and sometimes by use of
pagan traditions—is threatening to many evangelicals. But it should
be recalled that "we are told more than once in the New Testament
that the disciples of Jesus understood some word of his, or of Scripture, only at a later time. We are told also that a function of the Spirit
is to lead the disciples into all truth, and bring his words back to their
memory."[19] To deny this divine pattern in history is to risk substitut-
ing ideology for theology—which we do when we think that the God
of the Bible cannot be *more* than the God of the Bible (active in cultures not described by the Bible),[20] or when we think that what we
know about God in Christ is all we can or need to know. When we fail
to recognize the development of doctrine both within Scripture and
by the Spirit's gradual illumination of Scripture in church history, we
begin to think we are in control of the gospel. We fail to see that Scripture is vast and rich, unsystematic and various, often figurative and
indirect, so that "to the end of our days and the church, it will be unexplored and unsubdued land."[21] When we fail to recognize the devel-

18. McDermott, *Can Evangelicals Learn?* chap. 5.
19. Walls, *Missionary Movement*, 50.
20. For this expression, and for my understanding of Luther's interpretation of matters discussed in footnotes below, I am indebted to my colleague Paul Hinlicky.
21. Newman, *Christian Doctrine*, 71.

opment of doctrine, we think we need only apply our previous understandings to new situations rather than continually listening to God
through fresh readings of God, Scripture, and world. Such listening
is open to new understandings of the gospel, not just application of
old understandings.

Without that listening we are in danger of hearing not the gospel
but ourselves, and at that point theology becomes idolatry. God
may have been waiting to prompt us through other cultures and religions to greater holiness, truth, and goodness, but we failed to
recognize that when something comes into the Christian faith from
the outside, it may be the process by which God brings truth to us.
The apostle Paul recognized this; he was not afraid to use concepts
such as *pleroma* and *musterion* from Hellenistic culture to understand Christ and his redemption, while at the same time guarding
against Hellenistic misconceptions. We need to return to the principles that Gregory the Great commended to Augustine of Canter-
bury—that missionaries should not transport France, Spain, and
Italy with them. Otherwise we can make the mistake of imposing,
"in the name of some universal and historic orthodoxy, a set of re-
quirements and inhibitions that arise from the Christian history of
another community."[22]

## The History of Revelation Is the History of Redemption

If we are to accept this pattern of the gradual unfolding of divine
revelation in history, we need to look more carefully at what it
means. But first, what does it not mean? Now that the incarnation
has become part of human history, it does not mean that there will
be a new revelation beyond what has been revealed by God in
Christ—for the simple reason that the history of revelation *is* the
history of redemption in and through Jesus Christ. All true manifestations of God in the history of religions are by Jesus Christ, as we
will see below. Therefore, we will not discover anything new through
non-Christian religions that is ontologically unrelated to or contradictory to Christ. We will not discover, for example, that there is an
impersonal God beyond the Triune God revealed in Christ. Nor will
we find that God has other means of saving, parallel to what he has
done in Christ. The history of revelation *is* the history of the work of
redemption by Jesus Christ. Evangelical theology, therefore, must
insist on a constitutive rather than representative Christology—the
notion that without Jesus God's salvific love would not be active in

22. Walls, *Missionary Movement*, 54.

the world. Hence, all experiences of the Divine Presence are caused by Jesus Christ; the signifier is the signified.[23]

If there is no new revelation behind or beyond the Triune God, there is, nevertheless, new development in the history of revelation as Christ makes himself more fully known by the progressive illumination of the Holy Spirit. What begins as an act of translation becomes a discovery of a new dimension of Jesus Christ. The attempt to transmit faith in Christ across linguistic and religious frontiers reveals that the Spirit of Jesus Christ has unveiled meaning and significance never known before. In this unveiling, there are new glimpses of the Trinity's glory.

Walls suggests that this growth in knowledge of Christ is at the same time growth in the very Triune God: "It is as though Christ himself actually grows through the work of mission—and indeed, there is more than a hint of this in one New Testament image (Eph. 4:13). As he enters new areas of thought and life, he fills the picture (the Pleroma dwells in him)."[24] In other words, as Christians seek to relate Christ to other visions of life and new worldviews (in the sort of "translation" described earlier), Christ's fullness in his body grows.

Jonathan Edwards expressed a similar (daring!) conception of a certain kind of ontic[25] growth in God through the history of redemption. Just as Jesus increased in holiness through the course of his sufferings (God made Jesus "perfect through suffering" [Heb. 2:10]), so too, in a certain sense, God enlarges his being by the creation and through the progress of the work of redemption.

> God looks on the communication of himself, and the emanation of the infinite glory and good that are in himself to belong to the fullness and completeness of himself, as though he were not in his most complete and

23. In contrast, representative Christology maintains that Jesus is simply one of many representations of God's saving activity. See Gavin D'Costa, *The Meeting of Religions and the Trinity* (Maryknoll, N.Y.: Orbis, 2000), 34–35. This also means that evangelicals, with other orthodox in the historic theological tradition, must reject the idea that we can know anything about God *in se*, beyond or behind what has been revealed through creation, Israel, and Jesus Christ. It is in these events and words about these events that the "essence" of God has been revealed. Robert Jenson and Catherine Mowry LaCugna have argued that this quest for a God behind the God of Christian revelation posits a transcendent God at the expense of separating God's so-called inner being from God's actions in history. LaCugna, *God for Us: The Trinity and the Christian Life* (San Francisco: Harper-SanFrancisco, 1991); and Jenson, *The Triune Identity* (Philadelphia: Fortress Press, 1982).

24. Walls, *Missionary Movement*, xvii.

25. I use this word rather than *ontological* to denote expansion in God's relations to other beings rather than change in God's essence, which could be suggested by *ontological*.

glorious state without it. Thus the church of Christ (toward whom and in whom are the emanations of his glory and communications of his fullness) is called the fullness of Christ: as though he were not in his complete state without her; as Adam was in a defective state without Eve.[26]

In one sense, God is eternally complete and perfect, fully actual and self-sufficient. Yet at the same time, Edwards argues, God *ad extra* (God acting in creation and history) is God's external *repetition* of his own being, and therefore a kind of ontic self-enlargement, just as the beams of light from the sun are an "increase, repetition or multiplication" of its glory: God, "from his goodness, as it were enlarges himself in a more excellent and divine manner . . . by flowing forth, and expressing himself in [his creatures], and making them to partake of him, and rejoicing in himself expressed in them, and communicated to them."[27]

The temporal extension of God's actuality repeats in time God's internal actuality without improving it. Another way of putting this is to say that the external exercise of God's internal disposition is the temporal repetition of the divine fullness. What happens in space and time, therefore, is really and integrally related to God's own life—not by adding to God's being *ad intra* but by constituting the external extension of God's internal fullness.[28]

"Self-enlargement" represents not spatial expansion but real involvement in history through the creation of new relationships. In other words, God is a God of history, through which he truly acts and does new things. God is not timeless self-identity, as in some Platonic versions of the Christian deity, but the infinite sum and comprehension of all being and beauty for whom the incarnation was something new.[29]

26. Jonathan Edwards, *The End for Which God Created the World,* in *Ethical Writings,* vol. 8 of *The Works of Jonathan Edwards,* ed. Paul Ramsey (New Haven: Yale University Press, 1989), 439.

27. Ibid., 433, 461–62.

28. For fuller development of this theme, see Sang Hyun Lee, *The Philosophical Theology of Jonathan Edwards* (Princeton: Princeton University Press, 1988), chaps. 7, 8.

29. This idea of God's self-expansion through the history of the work of redemption is akin to Martin Luther's insistence that the history of Jesus is the history of God, so that when Jesus changed by dying, God too participated in this change. New developments in Jesus' life were new developments in God, so that expansion of Jesus' ministry in redemption represented expansion in the life of God. See Robert H. Fischer, ed., *Word and Sacrament III,* vol. 37 of *Luther's Works* (Philadelphia: Muhlenberg Press, 1961), esp. 63–64, 222. For a contemporary expression of this view, see Eberhard Jüngel, "God's Unity with Perishability as the Basis for Thinking God," in *God as the Mystery of the World: On the Foundation of the Theology of the Crucified One in the Dispute between Theism and Atheism,*

If God's glory is self-enlarging, it enlarges in part through the history of redemption, which becomes the history of revelation. Providence makes a continual progress, continually bringing forth new and different things. This is why, Edwards proposed, the church is said by Scripture to be the completeness of Christ (Eph. 1:23), as if Christ were not complete without the church. The church is the fullness of Christ and therefore adds to the completeness of Christ as the further increase of that completeness. Hence, the church, even in its progressive understanding of the *meaning* of Christ by Christ's expansion of his work of redemption, continues to enlarge the actuality of God's self-repetition in time. Therefore, the church's translation of Christ, as it seeks to relate Christ to non-Christian religions while listening sensitively to the religions, is a significant part of God's self-enlargement through time.

## Revealed Types in Non-Christian Religions

At this point we must circle back to look more precisely at what we mean by the church's progressive understanding of the meaning of Christ, and what this understanding has to do with revelation and non-Christian religions. Traditionally, Christian theology has understood that the Holy Spirit imparts illumination to believers to help make clear the meaning of Scripture. Illumination has included, among other things, varying degrees of perception into the deep things of God that are mentioned but not explicated by Scripture (1 Cor. 2:9–10). The church's use of other religious systems to help explicate and understand the deep things of God limned by Scripture can also be conceived as part of the Holy Spirit's work in the church to progressively illuminate Scripture. This illumination, in turn, should be considered part of the general history of revelation in which Jesus Christ progressively unfolds God's Triune reality in the history of redemption.

More specifically, I have argued elsewhere that this illumination sometimes proceeds by the use of "revealed types" in non-Christian religions.[30] These types are neither part of general revelation (for they are not ideas generally available to all human beings) nor special revelation (they do not reveal salvation through Jesus Christ). They are akin to the types that Jonathan Edwards found in many world religions and

---

trans. Darrell L. Guder (Grand Rapids: Eerdmans, 1983), 184–225, esp. 191: "In this *existence* of God with the man Jesus, the divine *being* is realized."

This notion of God's self-expansion rejects process theology, which sees God as an instance of the process of becoming. Nor does my notion of God's extension through the work of redemption mean that God improves in character through time. It means instead that God manifests his character in and through time.

30. McDermott, *Can Evangelicals Learn?* chap. 4.

the "good dreams" and "great stories" that C. S. Lewis saw scattered throughout the myths of the world.[31] Edwards suggested that animal sacrifices, found in almost all world religions, were "shadows" or "images" of the great and final sacrifice of Jesus that would eliminate the need for all subsequent sacrifices. Even human sacrifice and idol worship were hints of the Father's sacrifice of the Son and the incarnation. While each of these pagan practices pictured divine realities in distorted (and sometimes horrific) fashion, they nevertheless contained enough truth to point truly to aspects of God's Triune identity. Furthermore, they were not merely human insights[32] but developments (albeit twisted and broken) of original perceptions granted by Jesus Christ himself.[33]

31. See C. S. Lewis, *Mere Christianity* (New York: Macmillan, 1967), bk. 2, chap. 3; idem, *Miracles* (New York: Macmillan, 1963), chap. 14; and idem, *The Problem of Pain* (New York: Macmillan, 1962), chap. 6.

32. James Dunn has shown that neither the Old Testament nor Jesus clearly distinguished between human wisdom and divinely given wisdom (Dunn, "Biblical Concepts of Revelation," 8). Theologians have typically placed under the umbrella of general revelation phenomena often ascribed to human wisdom: moral consciousness, appreciation for the abundance of nature's provisions, recognition of God acting in history, insightful lessons about right living, prophecy as inspired speech, dreams and visions. They have done so for good reason: If there is knowledge of God that can be gained by human insight alone, God would seem to be uninvolved. There is a sphere, this presumption suggests, of human knowing in which human beings by their own unaided powers speculate (accurately) about the divine, so that there is a way apart from God to come to know the true God. Then there is a special sphere, rare and extraordinary, in which God enters the picture and communicates awareness of his person and nature. God apparently is not the source and sustainer of all being and knowing: He is not the sovereign Lord of all history but a deistic deity occasionally intervening in human affairs. God is not the foundation and fountain of all being and beauty, the glorious One "in whom we live and move and have our being," but a cause agent who operates on us from the outside of our own autonomous spheres.

Therefore, this notion of some true awareness of God coming from mere human insight does not seem to me to cohere with the biblical portrait of the sovereign God. All recognition of the identity of the true God comes only from God. It is a participation in God's own self-knowledge.

33. Neither Edwards nor I would deny that some elements in the religions, and perhaps some religions entirely, are demonic. But the strength of this point, particularly for evangelicals, is to question facile dismissals of religions as bereft of truth and God's hidden activity. This has implications for Christian missions: Kosuke Koyama tells of a missionary couple arriving in Bangkok who told their host that all Thai religion (composed chiefly of Theravada Buddhism) is the worship of demons (thirty million people and seven hundred years of tradition brushed aside in one instant, Koyama notes), and that the People's Republic of China, with her (then) eight hundred million who—according to the missionaries—were all atheists and therefore unsaved, was an enemy of the gospel. Kosuke Koyama, *Waterbuffalo Theology* (Maryknoll, N.Y.: Orbis, 1974), 213. Thankfully, most missionaries I know do not display such cultural insensitivity. But this kind of

The word *type* is used purposely to recall the types of Christ found in the Jewish covenant. The Old Testament types reveal Christ obscurely, partially, and indirectly—but nevertheless truly—in times and places when and where Christ's name was not known. They contain developments and applications of divine imperatives that sometimes confound and horrify, such as Joshua's extermination of what seem to be innocent women and children.[34] So if the types in non-Christian religions give only broken and partially distorted access to divine realities, they are similar to Old Testament types—which point to truth but sometimes obscurely.

This is not to equate the Christian Scriptures, which contain types, with other scriptures that may contain types. The Bible is in a different category of revelation from that of non-Christian religions, since it alone mediates the reality of the Triune God as incarnate in Jesus of Nazareth. But the Bible itself suggests that there are "little lights" in non-Christian religions that help illuminate the realities that the Light of the World more clearly displays. Indeed, as Edwards argued, it suggests that all the world is full of types that point to the Triune God—just as traditional theology has claimed that all the world is full of general revelation. My claim is that among non-Christian religions there are scattered promises of God in Christ and that these promises are revealed types planted there by the Triune God.[35]

In fact, the revealed types in non-Christian religions are instances of Jesus Christ speaking and imaging the Triune God. Edwards argued that Jesus Christ has been revealing God through types ever since the fall. At that point "Christ the eternal Son of God clothed himself with his mediatorial character" and stepped in between a holy but offended majesty and offending humankind to begin his work as ruler of the world and caretaker of the church.[36] God the Father would have no more to do with humans directly but delegated all communication of

---

evangelistic approach, which ignorantly assumes that non-Christians have no knowledge of God and their traditions are worthless and pernicious, may do more harm than good to the name of Christ. It tells non-Christians that Christians are not interested in learning about them and have no respect for their cultures. Often it communicates the message that we are interested not in people as human individuals but only as representatives of systems of thought. In the language of Martin Buber, we regard the other person not as a Thou demanding respect but as an It to be accepted only conditionally.

34. This suggests that it is within God's providential designs to reveal his truth sometimes obscurely, partially, and indirectly. It also indicates that the Spirit of Jesus may be at work revealing God even when the name of Christ is not known. See McDermott, *Can Evangelicals Learn?* 96–104.

35. For a fuller argument for the world as full of types, see chapter 6 in Gerald McDermott, *Jonathan Edwards Confronts the Gods: Christian Theology, Enlightenment Religion, and Non-Christian Faiths* (New York: Oxford University Press, 2000).

36. Jonathan Edwards, *A History of the Work of Redemption*, ed. John F. Wilson, vol. 9 of *The Works of Jonathan Edwards* (New Haven: Yale University Press, 1989), 130.

his being and truth to the great Mediator, Jesus Christ. Hence, whenever we read in the Bible that God spoke or revealed himself to human beings, we are to understand these to be actions of the Second Person of the Trinity. This is why John declares that "no one has ever seen God, but God the One and Only, who is at the Father's side, has made him known" (John 1:18 NIV), and Colossians calls Jesus Christ "the image of the invisible God" (1:15). The intimation is that God the Father is invisible, but Jesus Christ is his image or symbol (in the most profound sense) that makes tangible what cannot be perceived.[37]

Hence, it was Jesus Christ who appeared in the burning bush, Jesus Christ who redeemed Israel through the Red Sea, Jesus Christ who sent Moses to deliver his people, and Jesus—the captain of the Lord's hosts—who went before the Israelites in a pillar of cloud and fire. Thus, the Second Person of the Trinity appeared in human form *before* his birth in Bethlehem. It was "the back parts of a glorious human form" in which Christ appeared to Moses, and in "the form of his glorified human nature" that he appeared to the seventy elders and Joshua and Gideon and Manoah. Edwards explained that in his revelations to these Old Testament figures, Jesus Christ appeared in the form of the same human nature that he assumed in the incarnation because his purpose and work were the same in all these appearances: the redemption of humanity.[38]

37. Ibid., 130–31.

38. Ibid., 175–76, 196–98. Martin Luther had a very similar conception of the presence of Jesus Christ in Old Testament theophanies: "[Christ] was not only prophesied in the Old Testament; he was himself present everywhere. The God who turned to us, the Word that created the world and spoke to the patriarchs and to the prophets, is Jesus Christ" (Heinrich Bornkamm, *Luther and the Old Testament*, trans. Eric and Ruth Gritsch [Philadelphia: Fortress Press, 1969], 200). Based on the inseparability of Christ's two natures and therefore the "communication of attributes" from the divine to the human nature, Luther believed that "wherever God spoke in the Old Testament Jesus Christ spoke." The Old Testament messianic promises were not merely symbolic or sensed in advance but spoken actually by the Son of Mary. So the protevangelium of Genesis 3:15 was spoken by Jesus Christ, and the rock in the wilderness, as Paul confessed, was Christ. From the very beginning of the Bible Christ was present and already bound to his future earthly body (Bornkamm, *Luther and the Old Testament*, 200–207). In Luther's words: "Thus it follows powerfully and irrefutably that the God who led the people of Israel out of Egypt and through the Red Sea, who guided them in the wilderness through the pillars of cloud and fire, who nourished them with heavenly bread, and who performed all the miracles Moses describes in his book, who also brought them into the land of Canaan and then gave them kings and priests and everything is therefore God and no other than Jesus of Nazareth, the Son of the Virgin Mary, whom we call Christ our God and Lord. . . . Again, it is he who gave Moses the Ten Commandments on Mount Sinai, saying, 'I, the Lord, am your God who led you out of Egypt; you shall have no other gods.' Yes, Jesus of Nazareth, who died for us on the cross, is the God who says in the First Commandment, 'I, the Lord, am your God'" ("On the Last Words of David," *Weimar Aufgabe*, 54, 67:1ff.; quoted in Bornkamm, *Luther and the Old Testament*, 204).

There seem to be two advantages to this view of the history of revelation *as* the history of redemption by Jesus Christ. First, it liberates the history of revelation from a view that would limit the Trinity's presence to those who recognize Jesus explicitly, and it opens up a vaster economy of the eternal Word in Jesus Christ relating to the religious history of humankind.[39] Justin Martyr and Clement of Alexandria rightly noted that God revealed himself to the heathen world as well as to the Jewish people—and that he did so not merely through a subordinate process in external nature but through his Son, who is the divine Reason in every person.[40]

Yet this history of revelation and redemption by Jesus Christ avoids the danger of separating Jesus' redemption on the cross from the work of the Spirit in non-Christian religions—the Nestorian mistake that the logos theology of the early apologists risked when they distinguished between the *logos asarkos* (the eternal Logos apart from its incarnation) and *logos ensarkos* (the enfleshed Logos).[41] John Paul II rightly insists that every manifestation of divine presence in human history, both before and after the incarnation of the first century, "bears within itself both a Christological aspect and a pneuma-

39. Amos Yong has provided a richly suggestive argument that Word and Spirit are inseparable features of all things in his chapter in this book.

40. Justin, *First Apology*, 46; *Second Apology*, 8, 10; Clement, *Stromateis*, I, V–VII.

41. See Aloys Grillmeier, S.J., *Christ in Christian Tradition*, vol. 1, *From the Apostolic Age to Chalcedon*, trans. John Bowden (Atlanta: John Knox Press, 1975), 108–344, esp. 108–17, 133–38. Nestorianism tended to separate the eternal Logos from the human Jesus, following Nestorius's rejection of *Theotokos* (God-bearing) as a title for Mary.

Karl Barth rightly protests that talk of a *logos asarkos* is speculation about "some image of God which we have made for ourselves." The only God we know is that revealed in Jesus of Nazareth; we know nothing of the Second Person of the Trinity apart from his incarnation. But we do know that the Lamb was slain "from the foundation of the world" (Rev. 13:8), which suggests that the incarnate Lord was somehow present before the first-century incarnation (Barth, *Church Dogmatics*, 4/1 [Edinburgh: T & T Clark, 1956], 52–53).

It may boggle the mind to think of how Christ's human nature before the incarnation relates to his human nature *during* the incarnation, but we must not let such a mystery forbid us from affirming the apostles' vision of this unity (John 1:18; 1 Cor. 10:4; Col. 1:15) or tempt us "to ascribe to [Christ] another form than that which God Himself has given in willing to reveal Himself and act outwards." Barth warns that the dangerous alternative ("indeed we can hardly escape it") is to ask "whether the revelation and activity of this 'Logos in itself' can altogether and always be confined to this phenomenon, the incarnation in Jesus Christ. If this is not as such the content of the eternal will of God, if Jesus Christ is not the one Word of God from all eternity, why are we not free, or even perhaps obliged, to reckon with other manifestations of the eternal Word of God, and to look at Him in the light of such manifestations?" Barth suggests that the inability or unwillingness to see the incarnate Word acting before the first century is a failure of theological imagination (ibid.).

tological one."[42] The "Christological aspect" is, as Edwards would put it, Jesus Christ exercising his prophetic, priestly, and kingly offices by speaking words (prophet), pointing through pagan sacrifices to his own true sacrifice (priest), and actually redeeming souls from the devil in non-Christian religions (king).[43] Hence, when there is a revealed type of Christ in non-Christian religions, it is Jesus Christ speaking and acting.[44]

## Can Christians Learn from Non-Christian Religions?

Why does God work this way? Why would Jesus Christ use revealed types in non-Christian religions? One answer is that they can lead to salvation. For almost two millennia Christian thinkers have argued that foreign systems of thought—both philosophical and religious—can be stepping-stones or schoolmasters to lead the heathen to Christ. Perhaps the religions will serve this function: as providential preparations for future peoples to receive the full revelation of God in Christ. This does not mean that there is direct continuity from the religions to Christ, but it does mean that the religions may be used by Jesus to prepare their devotees to understand and receive himself—just as the practice of animal sacrifice instituted by the Triune God (and copied by nearly every world religion thereafter) prepared the Jews to be able to understand and receive Christ as the Lamb of God who takes away their sins.

There are several ways in which the types may aid Christians. To use a metaphor from C. S. Lewis, it is easier to see the stars that way. Lewis

42. Encyclical "Dominum et Vivificantem" (1986), no. 53; cited in Jacques Dupuis, S.J., *Toward a Christian Theology of Religious Pluralism* (Maryknoll, N.Y.: Orbis, 1997), 221.

43. Edwards, *History of the Work of Redemption*, 137.

44. Luther had a similar view of the true God operating under a mask in other religions. According to Bornkamm, "Luther had no compunctions at all in applying his general conviction that God's name is hidden in the idols to particular idols in a concrete way. Thus he was convinced that the Moabites prayed to the real God under a false name *(Baal Peor)* and a false cult, as did the Israelites who worshiped Baal. 'Hence, I believe that the true God was honored under this lying name and false worship by the Moabites; and by the children of Israel he was called *Baalim*, as the prophet Hosea testifies [Hosea 2:8]'" (Bornkamm, *Luther and the Old Testament*, 49); the quote is from *The Deuteronomy of Moses, with Notes*, vol. 9 of *Luther's Works*, 55. Bornkamm refers also to Luther's comment on the ancient faith in fortune, "in which true perceptions can be contained in a hidden manner. The ancients knew that in case of war one should not depend solely upon the just cause or upon other human advantages. Instead, they sensed in the work of fortune something of the boundless omnipotence of God, who demands the complete and unconditional trust of man (Bornkamm, *Luther and the Old Testament*, 53; he cites "Whether Soldiers, Too, Can Be Saved," *Luther's Works*, vol. 46, 124).

compared the riches of human culture to moonlight. He was defending Christians' use of pagan culture by claiming that it contained "ante-pasts and ectypes of the truth," which we gain thereby second hand.[45] I would go one step further to say that we can see things in moonlight (such as the stars) that we generally cannot see in daylight.[46] And that Lewis is a good illustration of this: His lifelong immersion in pagan my-thology enabled him to see things in Scripture that have opened up new vistas for Christians ever since.

Another way of putting this is to say that truth in non-Christian reli-gions can help us better comprehend what we already have appre-hended. Jesus' types in the religions can help us see more clearly the great anti-types in the biblical narrative of redemption. A theologian who likes Edwards's conclusion that there is no independent sub-stance, for example, may be better able to articulate that theological position after reading the Buddhist thinker Nagarjuna, who came to the same conclusion.[47] The apophatic strain in Theravada Buddhism may remind us Christians of our own tendency toward anthropomor-phism (attributing our own form and attributes to God), for Buddhists recognize the inadequacy of the human mind to grasp ultimate reali-ties in their own being—something that good Christian theologians also recognize but sometimes need to be reminded of.

Another providential purpose for revealed types may be that non-Christian religions contain aspects of the divine mystery that the Bible does not equally emphasize—for example, the Qur'an's sense of divine majesty and transcendence, and the human being's submission to the holiness of God's eternal decrees. Hindu traditions can help remind Christians of God's immanence in an era in which deistic tendencies have obscured it.

Or we may see an illustration of a Christian principle in someone of another religion. Martin Luther King, Jr., for instance, worked out his philosophy of nonviolent resistance by studying Gandhi's methods, which were influenced in turn by the Sermon on the Mount. King may

45. C. S. Lewis, "Christianity and Culture," in *Christian Reflections* (Grand Rapids: Eerdmans, 1967), 24.

46. To extend the metaphor, eventually we will need neither sun nor moon to see what is real (Rev. 21:23). But in the meantime, given our finite and fallen natures, some things are able to be seen *only* in moonlight, such as the planets (and moonbeams!).

47. Edwards argued that substances are nothing other than God's activity; Nagarjuna insisted that all things are interdependent and lacking in substantial nature. See Jonathan Edwards, *Scientific and Philosophical Writings*, ed. Wallace E. Anderson, vol. 6 of *The Works of Jonathan Edwards* (New Haven: Yale University Press, 1980), 61–69, 113–14, 135–36, 342–43; and David Burton, *Emptiness Appraised: A Critical Study of Nagarju-na's Philosophy* (Richmond, Surrey, U.K.: Curzon Press, 1999).

not have learned the concept originally from Gandhi, but Gandhi helped him understand how such a principle could be practiced in a movement for social change. For both Gandhi and King, nonviolence was not simply a strategy to achieve desired ends but the embodiment of religious principles.

George Lindbeck has gone further by suggesting that Christians can learn from other religions new truths of which Christians were not formerly aware. Partly false religions, he argues, may contain truths of an important but subordinate nature that are not initially present in the highest religion (which for him is Christianity) and can therefore enrich it. Hence, other religions may contain realities and truths of which Christianity to this point knows nothing and by which it could be greatly enriched. Other religions can teach Christians just as geocentrists taught heliocentrists certain things, even though the latter knew the former were wrong in their overall interpretation of the data.[48] As I have indicated in my book *Can Evangelicals Learn from World Religions?* Theravadin Buddhists may be able to show us dimensions of the fallen ego that will shed greater light on what Paul meant by "the old man." Philosophical Daoists may have insights into nonaction that can help Christians better understand "waiting on God." Confucius's portrayal of virtue may open new understanding of radical discipleship, and the Qur'an's attention to the world's "signs" of God's reality can enrich our belief that the cosmos is the theater of God's glory.[49]

The Spirit of Jesus has revealed to the church in the last two centuries implications of the gospel for slavery and women that were not seen by most in the church in the first eighteen centuries of its history. We now believe that the Spirit gave the church understanding of what was implicit in the gospel but remained hidden for centuries. There is no reason to think that there is not more truth and understanding of Christ and the history of redemption yet to be illuminated by his Spirit, perhaps with the aid of insights from other religions.

Of course, the Christian doctrine of objective revelation (having been finalized with the closure of the biblical canon) puts limits on what we can expect. "New truths" are new understandings of God's redemption in Jesus Christ—ideas that Christians in the history of the church did not think of, or at least ideas that did not survive in written form, rather than ideas that go beyond what could possibly be suggested by Scripture. The history of revelation is a history of Jesus Christ's ever expanding work of redemption. Since the only truth they ever suggest has come through

48. George A. Lindbeck, *The Nature of Doctrine: Religion and Theology in a Postliberal Age* (Philadelphia: Westminster, 1984), 49, 54, 67.
49. McDermott, *Can Evangelicals Learn?* chaps. 6–9.

Jesus' revealed types, non-Christian religions can provide insight only into the anti-type—Jesus' work of redemption.

Finally, the Spirit can use non-Christian religions to induce repentance and awareness of God's judgment. Gavin D'Costa and others who have worked in missions warn that those of other religions can show Christians—if they are open to it—the poverty of their own commitment. Christians may also see or hear God in the encounter. According to D'Costa, there is always a moment in missions when the Christian realizes that the evangelized may already implicitly or explicitly know God and that from this person the Christian may learn and hear God's word, as Peter learned from Cornelius's religious experience and heard God's word through him.[50]

The modern missions movement was one of the great turning points in church history. The shape of Christian faith was forever altered, and the demographics of the church were radically realigned. A century ago, for example, tropical Africa was marginally Christian, and 80 percent of professing Christians lived in Europe or North America. Today more than 65 percent of the church inhabits the Southern Hemisphere, and some of its most vibrant expressions and creative thinking are African.[51]

We may be on the verge of another, perhaps even more transforming, turning point. Just as an encounter with competing visions has traditionally stimulated the church's growth in self-understanding and understanding of the Triune God—as Jesus Christ has expanded his work of redemption through the nations—a careful and respectful engagement with what Jesus is doing in non-Christian religions may trigger a quantum leap for evangelical theology. Just as medieval Christian theology (with the help of Muslim thought, interestingly enough) co-opted Greek philosophy so that Christian theology emerged as the pre-eminent vision in the West until the Enlightenment, so too can serious and humble encounters with the great world religions produce a Christian theology that becomes recognized as the only truly global religious vision. In other words, while evangelical theology has recently joined Catholic, Orthodox, and Protestant endeavors to regenerate and baptize the best of Western thinking, it has the potential, if it appropriates the fruits of missions encounters with Africa and the East, to develop a vision that enlarges our view of God in Christ, makes Christ more intelligible to billions of other religionists, and participates in the expansion of Jesus' work of redemption.

50. On Peter's learning, see section 1 above; see also Gavin D'Costa, "Revelation and Revelations: Discerning God in Other Religions: Beyond a Static Valuation," *Modern Theology* 10 (April 1994): 171–72.

51. Walls, *Missionary Movement,* 143, 239.

# 2

# Discerning the Spirit(s) in the World of Religions

*Toward a Pneumatological Theology of Religions*

AMOS YONG

I have previously sketched in some detail a pneumatological approach to Christian theology of religions within the context of global Pentecostalism.[1] While global Pentecostalism has certain affinities with evangelicalism in some respects, it is arguable that the differences between the two movements are much deeper. I hope to bridge part of that gap by outlining a pneumatological theology of religions motivated by evangelical commitments. The argument moves from the biblical bases to theological rationale, methodology, and tasks, and concludes with objections and answers to them. In the process of defending a pneumatological approach to theology of religions, I suggest that this proposal

---

1. See my *Discerning the Spirit(s): A Pentecostal-Charismatic Contribution to Christian Theology of Religions,* Journal of Pentecostal Theology Supplemental Series 20 (Sheffield: Sheffield Academic Press, 2000), esp. chaps. 4, 6, 7.

will play an important part in the further renaissance of contemporary trinitarian theology, that it will have the practical benefit of contributing to the formation of a more dynamic evangelical missiology, and that it will enable a more genuine and effective evangelical engagement with the post-Christian and postmodern cultures of the twenty-first century. My central claim, however, is a methodological one: A pneumatological theology of religions not only commits but also enables Christians to engage empirically the world's religions in a truly substantive manner with theological questions and concerns.

One item of clarification before proceeding. I was tempted to subtitle this essay "Evangelical Inclusivism in Pneumatological Perspective." That I have chosen not to do so is indicative of two assumptions underlying what follows. First, as a Pentecostal I do not wish to be presumptuous in defining "evangelicalism." That would take me well beyond the scope of this chapter. In defense of my decision, I proceed believing that what follows is truly evangelical and that evangelicals will recognize the evangelical heart, mind, and soul when they see them. Second, I am unsure that the theological position to be developed is best categorized by the label "inclusivism." I certainly am not an exclusivist if one means by this label a person who believes not only that salvation is dependent in an ontological sense on the person and work of Christ but also that one has to cognitively recognize that dependence. I am also not a pluralist who would deny both the latter epistemic conditional as well as the former ontological premise. Perhaps I am close to the inclusivist position that affirms the decisive importance of the saving work of Christ without insisting that persons must hear the gospel and verbally confess Christ to be saved.[2] Yet these exclusivist-inclusivist-pluralist categories are more concerned with the question of salvation with regard to those who have not heard the gospel than with the question of religious others and the world's religions. Further, they proceed from a christological starting point and are therefore closely intertwined with christological assumptions. But what if one begins with pneumatology rather than Christology? I will argue that a pneumatological paradigm transcends just these categories. Those who insist one must be an exclusivist or an inclusivist in order to be evangelical may then wish to take issue with my claim to provide an evangelical

2. In this case, I am in broad agreement with giants of the faith such as John Wesley and C. S. Lewis and with contemporaries such as Norman Anderson, *Christianity and World Religions: The Challenge of Pluralism* (Downers Grove, Ill.: InterVarsity Press, 1984); Clark Pinnock, *A Wideness in God's Mercy: The Finality of Jesus Christ in a World of Religions* (Grand Rapids: Zondervan, 1992); and John Sanders, *No Other Name: An Investigation into the Destiny of the Unevangelized* (Grand Rapids: Eerdmans, 1991), esp. 217–24, 249–57.

*theologia religionum*. For these, I will later affirm an inclusivist vision, albeit one that is more methodological and hermeneutical than theological, vis-à-vis the question of the religions. In any case, I leave it up to my readers to determine the appropriate evangelical boundaries for theological reflection and discourse. Now, on with the argument.

## A Pneumatological Approach to the Religions: A Biblical Overview

Evangelical theology begins with Scripture. In developing a theology of religions, one should look to see what the Bible says about religion in general and religions more specifically. While there is not an overwhelming number of references to these topics in the Bible, it is fair to conclude that religion and the religions are presented as being divinely providential on the one hand and demonically inspired to deceive and turn human beings away from the truth on the other.[3] My goal, however, is to develop a theology of religions that proceeds from a pneumatological starting point. The primary questions that emerge, then, are who is the Holy Spirit and what is his function[4]—that is, what has he done, what is he doing, and what will he do?[5] I propose to explore the notion that the Holy Spirit is God present and active: the power of God in creation, re-creation, and final creation. Let us look at each of these categories briefly.[6]

3. For biblical surveys that support this conclusion, see Pinnock, *Wideness in God's Mercy*, 85–110; and Daniel B. Clendenin, *Many Gods Many Lords: Christianity Encounters World Religions* (Grand Rapids: Baker, 1995), 117–40.

4. This, I think, is the proper hermeneutical strategy. Pinnock has proceeded in this way with powerful results. His *Flame of Love: A Theology of the Holy Spirit* (Downers Grove, Ill.: InterVarsity Press, 1996) is a robustly trinitarian theology and vigorous pneumatology that sets the stage for reconceiving the various theological loci—Christology, soteriology, ecclesiology, eschatology—thus enabling the brief discussion of theology of religions to rest within this much larger systematic framework. My project has been stimulated by Pinnock's theological exegesis and vision. But I also endeavor to answer the next question following Pinnock's evangelical theology of religions: Now what?

5. Donald Gelpi, *The Divine Mother: A Trinitarian Theology of the Holy Spirit* (Lanham, Md.: University Press of America, 1984) presents many valid reasons why theologians should use the feminine pronoun with regard to the Holy Spirit, with the recognition that the Spirit is not female—or male, for that matter. However, I will use the conventional masculine pronoun since I am addressing a controversial topic for evangelicals—the religions—and there is no need to complicate further an already difficult task.

6. The Spirit as God present and active comes from the biblical scholar Gordon Fee, *God's Empowering Presence: The Holy Spirit in the Letters of Paul* (Peabody, Mass.: Hendrickson, 1994), xxi and passim. Besides those mentioned in previous notes, what follows is also indebted in various ways to Jürgen Moltmann, *The Spirit of Life: A Universal Affirmation*, trans. Margaret Kohl (London: SCM Press, 1992); Michael Welker, *God the*

### The Spirit of God in Creation

God's presence and activity in creation speak to the universality of the Holy Spirit. In fact, it is important to emphasize that all things are created by God's word *and* God's Spirit. The creation narratives clearly portray God as speaking the world into existence (Gen. 1:3ff.). Yet sometimes overlooked is the fact that speech (as we know it) requires breath, and it is the breath of God that is first said to have "swept over the face of the waters" (Gen. 1:2 NRSV). Elsewhere, the psalmist extols the creative and sustaining power of God through the Spirit for both the heavens ("By the word of the Lord the heavens were made, and all their host by the breath *[ruach]* of his mouth" [Ps. 33:6 NRSV]) and the earth ("When you hide your face, they [the creatures of the world] are dismayed; when you take away their breath, they die and return to the dust. When you send forth your Spirit, they are created; and you renew the face of the ground" [Ps. 104:29–30 NRSV]). It is this same breath of God that also bestows *life* to certain creatures formed of clay, thus enabling *ha adam* to become "a living being" (Gen. 2:7; cf. Job 33:4).

Recognition of the Spirit's omnipresence follows from this pneumatological vision of creation and providence. Certainly, there is no place one can go to escape the Spirit of God:

> Where can I go from your Spirit?
>      Or where can I flee from your presence?
> If I ascend to heaven, you are there;
>      if I make my bed in Sheol, you are there.
> If I take the wings of the morning
>      and settle at the farthest limits of the sea,
> even there your hand shall lead me,
>      and your right hand shall hold me fast.

Psalm 139:7–10 NRSV

This is a remarkable portrait of the ubiquitous presence of the divine Spirit. Even more striking is that in the context of this psalm, the psalmist affirms the Spirit's universal presence by declaring God's exhaustive knowledge of the psalmist himself—both in the depth of his personal subjectivity (vv. 1–6) and in the breadth of his life from conception to last days (vv. 13–16). In other words, the Spirit's universality is intimately connected with God's knowledge of and activity in the

---

*Spirit*, trans. John F. Hoffmeyer (Minneapolis: Fortress Press, 1994); and Lee Snook, *What in the World Is God Doing? Re-imagining Spirit and Power* (Minneapolis: Fortress Press, 1999). The categories of creation, re-creation, and final creation, however, are mine.

world of human beings—and these by the same Spirit. This receives confirmation by Paul in his sermon at the Areopagus:

> The God who made the world and everything in it, he who is Lord of heaven and earth . . . he himself gives to *all* mortals *life and breath* and all things. From one ancestor he made all nations to inhabit the whole earth, and he allotted the times of their existence and the boundaries of the places where they would live, so that they would search for God and perhaps grope for him and find him—though indeed he is not far from each one of us. For *"In him we live and move and have our being";* as even some of your own poets have said, "For we too are his offspring."
>
> Acts 17:24a, 25b–28 NRSV, my emphasis

From this it is clear that human life—even that of the pagan poets (or philosophers) quoted here by Paul—is animated by the presence and activity of God by and through the divine Spirit.

### The Spirit of God in Re-creation

It is precisely because the divine Spirit is universally present and active that God is not only creator but also re-creator, or redeemer and savior.[7] This is evident most concretely in the life, work, death, and resurrection of Jesus Christ—the ultimate pneumatological event in history. Notice the prevalence of the Spirit at key events in the Lukan version of the life of Jesus: conception (1:35), fetal development (1:39–44), dedication (2:25–34), baptism (3:21–22), temptation (4:14), ministry (4:18–19; cf. Acts 10:38), and death (23:46; cf. Heb. 9:14). While I believe in the importance of Spirit-Christology to the task at hand, space constraints prohibit any further development of this theme.[8] Yet the events of this life are paradigmatic for the ways in which God redeems and saves humankind individually and as a whole. It is pneumatology that provides for Luke the thread of continuity between his two books—volume 1 on the life of Jesus and volume 2 on the life of the church, those who are being saved.

The centrality of the day of Pentecost to Luke's story of the early church should therefore not be overlooked. At Pentecost, God enacted the first step of the divine plan to extend the boundaries of those who could be the people of God to include the Gentiles. The presence in Jerusalem of "devout Jews from every nation under heaven" (Acts 2:5,

---

7. It could also be argued that re-creation as a pneumatological motif is typologically prefigured in the Hebrew Bible in the sending of the wind *(ruach)* that causes the receding of the flood waters from the earth (Gen. 8:1).

8. Cf. Ralph Del Colle, *Christ and the Spirit: Spirit-Christology in Trinitarian Perspective* (Oxford: Oxford University Press, 1994).

8–11) was the occasion of the outpouring of the Holy Spirit and the re-constituting of the "new" people of God. Recognizing this kairotic moment, Peter announces that this event signifies the beginning of fulfillment of the words spoken through the prophet Joel:

> In the last days it will be, God declares,
> that I will pour out my Spirit upon all flesh,
>     and your sons and your daughters shall prophesy,
> and your young men shall see visions
>     and your old men shall dream dreams.
> Even upon my slaves, both men and women,
>     in those days I will pour out my Spirit;
>         and they will prophesy.
> And I will show portents in the heaven above
>     and signs on the earth below,
>         blood, and fire, and smoky mist.
> The sun shall be turned to darkness
>     and the moon to blood,
>         before the coming of the Lord's great and glorious day.
> Then everyone who calls on the name of the Lord shall be saved.
>
> Acts 2:17–21 NRSV, quoting Joel 2:28–32

Two points deserve more extended comment. First, this passage features the centrality of the Holy Spirit to the new work of God and clearly emphasizes the pneumatological character of the new covenant. What needs to be underscored is the extensiveness of the work of the Holy Spirit among the new people of God. At first glance, the text appears to limit the "effects" of the Spirit's work to that of prophecy, visions, and dreams. The divine objective expressed in Peter's sermon, however, is to prepare the way for the day of the Lord; more specifically, it is the full salvation of "everyone who calls on the name of the Lord" (Acts 2:21). As with the life of Jesus, this full salvation is a pneumatological work from start to finish. The Spirit is not only sanctifier of those already "saved," as it is commonly recognized, but also the one who actually brings about the new birth itself (John 3:3–7; Titus 3:5). More than that, it is the Spirit who is at work in the hearts and lives of individuals, preparing them for that new birth (John 16:8–11). Apart from that presence and activity of the Spirit of God, no one would ever be convicted of his or her sin or need to repent and turn to God.

On one level, then, the pentecostal experience and event were ecclesiological: The work of the Holy Spirit was to birth and nurture Parthians, Medes, Elamites—the Gentiles—in the body of Christ. On another level, however, Pentecost anticipated, as Peter clearly proclaimed, the day of the Lord (Acts 2:21). This, along with the references to the many peoples present in Jerusalem, should caution us against reading the "all" of Acts 2:17 in an exclusively ecclesiological sense.[9] The Spirit's activity across the dimensions of both space (the Spirit's being poured out upon all people) and time ("in the last days," stretching from the day of Pentecost to the coming of the kingdom of God) begs to be understood in a universal sense that transcends (at least the institutional boundaries of) the church.[10]

### The Spirit of God in Final Creation

This leads to the second point regarding the events of Pentecost: the eschatological character of the Spirit's activity. The work of the Spirit of God covers not only original creation and re-creation (salvation) but extends also to final creation—the new heavens and the new earth. The diversity of peoples present in Jerusalem on the day of Pentecost not only represents the configuration of the body of Christ but also anticipates the scope of the kingdom of God. The seer of the Apocalypse confirms that the saints are those from every tribe, language, people, and nation (Rev. 5:9; 7:9; 13:7; 21:24). This testifies further to the universal presence and efficacious activity of the Spirit. Clearly, it is the Spirit who not only extends the divine invitation to the new heavens and new earth (Rev. 22:17) but who also accomplishes the transition for the people of God. This is true not only in a symbolic sense (Rev. 4:1–2; 21:10) but also in the sense that it is the Spirit who is the power of resurrection life (Ezek. 37:1–14; Rom. 1:4).

Yet it is also important to note that the eschatological work of the Spirit of God involves not only the people of God but also the entirety of the creation itself. The Spirit is that power of God that both renews the face of the earth (Ps. 104:30) and also finally re-creates it. I refer here not so much to the emergence of the new heavens and new earth out of the fiery destruction of the initial created order (2 Peter 3:12–13), even if the Spirit is symbolized throughout Scripture as God's purifying fire. Rather, I am thinking more specifically about the Spirit who groans in, with, and through us in order to bring about the liberation of the creation itself (Rom. 8:18–27). This final creation will deliver the creation "from its bondage to decay and [bring it into] the freedom of the glory of the children of God" (Rom. 8:21 NRSV). And, of

9. Even the classical, exclusivist Pentecostal exegete Stanley M. Horton says that the "all" in this passage refers to "all mankind" (see Horton's commentary on Acts 2:17 in *The Book of Acts* [Springfield, Mo.: Gospel Publishing House, 1981], 38; cf. Welker, *God the Spirit*, 228–78 for a much more extended argument for this reading).

10. This universality is explicitly confirmed later by Peter in his sermon to the household of Cornelius: "I truly understand that God shows no partiality, but in every nation anyone who fears him and does what is right is acceptable to him" (Acts 10:34b–35 NRSV).

course, the Spirit is the Spirit of freedom, and life in the Spirit is salvation, deliverance, and liberation (Rom. 8:1–17).

The Spirit at work in original creation, re-creation, and final creation thus highlights the dynamic character of the divine plan. It also explains the tension that exists in our time, one that is "between the times"—already but not yet, to use eschatological language. We not only eagerly anticipate the coming of the kingdom but also celebrate its presence in our midst (Luke 17:21), and that precisely because of the presence and activity of the Spirit (Luke 11:20).[11] The goal of the Spirit's activity, however, is not only a manifestation of what some call the *charismata* but the establishment of righteousness, peace, and justice. In the words of the prophet Isaiah:

> until a spirit from on high is poured out on us,
> and the wilderness becomes a fruitful field,
> and the fruitful field is deemed a forest.
> Then justice will dwell in the wilderness,
> and righteousness abide in the fruitful field.
> The effect of righteousness will be peace,
> and the result of righteousness, quietness and trust forever.
>
> 32:15–17 NRSV

The Spirit is thereby the universal presence and activity of God. It is a universality that permeates both the external structures of the natural and human world and the internal realms of human hearts. It is also a universality that spans the entirety of God's work from original creation, to re-creation, to final creation. Having established this pneumatological framework, the question that now needs to be asked is this: How does this pneumatological vision enable theological understanding of the phenomenon we today call the diversity of religions?

## Contours of a Pneumatological *Theologia Religionum*

Three broad objectives need to be accomplished in this section. First, having laid the biblical foundations for a pneumatological approach to the religions, I will now articulate the theological rationale for this project. Then I will set forth the basic axioms of a pneumatological approach and suggest where these get us theologically. Finally,

---

11. In the NRSV Luke 11:20 reads, "the finger of God." Most scholars agree that Jesus' reference here to casting out demons by the "finger of God" refers to the Spirit of God, which is Matthew's language (Matt. 12:28); cf. the comments on these passages by D. A. Carson (on Matthew) and Walter Liefeld (on Luke) in vol. 8 of *The Expositor's Bible Commentary* (Grand Rapids: Zondervan, 1984), 289 and 951 respectively.

I will identify the goals, tasks, and methodology of a pneumatological theology of religions.

### Why a Pneumatological Approach to the Religions?

I see numerous advantages to a pneumatological approach to theology of religions. The most important of these is that such an approach is both motivated by and invigorates trinitarian theology. To put it bluntly, only a genuinely pneumatological theology is a fully trinitarian theology. This is in part because Christians cannot speak of the Holy Spirit apart from either the First or the Second Persons of the Triune God. The Spirit is the supremely mediational and relational symbol. Augustine, for example, understood the Spirit as the love that existed between Lover (Father) and Beloved (Son). For Karl Barth, the Spirit reveals to us (i.e., is the "revealedness" of . . .) what the revealer (Father) has revealed (Son). Another trinitarian analogy includes the Spirit as the breath that mediates speaker (Father) and the spoken Word (Son) (Gen. 1:1–3). Theological schemes that explicate this same idea are the Spirit as mediating between the mystery of the transcendent Father and the revelation of the immanent Son; between the primordial Alpha and the eschatological Omega; between creation and redemption; between world and church; between nature and the kingdom of God; and so on. Certainly, at any number of levels, one can easily succumb to an idolatrous exaltation of the Spirit to the neglect or subordination of the Word, even as another can succumb to an idolatrous devotion to Jesus apart from Father or Spirit. However, I am convinced that serious theological reflection today has to capitalize on the relational and mediational resources of pneumatology rather than forget the "silent member" of the Trinity as previous generations have done.

I would suggest that one way to forge a robust trinitarianism is to revisit the patristic metaphor of Word and Spirit as "the two hands of the Father."[12] Briefly stated, the Word represents concreteness—as in, for example, Jesus of Nazareth and the written Scriptures—historical particularity, and the human experience of objectivity; the Spirit represents the dynamism of the anointed one—as in, for example, the Christ, and the living, inspired, and illuminating Word of God—cosmic relationality, and the human experience of subjectivity. Rather than being

---

12. The origins of this metaphor go back to Irenaeus (*Against Heresies* 4, preface, 4). I prefer this trinitarian model over the communitarian model currently advocated by social trinitarians because it seems capable of preserving the centrality of the notion of community inherent in the social doctrine without the latter's tendencies toward tritheism.

understood literalistically, these categories are meant to function heuristically and metaphorically. Their objective is to enable us to envision the truth that God works all things with the divine hands: by and through *both* Word and Spirit.[13] If that is the case, then any assessment that neglects either aspect of what God does fails truly to capture the heart or essence of that work or reality.

This togetherness of Word and Spirit means that the advantages of a pneumatological approach to the theological task can be assessed from a number of angles. Theologically, it means that reflection should bring together the biblical context and horizon with the contemporary context and horizon. Doctrinally, it means that articles of faith should be articulated in terms of faithfulness to past witnesses and relevance to contemporary needs and concerns. Most important, however, are the methodological implications: The doing of theology involves Scripture, tradition, reason, and experience, each considered as the conjunction of both Word and Spirit.[14] Scripture, for example, is the Word of God, even as it testifies to Christ as the Logos; at the same time, Scripture as a product is inspired and illuminated by the Spirit as well. Tradition is the interpreter of Scripture, even as it is led by the Spirit in that process of interpretation (e.g., as in the New Testament canonical process). Reason is both Logos (John 1) and Spirit as the mind and interpreter of God (1 Cor. 2:10b–11). Experience is both concrete (of Christ) and dynamic (of the Spirit), even while ultimately being of God (Christ as the representation of the Father and the Spirit as the presence of the Father). The point is that the dualism between Word and Spirit is bridged, and relational connections are seen and reasserted within a trinitarian framework. To better appreciate these aspects of a pneumatological approach, however, we need to examine its controlling axioms.

### Basic Axioms of a Pneumatological Theology of Religions

To reiterate, a pneumatological theology of religions is a robustly trinitarian approach that holds great promise but has been, for the

13. This means not that some things are to be considered manifestations of Word and other things of Spirit, but that Word and Spirit are inseparable features of *all* things. Thus, there is the universality of Word (the cosmic Christ) as well as a particularity of Spirit (that accentuates and values the differentiated order of determinate things) precisely because both aspects inhere—as in the patristic notion of *circumincessio* and the Greek notion of *perichoresis*—and inform each other. On the notion of the particularity of Spirit, see Colin Gunton, *The One, the Three, and the Many: God, Creation, and the Culture of Modernity* (Cambridge: Cambridge University Press, 1993), 180–209.

14. This is congruent with what has come to be called the Wesleyan quadrilateral. I defend the viability of the quadrilateral for evangelical theological method in part 2 of my article, "The Demise of Foundationalism and the Retention of Truth: What Evangelicals Can Learn from C. S. Peirce," *Christian Scholar's Review* 29 (2000): 563–88.

most part, relatively unexplored.[15] Again, if we grant that the works of God are by Word and Spirit, then the following three theses can be developed within a trinitarian framework.

*Thesis 1: God is universally present and active by the Spirit.* Articulating this universal presence and activity is the task of foundational pneumatology—the investigation of the pneumatological features of the entire created order.[16] The questions that arise here include, but are not limited to, the following: In what ways is the Spirit identifiable in creation—in the cosmos, in nature, in human history, and in human experience? If human society includes politics, economics, and so on, what is the Spirit doing in those arenas of human life? If human culture includes the arts and the religions, what are the purposes of the Spirit in those domains of human experience? How does the Spirit sustain these dimensions of human life, and how do they reflect the presence and activity of the Triune God?[17]

*Thesis 2: God's Spirit is the life-breath of the* imago Dei *in every human being and the presupposition of all human relationships and communities.* This means that there is a pneumatological dimension to each human individual that sustains intersubjective communication, interpersonal relationships, and intentional, rational, moral, and spiritual life.[18] All human engagements with the "other"—whether that other be human others, the world, or the divine—are pneumatologically mediated. This is first and fore-

15. See, for example, Kevin Vanhoozer, "Does the Trinity Belong in a Theology of Religions? On Angling the Rubicon in the 'Identity' of God," in *The Trinity in a Pluralistic Age,* ed. Kevin Vanhoozer (Grand Rapids: Eerdmans, 1997), 41–71; and the three essays by Rowan Williams, Gavin D'Costa, and Christoph Schwöbel on the promise of trinitarian theology for theology of religions in part 1 of *Christian Uniqueness Reconsidered: The Myth of a Pluralistic Theology of Religions,* ed. Gavin D'Costa (Maryknoll, N.Y.: Orbis, 1990). D'Costa advances the discussion substantively in his recent book, *The Meeting of Religions and the Trinity* (Maryknoll, N.Y.: Orbis, 2000). An older, much smaller, but still suggestive work is Raimundo Panikkar, *The Trinity and the Religious Experience of Man* (Maryknoll, N.Y.: Orbis, 1973).

16. For an explication, see my "On Divine Presence and Divine Agency: Toward a Foundational Pneumatology," *Asian Journal of Pentecostal Studies* 3 (2000): 163–84.

17. The trinitarian character of this pneumatological proposal that defines Spirit not only in relationship to God but also in relationship to the Word should not be underestimated. It is this trinitarian framework that makes this pneumatological theology of religions *Christian* and distinguishes it from a Hindu theology of religions whereby all things are Atman vis-à-vis Brahman, or a Buddhist philosophy of religions emphasizing the interdependence of all things, or a Neo-Confucian metaphysic of the ten thousand things derived from the Great Ultimate.

18. This is the thesis of Steven G. Smith, *The Concept of the Spiritual: An Essay in First Philosophy* (Philadelphia: Temple University Press, 1988), who builds on the work of Martin Buber; cf. also D. Lyle Dabney, "Otherwise Engaged in the Spirit: A First Theology for the Twenty-first Century," in *The Future of Theology: Essays in Honor of Jürgen Moltmann,* ed. Miroslav Volf, Carmen Krieg, and Thomas Kucharz (Grand Rapids: Eerdmans, 1996), 154–63.

most an ontological claim (thus, Gen. 2:7 regarding our breath of life and Acts 17:28 regarding our life together in God) rather than a soteriological one.[19] It is also a claim about the fact that human beings are nothing but individuals-in-communities, and that enabled by the Spirit of God. In other words, we live, think, communicate, and relate as spirit-beings, and our quest for ultimate reality proceeds from our being in communities (all of us belonging to multiple communities with varying degrees of commitment). I will return later to the importance of understanding the communal context of all religious quests. For the present, however, what needs to be emphasized is the fundamental human commonality—as pneumatologically situated individuals-in-communities—that transcends human differences of gender, race, ethnicity, class, and, of course, religion. At the same time, the constitution of human beings by Word and Spirit points to the objective *and* the subjective nature of human being-in-the-world. This calls for a recognition of human fallibility, and for human openness to each other in humility, as seeing through a glass dimly (1 Cor. 13:12).[20]

Following from these two is *thesis 3: The religions of the world, like everything else that exists, are providentially sustained by the Spirit for divine purposes.*[21] While I will qualify this thesis in important ways later, it is important to state it boldly here. Unless one is prepared to say that all forms and expressions of human culture are anti-theistic, one cannot arbitrarily separate out one dimension of culture—the religious aspect— and so label it, as previous generations of theologians have, as either a solely human effort to reach God or as demonic. Rather, all human endeavors reflect either God's permissive or active will toward ultimately divine purposes centered around the full revelation of Jesus Christ and the impending kingdom of God. This should be no different with regard to the religions. As Clark Pinnock has observed, "It would seem strange if the Spirit excused himself from the very arena of culture where people search for meaning. If God is reaching out to sinners, it is hard to comprehend why he would not do so in the sphere of religion."[22] In short, a

19. Might this not also connect with the Johannine claim that the Logos is "the true light, which enlightens *everyone*" (John 1:9, my emphasis)? I take passages describing the departure of the Spirit of God from individuals (e.g., 1 Sam. 16:14) as functionally descriptive of their relationship with God rather than being an ontological statement regarding their humanity as such.

20. James K. A. Smith, *The Fall of Interpretation: Philosophical Foundations for a Creational Hermeneutic* (Downers Grove, Ill.: InterVarsity Press, 2000) understands this epistemic dimness as connected to the distance between subject and object. His primary contribution, however, lies in his argument that this distance is inherent to creation itself—a creation pronounced good by the Creator—rather than being the result of the fall.

21. This is the proposal of J. A. DiNoia, *The Diversity of Religions: A Christian Perspective* (Washington, D.C.: Catholic University of America Press, 1992), 65–107.

22. Pinnock, *Flame of Love*, 203.

pneumatological approach to the religions enables an inclusive methodology and hermeneutic rather than a monological one that assumes in
an a priori sense that the religions lie beyond the pale of divine presence
and activity. I submit that this inclusiveness represents the latent power
of a pneumatological (read: trinitarian) theology to overcome the traditional impasses that have hindered developments in *theologia religionum*.
Let me briefly identify three.

First, pneumatology is the key to overcoming the dualism between
christological particularity and the cosmic Christ. When it is recalled
that the historical Jesus was who he was precisely by the Spirit of God
and that the risen Christ was resurrected by the power of the Spirit,
then the either/or of particularity/universality dissolves. Rather, in consistent trinitarian fashion, all things have to be seen as the conjunction
of Word and Spirit, including both the historical Jesus and the coming
Christ, and the dynamic presence and activity of God in the world. In
this framework, the Spirit is certainly the Spirit of Jesus, even as Jesus
is the one anointed by the Spirit of God (Acts 10:38). Yet this mutuality
should not obscure the broader trinitarian framework in the sense that
the Spirit is also the Spirit of God, even as Jesus is the Son of God.

Second, pneumatology is the key to understanding the tension between what has traditionally been termed specific and natural revelation—namely, between the sacred and the profane, or the church and the
world. These categories have previously been correlated with those who
are saved and those who are lost: specific revelation being necessary for
salvation, and natural theology being sufficient only for damnation. A
pneumatological understanding of salvation, however, is dynamic, requiring triadic recategorization of "was saved," "am being saved," and
"will be saved." (I leave aside the questions regarding the salvation of infants, the mentally incapacitated, and so forth.) In this framework, conversion itself needs to be understood as a multifaceted process involving
cognitive, moral, affective, spiritual, sociopolitical, religious, and other
dimensions of human experience.[23] My point is that with both revelation
and salvation, a pneumatological perspective emphasizes process and

---

23. Here I build on Donald Gelpi's categories (see Gelpi, *The Turn to Experience in Contemporary Theology* [New York: Paulist Press, 1994], 134–36), which are, in turn, appropriated
from the ideas of Bernard Lonergan; see the latter's *Method in Theology* (New York: Seabury
Press, 1972), 237–44. It is arguable that my connecting a processive soteriology to a pneumatological *theologia religionum* was anticipated by Jonathan Edwards. Gerald McDermott
suggests that the doctrines of original and progressive revelation (the *prisca theologia*), creation as typological or semiotic pointers to divinity, and salvation as dispositional were central to the Puritan theologian's eighteenth-century fascination with the non-Christian
religions; see McDermott, *Jonathan Edwards Confronts the Gods: Christian Theology, Enlightenment Religion, and Non-Christian Faiths* (Oxford: Oxford University Press, 2000).

dynamism rather than intractable dualisms. This does not deny the value of understanding revelation as "natural" or "specific," nor does it reject the ancient *extra ecclesia nulla salus* ("no salvation outside the church") formula. It does relativize the meaning of theological categories vis-à-vis the historical frameworks within which they emerged and demands a reassessment of their meanings within both the wider contexts of Scripture, the entire historical and dimensional scope of human life and experience, and the eschatological horizon.

Last but not least, I need to return to the view of religion mentioned above. Traditionally, evangelical Christianity has been identified as the individual's cognitive awareness of a living relationship with Jesus (whether mediated sacramentally or otherwise). By implication, all other religions were false, being either failed human efforts to reach God or inspired by the devil and his demons. This disregards both the universality of Spirit and the dynamic nature of divine activity. With regard to the religions, this means that religious traditions are dynamic, evolving realities and that hard-and-fast lines between religion and culture and between one religious tradition and another are difficult to draw.[24] Given this, it is better to see religious traditions as serving divine purposes in greater or lesser degrees at each stage of their evolution. The Christian tradition, as Barth noted, is also not exempt from either the vicissitudes of history or the presence and activity of the Spirit of God. There is as much human frailty and demonic activity within Christianity as there is without. Further, where Judaism stops and where Christianity starts is difficult to determine in some respects—for example, as in their monotheistic commitments or their ethical codes. Pneumatology enables us to transcend these categories even while recognizing their contextual, rather than absolute, validity.

My point is that a pneumatological approach to the religions offers alternatives to the traditional impasses and enables new, relational categories to sustain further inquiry.[25] It does this negatively and posi-

---

24. See the fascinating story of the movement of a New Age group toward Eastern Orthodoxy from the 1960s to the 1980s described by Phillip Charles Lucas, *The Odyssey of a New Religion: The Holy Order of MANS from New Age to Orthodoxy* (Bloomington and Indianapolis: Indiana University Press, 1995). On an empirical level, the Holy Order of MANS can be described only as a dynamic convergence of various cultural and religious influences with different manifest trajectories at different times. And, of course, the history of religion is filled with the cross-fertilization of religious traditions, the emergence of new movements from older ones, and the dying out of traditions.

25. This is elaborated at length in my "The Turn to Pneumatology in Christian Theology of Religions: Conduit or Detour?" *Journal of Ecumenical Studies* 35 (1998): 437–54; a complementary recent discussion on the centrality of pneumatology to a trinitarian theology of religions is D'Costa, *Meeting of Religions and the Trinity*, 109–32.

tively—the former by enabling the surmounting of static dualisms erected by traditional theological frameworks, and the latter by vitalizing and animating a robust trinitarian (read: relational, holistic) framework for theological reflection. Spirit is supremely mediational and relational.

### The Goals, Tasks, and Methodology of a Pneumatological Theology of Religions

The preceding theological rationale creates the necessary space for conceiving and executing a pneumatological approach to the religions. The overarching categories for reflection derive from the pneumatological symbol itself. As noted above, the Holy Spirit is the primary theological symbol for the presence and activity of God in the world. Pneumatology in its broadest sense, however, includes the diversity of human, social, and even demonic "spirits." This requires a third category flexible enough to accommodate this pluralistic realm of the spiritual. I propose that in addition to the categories of divine presence and divine activity, a pneumatological theology of religions also has to engage this reality of greater or lesser divine presence and activity, or, alternatively, divine absence.

In order to demarcate with greater precision just what these categories—divine presence, divine activity, and divine absence—do and do not accomplish, let me insert a caveat at this point. The goal of a pneumatological theology of religions can never be to state dogmatically or precisely: "This is where the Spirit of God is!" This is not because of the fallibility and finitude that accompanies both all human relationship with the divine and all human knowledge in general. Certainly, evangelicals who believe in the charismatic gift of discernment of spirits can and should utilize this gift. But even if it is the case that God does all things through Word and Spirit, it is also surely the case that the full manifestation of Word and Spirit in the world has been distorted, muted, and even effaced by sin. In other words, things in the world—including the rituals, doctrines, myths, texts, communities, practices, morals, and so on of all religious traditions—do not reflect Word and Spirit in a pure manner. Rather, every thing, and more specifically, every religious reality and event, reflects not only Word and Spirit to a greater or lesser degree but also human and perhaps even demonic spirits to various degrees as well. Not only epistemologically and ontologically but also phenomenologically, divinity, humanity, and the demonic cannot be understood apart from each other; each derives part of its significance and reality from the other two. Spiritual discernment, therefore, cannot stop at labeling any religious reality only as divine, human, or demonic since none of these features inheres purely in the events of human history.[26] Rather, incisive discernment should be able to point out not only where God the Spirit is or is not at work but also where other spirits are at work in the same thing.

The importance of the pneumatological categories can now be clearly stated. Whereas the category of *divine presence* marks the truth, goodness, beauty, and holiness that characterize the reality of God, that of *divine absence* registers the false, evil, ugly, and profane existence of the fallen world. The symbol of *divine activity* is thus dynamic and mediational, calling attention to the fact that things move continuously either toward or away from their divinely instituted reason for being. Clearly, given the nature of the world's religions, it is imperative that all three pneumatological categories should be kept in play. Needless to say, the object of theological discernment is to identify the presence or absence of divinity at various levels of any religious phenomenon at any particular point of space-time. As important, however, is the capacity also to follow the trajectory of that phenomenon's historical transformation—whether that be identified in moral, religious, spiritual, or theological terms. I am convinced that it is the failure to discern adequately the Spirit and spirits in the religions in all of their dynamic complexity that becomes the Achilles' heel of any pneumatological approach to theology of religions.[27]

Discernment, however, requires criteria. At this point, the Christian norm of Jesus Christ reasserts itself: "No one can say 'Jesus is Lord' except by the Holy Spirit" (1 Cor. 12:3 NRSV). Here it may seem that those of us exploring a pneumatological approach to the religions are confronted once again with the particularity of Jesus Christ. On the one hand, one might admit that pneumatology is subservient to Christology after all, at least insofar as discerning the Spirit is concerned. On the other hand, does this "formula" serve finally to resolve the relationship between pneumatology and Christology by subordinating the former to the latter? Is it not the case that, like all formulas, even this one is not sacrosanct, especially insofar as it is understood in a legalistic and rigid fashion? After all, Jesus himself warned that there will be those who will call him "Lord" but who evidently do not know him since their lives

26. I expand on this notion in "Spiritual Discernment: A Biblical and Theological Reconsideration," in *The Spirit and Spirituality: Essays in Honor of Russell P. Spittler,* ed. Wonsuk Ma and Robert P. Menzies (Irvine, Calif.: Regnum Books International, forthcoming).

27. I have previously argued that this is the key to a robust evangelical *theologia religionum;* see my "Whither Theological Inclusivism: The Development and Critique of an Evangelical Theology of Religions," *Evangelical Quarterly* 71 (1999): 327–48. Of course, the inclusivism I now defend is more of a methodological and hermeneutical one than a theological one.

do not bear the appropriate fruit (of the Spirit of God, it should be added, according to Gal. 5:19–23; cf. Matt. 7:15–23). The formal norm of Jesus Christ is therefore applicable only by and through the power of the Spirit. So while discerning the Spirit is intimately connected with the Christ, this should not be understood in a way that subordinates the Spirit to Christ—as in, "Ah, here is a confession of Jesus as Lord, and therefore the presence and activity of the Spirit, period!" in a simplistic sense—or that renders the Spirit subservient to the Word. Rather, Word and Spirit are mutually defining as the "two hands of the Father."[28] This should alert us to the processive and ambiguous nature of discernment. The discernment of Spirit or spirits, in short, can never be complete.

The overarching goal of a pneumatological theology of religions, therefore, is the ongoing activity of discerning the Holy Spirit and the diversity of spirits in the world of the religions. This goal has three aspects, not necessarily in any particular order: to understand the religions as a human phenomenon; to understand the relationship between the divine and this human phenomenon in all of its diversity; and to distinguish, where possible, the divine and the human from the demonic. Getting at the phenomenon of religion is therefore at least in part an empirical task requiring an interdisciplinary approach. Interpreting the data theologically is an ongoing comparative project. Let me briefly expand on each.

Discerning the Spirit and the spirits in the world's religions has to begin with the empirical reality of these traditions and therefore requires an interdisciplinary methodology. Theologians who attempt to understand the phenomenon of religion rely on historians, anthropologists, sociologists, psychologists, and religious practitioners to familiarize them with the object of their reflections. On another level, theologians should also listen to those pastoral agents and missionaries who work within environments that sustain such traditions. Certainly this does not exclude personal observation and participation, even as theologians cannot ignore their own personal experiences with a religious tradition. For this reason, they should also heed the testimonies of those—both insiders and outsiders—who have firsthand experience of that tradition. Otherwise, one theologizes alone, in an ivory tower,

---

28. Here I confess my sensitivity to the Eastern Orthodox critique that the *filioque* clause has translated in the Western Church to a subordination of the third article of the creed to the second. Of course, the danger of reverse subordination presents itself as well, of which we need to be continuously mindful. The way forward, I suggest, is to extend pneumatology toward a robust trinitarian theology; see my *Spirit-Word-Community: Theological Hermeneutics in Trinitarian Perspective,* New Critical Thinking in Theology and Biblical Studies (Aldershot, Hampshire, U.K.: Ashgate Publishing, forthcoming).

far removed from the empirical reality of the world's religious traditions. Getting at that empirical reality is a complex and arduous task
beyond the capacities of any one human being. In short, our awareness
of the religiously plural world that characterizes our time requires that
theologians look to and learn from the work of other specialists in religion. A relevant and true theology of religions builds on an empirical
engagement with the world of the religions, and such has to be developed from diverse perspectives and approaches.

But what then does one do while gathering one's data? Inevitably,
one categorizes one's data as one proceeds. Fair categorization, however, requires that one pay attention to the categories emergent from
within the religious tradition one is engaging. In other words, a faithful
and true interpretation of Buddhism, for example, must pay close attention to the ways in which Buddhists understand and engage each
other, the world, and that which is, in their perspective, ultimately real.
One's depiction of Buddhism should be recognized and accepted by
Buddhist practitioners as authentic to their experience and tradition.
One should always be cautious of imposing foreign categories on religious others.

But the pneumatological categories themselves derive from specifically Christian reflection on the world's religions. And if from a pneumatological perspective the data is supposed to illuminate, finally, divine presence, activity, and absence, how then does one bridge the gap
between the categories of the religious other and the pneumatological
categories? One does so by doing comparative theology. My conviction
is that theology of religions can proceed only as a comparative enterprise. Now certainly one of the goals here is to identify points of convergence or divergence among religious traditions. And in this regard,
it is important to note that this generation of comparativists is finally
getting beyond the early comparative phenomenological work of previous thinkers such as Rudolph Otto and Mircea Eliade and engaging in
much deeper and more substantive hermeneutical, philosophical, and,
ultimately, theological comparisons and contrasts.[29] For Christian theo-

29. An example of what I mean by the current movement beyond or beneath the
former surface comparativism is Roger Jackson and John Makransky, eds., *Buddhist
Theology: Critical Reflections by Contemporary Buddhist Scholars*, Curzon Critical Studies
in Buddhism 7 (Richmond, Surrey, U.K.: Curzon Press, 1999). In previous generations
some have been too quick to assume that Buddhist reflection on ultimate issues is "theological" since that is what Western reflection on ultimate issues has been called. The contributors to this volume, however, are all Buddhists who not only recognize that many
branches of Buddhism are nontheistic but who also have been trained in theistic traditions. What they call "Buddhist theology," then, is not the acknowledgment that Buddhists are "anonymous theists" after all but the recognition of the need to explore how

logians, however, cross-cultural and cross-religious dialogue, hermeneutics, and comparison are all the more significant since they are part and parcel of our asking and attempting to answer questions regarding whether or not and how the Holy Spirit is present and active in the religions. And engaging this question itself has to be understood as a Spirit-led process of encounter with religious others who are not entirely devoid of the Spirit of God, according to the central axioms of a pneumatological theology of religions (so above). Theology of religions, therefore, needs to be comparative theology of religions that proceeds from multiple conversational starting points: that of the practitioners, that of a diversity of scholars from various disciplines, and that of a diversity of perspectives of theologians or intellectuals representing the various traditions, all of whom are reflecting from both within and without the traditions in dialogue. This multifaceted conversation is necessary to protect oneself against ideological or personal bias in interpreting and categorizing the religious other. It is also the process through which one translates the symbolic content of Christian faith into different religious (and cultural) contexts. In short, it is the means through which Christian theologians tentatively determine the presence and activity of the Spirit in the lives, practices, and beliefs of the world's religious traditions.

## Objections to a Pneumatological Theology of Religions

It is important for any major research program to face squarely the objections that may be raised, especially by the constituency to whom the project advocate is appealing for support. I want to briefly raise and respond to three complexes of potential objections to a pneumatological approach to Christian theology of religions: It is not distinctly *Christ*-ian, in the sense of subjecting Christ to the Spirit; its evangelical credentials are suspect; and it smacks of a more subtle form of theological imperialism.

---

the various Buddhist traditions should or should not engage the questions, concerns, and issues that are raised by theistic traditions. For more on the complexity, sophistication, and direction of the current comparative enterprise, see, e.g., David Tracy and Frank E. Reynolds, eds., *Myth and Philosophy*, SUNY Series, Toward a Comparative Philosophy of Religions (Albany, N.Y.: State University of New York Press, 1990); and Thomas Dean, ed., *Religious Pluralism and Truth: Essays on Cross-Cultural Philosophy of Religion* (Albany, N.Y.: State University of New York Press, 1995). My own comparativist vision is modeled after Robert Cummings Neville, *Behind the Masks of God: An Essay toward a Comparative Theology* (Albany, N.Y.: State University of New York Press, 1991).

### *Pneumatological* Theologia Religionum *as Sub-Christian*

In some respects, the project outlined in these pages is not new. I am thinking specifically about the spiritualist understandings of religious diversity characteristic of nineteenth-century American transcendentalism and the recent New Age movement. Influenced by the tradition of Western esoterica such as the Perennial Philosophy, Rosicrucianism, and theosophy, as well as by Eastern traditions, the category of "spirit" has also been central to how spiritualists then and now think about religion. For them, Christ is certainly important, but only as one of many religiously crucial personalities. He may be a master *avatar*, a profound teacher, or even a decisive spirit-guide, but he is understood, in effect, as having secondary importance in contrast to the transcendental unity all human beings enjoy through our spiritual connections. By virtue of the ever present and active divine spirit, all authentic religious traditions point to the truth and are ultimately salvific.

I say this to caution us, and especially myself, against being deluded with euphoria about finding *the* resolution to the impasse posed by christological approaches to Christian theology of religions. Clearly, a pneumatological *theologia religionum* is susceptible, over time, to diminishing the centrality of Christ to Christian theological reflection; this tendency should be recognized and admitted. But it is also clear that an energetically pneumatological theology of religions will be nothing less than a fully trinitarian theology of religions. It is the vigorous trinitarian character of a pneumatological theology of religions that not only distinguishes this project from that proposed by spiritualist thinkers but also holds promise for the foreseeable future. To repeat, a Christian theology that recognizes that God does all things through Word and Spirit is therefore doubly armed for reflective engagement with the world's religions. Word and Spirit provide the two poles through which all orthodoxy must pass. How both poles relate to each other and how to keep either pole from subjugating the other is part of the dialectical task that pneumatologists of religion have to work out continuously.

But the question still remains: Does not a pneumatological approach to the religions effectively undermine the Christian conviction regarding the centrality of Christ? Does not the universality of Spirit have to be understood within the context of Jesus Christ as being the way, the truth, and the life (John 14:6) apart from whom no one can be saved (Acts 4:12)? Does not Christian salvation depend on calling on the name of the Lord and verbally confessing Christ's lordship (cf. Rom. 10:9–15)?

I believe that an evangelical can affirm all of these truths within the contours of a pneumatological approach to the non-Christian faiths. It is important to note that theology of religions engages the question concerning the relationship of the religions to divine providence. Theologians of the religions are not called to check passports at heaven's gate. Certainly, to reflect on the religions with the proposed pneumatological categories raises questions of whether or not those in other faiths can be, or perhaps even are, saved. But pneumatologists of religion can affirm the place of the religions in divine providence, even as they affirm the absolute centrality of Jesus Christ's life, death, and resurrection for salvation. I believe that the issue of the religions and the issue of the unevangelized should be kept separate for the purposes of doing theology of religions. This leads to the more specific "evangelical" objection to the kind of pneumatological approach to the religions that I have sketched here.

### Pneumatological Theologia Religionum as Sub-Evangelical

I indicated at the beginning of this chapter that I would not attempt to define "evangelicalism," and I will not break that promise. As a Pentecostal, however, I am concerned not so much about evangelicalism per se but with the going forth of the Evangel—the Good News of Jesus Christ. How, it may be legitimately asked, is a pneumatological approach to the religions that emphasizes dialogue able to sustain the evangelistic enterprise? Does not a theology that emphasizes the universality of the Spirit's presence and activity undercut the motivation for missionary proclamation? If in fact the Spirit is already at work in the religions, then why bother with preaching to non-Christians at all? What is the object of theology of religions after all?

These are valid questions that concern evangelicalism. My initial response is to say that those who insist that theology of religions should motivate evangelical missions are presenting primarily a pragmatic rather than a theological argument. While I am committed to the notion that all truth is pragmatic in the sense that it "works" as it corresponds to reality, I am also concerned that pragmatism not become the sole or even dominant criterion for theological truth. In other words, I think it a weak argument to reject a pneumatological *theologia religionum* simply because one feels that emphasis should be placed on preaching the gospel rather than dialoguing with religious others.

Second, however, dialogue and proclamation are not mutually exclusive but intrinsically connected.[30] Genuine dialogue proclaims truth,

---

30. See, for example, Jürgen Moltmann, "Dialogue or Mission: Christianity and the Religions in an Endangered World," in *God and Secular Society: The Public Relevance of Theology,* trans. Margaret Kohl (Minneapolis: Fortress Press, 1999), 226–44.

and effective proclamation engages with others at a personal, dialogical level. From a missiological perspective, evangelicals already agree that lasting conversions are achieved best through the establishment of one-on-one relationships. Dialogue, rather than proclamation, characterizes such relationships. More important, mutual vulnerability is a feature of such relationships rather than attitudes of superiority. A pneumatological approach to the non-Christian faiths supports and encourages precisely such dynamics and enables us to cultivate just such virtues. It opens up the Christian to whatever is true, good, beautiful, and holy in the other tradition, even while nurturing an environment in which the non-Christian can come to appreciate the same in the Christian faith. What else is this besides grass-roots "evangelism"?

Evangelicals, however, might still be concerned that we are going too far. After all, "dialogue" seems too passive. Further, many would argue that the discontinuities between the Christian faith and the world's religious traditions are much more profound than the continuities. For such people, engaging in an interfaith conversation would be a betrayal of their commitments to the exclusive claims of the gospel. Many evangelicals don't even think that dialogue with Catholics, Orthodox, or non-evangelical Christians in general is all that valuable, much less dialogue with non-Christians or, more specifically, Jews, Muslims, Hindus, Buddhists, Confucianists, practitioners of indigenous traditions, and the like.

These concerns, however, may also be approached from another direction—that of how deep inculturation of the gospel occurs otherwise. Does not the process of translating the message of the gospel require prolonged engagement and exposure to the "foreign" cultural and religious milieu? Rather than being afraid of diluting evangelical truth, should not evangelicals be confident that the advance of the gospel rests not so much in our hands but in its universal relevance and explanatory power? Yes, there is always a fine line between syncretism and inculturation (indigenization, contextualization, acculturation, etc.). But recognition of this fine line should not produce withdrawal. Instead, it should translate into engagement through the discerning empowerment of the Holy Spirit. This kind of zeal, however, will no doubt raise the accusation that evangelical "dialogue" is actually motivated by polemical, apologetic, and expansionist concerns, all under the guise of taking the religious other seriously on his or her own terms. This, I think, is the most serious objection and requires somber reflection.

## Pneumatological Theologia Religionum *as Covertly Imperialistic*

Ours is a postmodern world. Whatever else postmodernity might mean, it means at least post-foundationalist, post-Enlightenment, post-Western, post-colonial, and perhaps also post-Christian. It also means the emergence and empowerment of local languages, local rationalities, and local ways of being human. The language and concepts undergirding a pneumatological theology of religions—foundational pneumatology, divine presence and activity, universality, and so on—will rightly seem to many postmodern critics to reveal a hegemonistic impulse. Such critics will point out that even the very use of the pneumatological categories themselves is an imposition of Christian notions on the practices and beliefs that religious others consider sacred. How then can a pneumatological *theologia religionum* proceed without being imperialistic?

First, theological reflection today can be post-foundationalistic only if by this the Cartesian sense of foundationalism is meant.[31] The postmodern turn, I am convinced, is largely valid. There is no neutral place from which unbiased engagement of the world's religious traditions can proceed. This is especially the case in theology, where the best words and concepts are ultimately symbols that enable truer and more meaningful engagement with the divine and with reality. Those who would advocate a pneumatological theology of religions should be cognizant of their sociohistorical location as interpreters, of the ambiguity of interpretation, of the polyvalence of reference, and of the subjectivity of interpersonal encounter. I would argue that such admission derives, at least in part, from the ambiguity of the core pneumatological symbols themselves—for example, wind, fire, or water, which are gentle, purifying, and life-giving on the one hand, but all of which can be destructive on the other hand.[32] Yet a pneumatological approach to the religions is also open to the Spirit and proceeds from the conviction that it is the Spirit who leads the quest for truth amid all those who are searching for it (John 14:17; 16:13; 1 John 2:27). In the postmodern context, then, a pneumatological *theologia religionum* legitimates rather than undermines interreligious dialogue as an appropriate arena for Christian inquiry after truth.

This means, second, that a pneumatological theology of religions is fallibilistic in the sense of being tentative and open to correction. In its

31. On this, see part 1 of my "Demise of Foundationalism and the Retention of Truth"; cf. F. LeRon Shults, *The Postfoundationalist Task of Theology: Wolfhart Pannenberg and the New Theological Rationality* (Grand Rapids: Eerdmans, 1999).

32. I develop the theological implications of these root metaphors for the Spirit in chapter 2 of my *Spirit-Word-Community*.

overall framework, it can be understood as a large-scale theological hypothesis to be tested. The tests are applied in the long-term, multidisciplinary, and multi-perspectival conversation in which theology engages. Criteria of truth (correspondence, coherence, and pragmatic value) operate not only to transform the theory in its details, as well as generally, but perhaps also to undermine the overall plausibility of the theory during the course of the dialogue. This is what true fallibilism at the theological level has to mean. My point is that a pneumatological *theologia religionum* is always *in via*, as is any pneumatological enterprise. It is always in quest, open to further investigation by continuously enlarging the borders of inquiry and by including in the conversation any and all who are interested in the subject matter. This proceeds, again, from the fundamental convictions undergirding a pneumatologically informed worldview: The Spirit of God is universally present and active. No voices or perspectives can, therefore, be excluded in an a priori fashion from the conversation.

The result, of course, is that a pneumatological theology of religions is a fully public enterprise.[33] Certainly, I agree that it should serve the church, as should all viable theology. But serving does not mean isolating, nor does it mean parochializing. Rather, part of the service rendered is energetic cultural and religious engagement wherever the Spirit blows (cf. John 3:8). Christians convinced of the importance and truth of Christian faith should not be hesitant to test even the most central of its claims against those of other religious traditions. This kind of fully public theology invites a pluralism of ideas, convictions, doctrines, claims, and even criteria—including the frameworks of interpretation and worldviews from which criteria derive—for testing such claims.[34] It is dialogue in the most comprehensive sense, including testimonials, arguments, and even apologetics.[35] And if conducted sincerely as they should be, such dialogues might result in conversions at

33. Here I follow David Tracy's proposal that theology is foundational in engaging the world, systematic for the church, and pragmatic for Christian life in the world; see his *The Analogical Imagination: Christian Theology and the Culture of Pluralism* (New York: Crossroad, 1981).

34. And as Gavin D'Costa points out, such an authentic pluralism is not only sustainable but is actually the outgrowth of a pneumatological approach to the religions because only the universality of pneumatology enables emphasis to be laid on the particularity and difference of all non-Christian Others ("The Resurrection, the Holy Spirit and the World Religions," in *Resurrection Reconsidered*, ed. Gavin D'Costa [Oxford: Oneworld, 1996], 150–67). Interestingly, D'Costa comes to his conclusions by following out the ecclesiological, evangelistic, missionary implications of the Paraclete pneumatology in John's Gospel.

35. See Paul Griffiths, *An Apology for Apologetics: A Study in the Logic of Interreligious Dialogue* (Maryknoll, N.Y.: Orbis, 1991).

various aesthetic, ethical-moral, cognitive, existential-spiritual, doctrinal/theological, and even religious levels. Without the rational kind of pseudo-certainty engendered by Cartesian foundationalism, there is always the risk that such mutual transformation will result in conversion not only of the non-Christian but also of the Christian at any of these levels. Yet, while possible on the theoretical level, I doubt that interfaith dialogue partners frequently leave their home religious traditions. Instead, their convictions are often deepened precisely because their core beliefs and practices are honed through the crucible of in-depth interpersonal encounter.[36] This said, however, is it too much to hope for the "conversion" of the non-Christian dialogue partner due to the presence and activity of the Holy Spirit in the conversation?

This, I submit, is possible in large part because of the pneumatological assumptions that motivate this kind of theology of religions. A Spirit-inspired evangelical vision is evangelistic and missiological in the best—that is, relational—sense of those terms. More important, it is (as it should be) genuinely humble in its quest for truth, especially since Christians should be among the first to confess their finitude and sinfulness. This approach is thereby open, honest, and sincere in engaging religious others precisely because it recognizes the *imago Dei* and the breath of life in each person, thereby enabling respectful listening, ongoing learning, and spiritual transformation. Christ is lifted up in this encounter precisely because it is the Spirit who accomplishes this through human forms, rather than us taking on this task ourselves. And that, I would submit, is exactly what evangelical Christianity is all about after all.

36. This is suggested also by William Placher, who writes that "to say that other folks are wrong about religion is not necessarily . . . to say that they are damned. . . . [Further,] even while arguing for the essential truth of one's own position, one can acknowledge [because of the fact that the divine mystery is beyond human comprehension and linguistic conceptuality] that the truth one holds is only partial, that others have hold of real truths too, and that one can learn from them in ways that will lead to correcting one's own position. . . . [In addition, as with, for example, J. A. DiNoia (see note 21)] Christians might even hold that some non-Christians best serve the providence of God by continuing to live in their particular non-Christian faiths. . . . [Finally, the special case of Judaism allows us to] recognize that adherents of other religions may well be saved, may well have hold of partial truths on matters where our own truths are partial as well, and may well be serving God's providential purposes in pursuing the depths of their own faiths" (*Narratives of a Vulnerable God: Christ, Theology, and Scripture* [Louisville: Westminster John Knox Press, 1994], 123–25). Whatever else may be said about Placher's latter statements—which, incidentally, are ultimately eschatological claims—it is certainly the case that those seasoned in the interreligious dialogue confirm my main point about what such dialogues have done for them as religious persons; see also the now-classic work by John B. Cobb, Jr., *Beyond Dialogue: Toward a Mutual Transformation of Christianity and Buddhism* (Philadelphia: Fortress Press, 1982).

# Part 2
## Points of Comparison:
## Discipleship and Community

# 3

# Rajah Sulayman
# Was No Water Buffalo

## *Gospel, Anthropology, and Islam*

### MIRIAM ADENEY

Zamboanga. Seen from the harbor, this city mirrors Philippine history. On the left is blue ocean. Then comes brown Rio Hondo, a town of several thousand Muslims who live in bamboo houses on stilts built over the sea. Next, one sees the grey stone Spanish bastion named Fort Pilar, a big coconut drying shed, and petrol silos. Magnificently painted, sail-bedecked Muslim fishing boats, ocean liners, and simple canoes bob in the waves. Sprinkled against the skyline are the domes and crescents of mosques and the spires and crosses of churches. Nearby lies a graveyard with carved wooden boat-of-the-dead figures, a motif dating back to 700 B.C. Pink and red bougainvilleas spill out of window boxes, and submachine guns and rifles dangle from shoulders.

Into this harbor in the 1300s sailed Muslim traders. Over centuries they had migrated down from the Arabian peninsula, through India, through the Malay peninsula, and up through Borneo. Neither warriors nor priests, these businessmen set up shops, often import/export exchanges. They married local women. And they practiced their faith. Locals were drawn to Islam for business connections, marriage connections, and political connections. They were drawn to the sophisticated, complex heritage of Muslim culture: the art, the books, the learning, and the philosophy. They were also drawn, often from animism, to the high concept of God, the ethical teachings, the international brotherhood of believers, and the immutable written Scripture.[1]

By 1571, when Magellan's men arrived, Muslims had spread as far north as Manila. A community leader in that settlement was Rajah Sulayman. Because I have lived in the Philippines, I have chosen Sulayman to represent the sincere Muslim, and I have chosen Muslim-Christian relations in the Philippines to serve as a microcosm of Muslim-Christian relations in general. Sulayman was not an ideal Muslim. Like millions of folk Muslims around the world today, he propitiated spirits. He represents the many whose religion is heartfelt but not pristine.[2] Nor are Filipino Muslim-Christian relations always rosy. Holy wars have ripped through Philippine society, mirroring jihads and armed crusades that have plagued Muslim-Christian encounters elsewhere.[3]

In this context, then, consider Sulayman. From a theological perspective, who is he? Clearly, he is created in the image of God. Clearly, he is a sinner. What more can we say? As a Muslim, is he totally benighted? Is he mired in a demonic slough? Can he discover God through nature and through conscience? If so, how far can he proceed toward God along these paths? And what is the role of Islam on this journey? Is it a bridge? A barrier? An irrelevance? Finally, if somehow Sulayman should experience regeneration through Christ while he is a Muslim, will Islam facilitate his discipleship? Discipleship is a fundamental part of Christian faith and life. Therefore, a Christian theology

---

1. Peter Gordon Gowing, *Muslim Filipinos: Heritage and Horizon* (Quezon City: New Day Publishers, 1979). See also Juanito Bruno, *The Social World of the Tausug* (Manila: Central Escolar University, 1973); Thomas Kiefer, *The Tausug: Violence and Law in a Philippine Moslem Society* (New York: Holt, Rinehart, and Winston, 1972); and "The Maranao Woman," special issue of *Mindanao Art and Culture* (Marawi City: University Research Center, Mindanao State University, 1979).

2. Bill Musk, *The Unseen Face of Islam* (London: MARC, 1989).

3. At this writing, twelve Filipino Christian evangelists are among the captives of the Abu Sayyif movement, a Filipino Muslim group. While the movement's European prisoners gradually are being released, there is no indication that the Abu Sayyif will let their own compatriots go free.

In the adjacent country of Indonesia, Muslims have been burning churches by the hundreds, raping women, and killing Christians in massacres. The fact that some of the Christians are relatively wealthy Indonesian Chinese has exacerbated the tension. In some places, Christians have responded with violence.

of religions must ask not only whether religions promote knowledge of God, or even allow for salvation through Christ, but also whether religions help people to be disciples of Christ.

## Anthropological and Christological Perspectives

> Any attempt to speak without speaking any particular language is not more hopeless than the attempt to have a religion that shall be no religion in particular. . . . Thus every living and healthy religion has a marked idiosyncrasy. Its power consists in its special and surprising message and in the bias which that revelation gives to life. The vistas it opens and the mysteries it propounds are another world to live in; and another world to live in—whether we expect ever to pass wholly over into it or not—is what we mean by having a religion.[4]

Religions are not merely doctrines. They are also lived. Thus, I write about Zamboanga, not disembodied Islam. A religion provides a cognitive map for relating to ultimate questions with coherence and commitment.[5] It includes beliefs and behaviors, experienced individually and communally, and expressed both ideally and imperfectly. Religious behaviors include both sacred rituals and ethically influenced everyday actions. In the life of an individual, a religion might fluctuate between a central and a peripheral role. Each major religion displays denominational, geographical, and generational variety. Sometimes religions overlap, when waves of missionaries of various religions deposit their messages one on top of another. Then people may practice several religions simultaneously.[6] Thus, Sukarno, legendary former president of Indonesia, could say, "I am a Muslim and a Buddhist and a Hindu and a Christian."

I bring anthropological perspective to the discussion, describing religions as parts of cultures. When I move to a Christian theological perspective, I continue to hold the assumption that religions are constructed by humans and reflect their makers. I propose, therefore, a theological approach to religions that is rooted in a theology of human nature.

---

4. George Santayana, *Reason in Religion,* quoted in Clifford Geertz, "Religion as a Cultural System," *The Interpretation of Cultures: Selected Essays by Clifford Geertz* (New York: Basic Books, 1973), 87.

5. See Geertz, "Religion as a Cultural System," for fuller discussion.

6. Of course, such syncretism is anathema to fundamentalists of most religions, who preach against it, and occasionally awaken people to distinctions between one religion and another. Political-religious radicals also accentuate these distinctions, although they do so for political ends. For ordinary adherents, however, although overlapping religions may be inconsistent doctrinally, they are integrated socially, each filling a different niche.

Classic Christian teaching on human nature affirms that humans are created in God's image and that humans are sinners. Religions reflect these polarized truths. On the one hand, religions contain patterns of wisdom, beauty, and caring, results of God's gift of creativity in his image. Therefore, I can learn from non-Christian religions. From Buddhists, for example, I have learned sensitivity to suffering, paradox, and ambiguity. From Confucianists, I have learned the importance of courtesy and the glory of the extended family. Primal religionists remind me that the transcendent supernatural breathes mystery immanently in every part of life, calling forth our awe and our ceremony. Jews encourage me to wrestle with God's world, and even with God himself. Mystics of various traditions inspire me to cultivate spiritual passion. Religious social activists, including Muslims, spur me to sacrifice for justice and righteousness.

On the other hand, since religions are shaped by sinners, the faiths are stained by sin. They seethe with idolatry and exploitation. Like the prophet Elijah on Mount Carmel, Christians are called to confront these idols, beginning with our own. While other religions' idols often appear obvious, our own are more elusive. Yet the ideologies we cherish are riddled with sin. Though the systems or powers of this world are not evil in themselves, since they were created by Christ and are held together in Christ (Col. 1:16), powerful systems can, nevertheless, become evil when they usurp the central place in ordering our values. In cultures greatly influenced by Christianity, such idols may be interwoven with Christian faith and practice.

Consider two examples. Theologian Hendrik Berkhof has described the "pull of the powers" in Germany in the 1930s:

> When Hitler took the helm in Germany in 1933, the powers of Volk, race, and state took a new grip on men. Thousands were grateful, after the confusion of the preceding years, to find their lives again protected from chaos, order and security restored. No one could withhold himself, without utmost effort, from the grasp these Powers had. . . . I myself experienced almost literally how such Powers may be "in the air." . . .
>
> The state, politics, class, social struggle, national interest, public opinion, accepted morality, the ideas of decency, humanity, democracy— these give unity and direction to thousands of lives. Yet precisely by giving unity and direction, they separate these many lives from the true God; they let us believe that we have found the meaning of existence, whereas they really estrange us from true meaning.[7]

Similarly, columnist George Will recently lambasted the worship of individual freedom in America. Freedom is an idol, Will writes. In the

7. Hendrik Berkhof, *Christ and the Powers* (Scottdale, Pa.: Herald Press, 1962), 32.

name of freedom, liberals promote abortion and pornography. In the name of freedom, they prohibit prayer in school or manger scenes on public property. Intriguingly, conservatives worship at the same altar:

> American conservatism's dominant strand shares modern liberalism's celebration of radical autonomy. Society, such conservatism says, is an aggregation of self-interested individuals choosing to associate not for the purpose of acquiring virtue, character and culture, but for liberty and property—security and prosperity. The mass consumption society that is capitalism's crowning success has a privatizing and community-weakening dynamic.[8]

Threads of idolatry and exploitation are woven through the fabrics of cultures and religions, as Berkhof and Will have illustrated. Even good values get bent. Since Islam has a number of admirable characteristics, this has special relevance. When *anything* exalts itself above the Lord Jesus Christ, Christians condemn it. When faced with *other* people's idols, however, they should not be hasty. Humility is called for, as well as a teachable spirit and a passion to learn from and work under indigenous leaders.

How, then, shall we encompass this tension in the world's religions between beauty and ugliness, sin and glory? Writing about culture in general, H. Richard Niebuhr observed that some Christians overemphasize the gifts of God's common grace evident in the patterns of culture. They condone and conform to the culture too much. Others overemphasize the patterns of idolatry and exploitation, and condemn too much.[9] The same is true with regard to religions. By contrast, a dynamic balance between radical critique and radical affirmation is better, rooted in a Christian theology of human nature.

A variety of evangelical approaches to world religions has enriched this model.

### Essential Error

Some theologians see truth so mixed with error in non-Christian religions as to make them of little value. Religions follow a cycle of "sin, repression and suppression, substitution, and more sin," according to Samuel Schlorff:

> Islam provides a perfect illustration. . . . The Quranic view of God, especially in its doctrine of absolute transcendence, cuts the Muslim off from the knowledge of God that he or she has by means of general revelation, and from a saving knowledge of Christ. God appears to be so distant, es-

---

8. George Will, "Making the World Safe for Filthy Lyrics," *Seattle Post-Intelligencer,* 15 September 2000, sec. B, p. 6.

9. H. Richard Niebuhr, *Christ and Culture* (New York: Harper & Row, 1951).

sentially unknown and unknowable, and the Trinity in unity impossible, because Islam has repressed the truth about God and substituted for it untruth. Islam has also repressed and suppressed the truth about ourselves . . . which we have received through general revelation. It attributes our separation from God and our sinful human condition to God's transcendence, and not our sin, and considers our present condition to be normal rather than abnormal. The Quran teaches that we are basically good and able to do the good; we are just weak.[10]

Following Karl Barth and Hendrik Kraemer, Schlorff sees a chasm between man's thoughts and God's, an absolute qualitative difference.[11] The gospel "falls from above like a stone into the water"[12] whereas—changing the metaphor—religions are "all *eros* steaming up, no *agape* darting down," in the words of C. S. Lewis. Religions are skewed. They are incorrigibly misdirected. They represent resistance rather than response. As a result:

the Quran and Islamic culture cannot be considered as neutral vehicles that may be used as a contextual or theological starting point, or source of truth, and filled with Christian meanings. These are used only as a communicational starting point to help the receptors connect to the biblical message.[13]

From a strictly theological point of view, there is no point within Islam that offers an unripe truth that can be simply taken over and utilized as a basis for Christian witness.[14]

*Stages of Truth*

Other theologians view religions much more positively. Religions contain ethical truth if not saving truth. The partial glimpses of God provided by various religions are like stages on the pilgrimage up Mount Fuji, according to Toyohiko Kagawa. Each rest stop yields a different vista.[15]

10. Samuel Schlorff, "The Translational Model for Mission in Resistant Muslim Society: A Critique and an Alternative," *Missiology* 28, no. 3 (July 2000): 319.
11. See Hendrik Kraemer, *The Christian Message in a Non-Christian World* (Grand Rapids: Kregel, 1956).
12. John Seamands, *Tell It Well: Communicating the Gospel across Cultures* (Kansas City: Beacon Hill Press, 1981), 45.
13. Schlorff, "Translational Model," 321.
14. J. H. Bavinck, *Introduction to the Science of Missions*, trans. David H. Freeman (Grand Rapids: Baker, 1960), 140.
15. Toyohiko Kagawa, quoted in Gerald Anderson, ed., *The Theology of the Christian Mission* (New York: McGraw-Hill, 1962), 146–47.

Christian faith "comprehends" and "fulfills" all the partial truths found in the other religions, while at the same time purging them from their errors and supplementing them with truths and values that they do not in themselves possess. In them, we see "broken lights," in the gospel, the full radiance of God's glory. This means that, much as Jesus came long ago "not to abolish the law and the prophets . . . but to fulfill them" (Matt. 5:17), so his gospel comes today to the laws and prophets of other religions.[16]

### Christ in World Religions

Still other theologians would go further and speak of "anonymous Christians" who have not heard the gospel and who would not identify themselves as Christians. Nevertheless, since Christ is omnipresent, and since it is his work that saves, the faith that people express within their own religions may be accepted by Christ.

> Christ is the only mediator, but he is not the monopoly of Christians and, in fact, he is present and effective in any authentic religion, whatever the form or the name, of the ever-transcending but equally ever-humanly immanent mystery. . . . The means of salvation are to be found in any authentic religion.[17]

By directing their adherents' attention to ultimate concerns and providing vehicles for reaching out to the transcendent, religions enable people to reach out to Christ, however unwittingly.

16. Seamands, *Tell It Well*, 43. This is taken further by J. N. Farquhar in *The Crown of Hinduism* (London: Oxford University Press, 1930), 45. Arguing that Christianity fulfills the Hindu scriptures, family system, asceticism, caste, and worship of idols, Farquhar exults, "Christ provides the fulfillment of the highest aspirations of Hinduism. . . . He is the Crown of the Faith of India."

17. Raimundo Panikkar, "The Rules of the Game," in *Mission Trends No. 5: Faith Meets Faith*, ed. Gerald Anderson et al. (Grand Rapids: Eerdmans, 1981), 122. See also idem, *The Unknown Christ of Hinduism* (London: Darton, Longman, and Todd, 1968).

Scripture texts offering support for universal salvation have been collated by Paul Sorrentino in an unpublished paper, "What Can We Know about the Salvation of the Unreached?" (April 2000). His research is rooted in John Sanders, *No Other Name: An Investigation into the Destiny of the Unevangelized* (Vancouver: Regent College Publishing, 1999). Sorrentino organizes scriptural support for this position in five categories:

1. God desires to save all humankind (1 Tim. 2:4; 4:10; 2 Peter 3:9).

2. Christ's atonement is unlimited (2 Cor. 5:19; Titus 2:11; Heb. 2:9; 1 John 2:2).

3. Just as all people participate in Adam's sin, so all people will come to participate in the Second Adam's righteousness (John 10:16; 12:32; Rom. 5:12–19; 9:22–23; 11:32; Col. 1:16, 20).

4. When God's salvation finally is consummated, all in creation will be restored and all people saved (Acts 3:19–21; 1 Cor. 15:22–28; Phil. 2:9–11).

5. Passages that seem to indicate damnation and separation are recognized and explained in a few different ways (Matt. 25:46; Mark 3:29; 1 Cor. 1:18; 2 Thess. 1:9; 2:9–11). The larger number of texts in the above four categories overrides the few passages that seem to communicate damnation.

### Sincere Seekers Will See

Some theologians would affirm the act of reaching while minimizing the particular religious avenue. If people seek after God, it is because God's grace is drawing them. Those persons' sincerity will be evident on judgment day, when they recognize Christ and worship him in joy.[18] A religion's role in this seeking is ambivalent. It may be either bridge or barrier.

### Christ in Movements That Liberate

Liberation theologians remind us that the God of creation, the exodus, and the cross is the source of freedom. He sets people free. Where people work for freedom and justice, Christ is present. By contrast, some religious groups, indeed some Christian groups, are constricting rather than freeing. Such groups are far from the true Spirit of Christ. One is most likely to meet Christ in a freedom movement.[19]

### Sincere Seekers Will Hear

J. Robertson McQuilkin, who holds a position close to Schlorff and Herman Bavinck, maintains that it is not enough to respond to an unknown God. Acts 4:12 is a key text: "Salvation is found in no one else, for there is no other name under heaven given to men by which we must be saved" (NIV). The word *name* indicates Jesus in his particularity. McQuilkin suggests that those who respond to the light that they have received eventually *will* hear the gospel. They will be given more light. This is a process with many steps, a dynamic interchange. "The repeated promise of additional light to those who obey the light they have is a basic and very important biblical truth concerning God's justice and judgment."[20]

In a broad sense, nearly all Christian theologians of religion would agree that God communicates to people in all cultures and religions through nature (Psalm 19), conscience (Romans 2), and dreams and vi-

18. Clark Pinnock, *A Wideness in God's Mercy: The Finality of Jesus Christ in a World of Religions* (Grand Rapids: Zondervan, 1992), 172.

19. Concluding a lengthy review of diverse liberation theologians, the venerable Orlando Costas says, "Salvation is viewed . . . as political liberation. . . . Christ is said to be found present in all mankind [cf. the thesis that "Christ is the neighbor" developed by Gustavo Gutierrez in his seminal book *Theology of Liberation* (Maryknoll, N.Y.: Orbis, 1972), 194]. Conversion takes place only in relation to one's commitment to the transformation of human reality, while the future can only be perceived in relation to the historical now. . . . The future kingdom exists to the extent that there is hope, and hope can only emerge from the now, from one's commitment to historical praxis" (*The Church and Its Mission: A Shattering Critique from the Third World* [Wheaton: Tyndale, 1974], 237).

20. Robertson McQuilkin, "Lost," in *Perspectives on the World Christian Movement: A Reader*, ed. Ralph Winter and Steven Hawthorne (Pasadena, Calif.: William Carey Library, 1999), 159. See Matthew 13:10–16; Mark 4:21–25; Acts 10.

sions (Acts 10). For the most part these phenomena are outside the sphere of specific religions. Theologians differ, however, when it comes to the question of whether a faith such as Islam is a bridge or a barrier to knowing God.

The model proposed in this paper allows for both and is rooted in classic theology of human nature.

## Does Islam Lead to God in Jesus?

Doctrinally and socially, a gulf yawns between Sulayman and the Christian faith. Consider the Islamic teachings that Jesus is not God, that Jesus did not die on the cross nor rise from the dead, that the biblical revelation has been corrupted, that humans are not so much sinful as ignorant and undisciplined, that salvation rests on keeping the precepts in the context of the sovereign will of God, that Muhammad is the greatest of the prophets, and that Islam deserves total loyalty in all spheres of life. Christians and Muslims turn toward different holy cities, celebrate different holy seasons, and are repelled by opposed histories of persecution and domination.

Nevertheless, Christians share much with Sulayman in their understanding of God, Christ, the world, human nature, the community of faith, prayer, and Scripture. In doctrine, Christians are closer to Jews and Muslims than to any other believers. With Muslim mystics, Christians share a longing for true spirituality. With Muslim political radicals, they hunger for justice and righteousness in society. Below are four areas in which much is shared.

### God

"A man without a sense of worship is like a water buffalo listening to an orchestra," say the Muslims of Java, just a few island hops to the south. Sulayman is no buffalo. He has a profound awareness of God the single Creator, Sustainer of the universe, Culminator of history, all-powerful, and holy. Sulayman encounters God through nature, Scripture, prophets, and the community of faith.

It is true that Sulayman's God would never lower himself to take on human form, much less to die for humans. Still, Muslim-background believers usually do not speak of coming to a new God when they meet God in Jesus. Rather, they feel that the One whom they worshiped in ignorance, inaccurately and incompletely, now has become their personal Father. They feel completed.[21]

21. This observation is based on the author's personal conversations with Muslim-background believers and missionaries who have worked with them.

## Human Nature

Adam and Eve were commissioned to be God's managers, or *khalifa*. Humans hold delegated authority to care for the earth and develop it. Islam does not agree, to be sure, that humans are created in God's image. "Orthodox belief is that man has no God-likeness. God breathing into man His spirit is explained by some scholars as the faculty of God-like knowledge and will, which if rightly used gives man superiority over all creation."[22] God simply is too transcendent, too totally other, to share his image.

The appropriate human response to such an awesome God is submission and worship, such as that of Rabia, a seventh-century Muslim mystic, who prayed:

> O Lord, if I worship You from fear of hell, burn me there
> And if in hope of paradise, exclude me from that
> But if for Your own sake, then withhold not from me Your eternal beauty.[23]

In an ideal construct, Sulayman is a man of prayer, worshiping his Creator five times a day. In theory, at least, Sulayman stands with Christians against idolatry and spiritism. He also stands with them against atheism. If he were alive today, he would want to discuss the integration of science and faith and how to raise godly children in the face of MTV and Internet pornography. He would welcome worshipful discussion of God's attributes.[24]

## Jesus

For Sulayman, Jesus is one of the greatest of the Muslim prophets. His birth was unique, comparable only to Adam's. His end was unique: He is the only man in history who never died, according to traditional interpretations. He will play a key role at the final judgment. He is mentioned in ninety-three verses in the Qur'an, generally with reverence. Titles awarded to Jesus in the Qur'an include prophet, messenger, ser-

22. Badru Katerrega and David Shenk, *Islam and Christianity: A Muslim and a Christian in Dialogue* (Nairobi: Uzima Press, 1980), 15.

23. Quoted in Kenneth Cragg, *The House of Islam* (Encino, Calif.: Dickenson Publishing, 1975), 68.

24. I am writing this on September 23, 2000, the "National Day" of the Kingdom of Saudi Arabia. When I opened my newspaper in Seattle this morning, I saw a quarter-page advertisement extolling that nation's progress. It began with this line: "In the last thirty years, the Kingdom of Saudi Arabia has, with the help of God, successfully undertaken a development programme of unique dimensions." Surely this humble, central acknowledgment of God in daily life may be a stepping-stone for the gospel.

vant, sign, witness, example, mercy, spirit of God, word of God, and, eleven times, Messiah, anointed princely messenger.[25]

Yet Jesus is not God. How could God become a baby, crying and colicky, diapered and nursed? How could the Ultimate become a point in time? How could he take on the features of a particular race? To say Jesus is God is the highest blasphemy, *shirk*, "making something like God."

### The Spirit World

Sulayman is Muslim to the core. He affirms the above doctrines fervently when he hears them. Yet if he is a typical Muslim Filipino, he may not hear them very often. This dichotomy was noted in a classic essay by Peter Gowing, "How Muslim Are the Muslim Filipinos?":

> It is possible to point to Muslims elsewhere in the world who are better informed about the Quran and the Hadith and the prescriptions of the Shariah than are most Muslim Filipinos. Doubtless Muslim groups can be found elsewhere whose faith in Allah, the Merciful and Compassionate, is less compounded with the worship of spirits and whose Islamic rituals and customs are less mixed with *adat* (customary law) than is the case with Muslim Filipinos. Certainly there are some Muslim groups elsewhere who are more faithful to the Five Pillars than the general run of Muslim Filipinos. But from the standpoint of their "disposition to be Muslim," their emotional and psychological allegiance to Islam as they understand it, there are no people on earth more Muslim than the Muslim Filipinos.[26]

Sulayman is likely to be preoccupied with spirits such as *diwatas, tonongs, hantus, salindagao, damipayag, lagtaw, balbalan,* and *Mangalit.* Although the prophet Muhammad inveighed against spirit worship, Allah remains distant from ordinary individual needs. Therefore,

25. Geoffrey Parrinder, *Jesus in the Quran* (New York: Oxford University Press, 1977).

26. Peter Gowing, "How Muslim Are the Muslim Filipinos?" *Solidarity* 4 (1969): 21–42. Consider this further example. One of the biggest groups of Filipino Muslims, the Maguindanao, enjoy all-night song debates called *dayang-dayangs.* The performers are two women and a man, or two men and a woman. The story line is a heroic, romantic narrative. Several years ago a group of Maguindanao returned from Egypt, where they had been studying on Egyptian scholarships. They came home charged with zeal to reform Filipino Islam. One of their targets was the *dayang-dayangs.* Men and women performing together? Romantic content? This is worse than pornographic movies, they said. Foreigners make those movies. That's not our fault. But we Maguindanao make the *dayang-dayangs.* Did they persuade their fellows to abandon the song debates? Not at all. Even when an imam was called in to mediate, he supported the song debates, remarking witheringly, "Allah revealed himself to the Arabs precisely because the Arabs were so wicked. Islamization is not Arabization."

like fifty million folk Muslims, when Sulayman gets sick he arranges a curing ceremony to bargain with the spirits. When he plants rice, when he harvests it, when he cuts down a tree, or when he names a baby, he propitiates spirits. In such a context, the Muslim preacher, the *khatib*, is low in the religious hierarchy. More significant is the *imam*, who leads prayers, and the pagan healer, who mediates with spirits.

Christians share with Sulayman an awareness of supernatural realities and spiritual battles. In Old Testament times, the prophet Elijah challenged the prophets of Baal. In advance, he drew on the power of Christ, who died to conquer the powers of evil, the powers that exalt themselves against God. In the 1980s, a Muslim-background Filipino, a Samal, dared to challenge local spirit powers in a contest. This began with a healing. It expanded to other areas of culture. The result was a rare "people movement" of Filipino Muslims to faith in Jesus Christ.

Given these differences and commonalities, two questions resonate: Is it *possible* for Sulayman to come to Christ as a Muslim? And will Islam *facilitate* that encounter? There is documentary evidence that many Muslims have come to know God in Christ through hearing or reading the Bible, through the lives and words of Christians, or through dreams and visions.[27] It is conceivable that Muslim understandings of God, human nature, Christ, the spirit realm, and other religious elements may have facilitated these pilgrimages. Such components of Islam may have been stepping-stones to faith in Christ.

Traditionally, however, Muslim teachings impede this pilgrimage. If Jesus is not God and did not die and rise, the gospel is thwarted. God in his grace does indeed bring people to new life in Christ while they are practicing Muslims. Yet as the next section will argue, Islam is not a context that promotes long-term spiritual health and growth.

## Does Islam Nurture Disciples of Jesus?

"All authority in heaven and on earth has been given to me. Therefore go and make disciples of all nations, baptizing . . . and teaching . . . and surely I am with you always, to the very end of the age" (Matt. 28:18–20 NIV).

If, as David Bosch asserts, the entire first Gospel points to and, in fact, springs from Jesus' final commission,[28] then a truly Christian the-

27. Miriam Adeney, "Why Muslim Women Come to Christ," in *Longing to Call Them Sisters*, ed. Frances Love et al. (Pasadena, Calif.: William Carey Publishers, 2000); and Jean-Maria Gaudeul, *Called from Islam to Christ: Why Muslims Become Christians* (London: Monarch Books, 1999).

28. David Bosch, *Transforming Mission: Paradigm Shifts in Theology of Mission* (Maryknoll, N.Y.: Orbis, 1991), 56–80.

ology of religion must ask, Is Islam conducive to discipleship? Does it foster growth toward maturity in Christ (Eph. 4:14–16)? Does it help people "rightly divide the Word" (2 Tim. 2:15)? If discipling is central in our Lord's last words, a Christian theology of religion surely must ask whether religions enhance discipleship of Christ.

Not only is discipling mandated biblically, it is urgent at this time. Superficiality infects Jesus' followers worldwide. "African Christianity is a mile wide and an inch deep," says Tokunboh Adeyemo, director of the Africa Evangelical Association. Much the same could be said of North American Christianity. Merely to name the name of Christ, however sincerely, is an incomplete, unbalanced, and ultimately unhealthy version of religion. Christ's followers are called to "grow up into him" (Eph. 4:15).

Can this occur inside Islam? At present, a ferment bubbles among evangelical missionaries regarding whether Muslim-background believers ought to stay within Islam. An article first published in a Southern Baptist newsletter, titled "Of 'Jesus Mosques' and 'Muslim Christians,'" observes:

> In one Muslim nation, more than 100,000 Muslims reportedly worship Jesus as Messiah in 100-plus mosques. Some "Jesus mosques" start from scratch. Others are traditional mosques transformed by Muslims who embrace Jesus as Lord. In still other cases, individual followers of Christ remain in typical mosques, quietly worshiping God as they seek to be "salt and light" among Muslims.[29]

The article goes beyond advocating the use of familiar forms so people will understand and appreciate what is shared. This position extends to supporting Muslim religious institutions.

Should Muslim-background believers call themselves Muslims? Should they worship in mosques? Should the Qur'an be cited positively in apologetics? In this discussion, fine lines have been drawn.[30] A friend who has forty years of experience sharing the gospel with Muslims says he never affirms the Qur'an as authoritative, yet he often starts a study session with Muslims with its stories, such as those of Abraham, Joseph, David, and Jesus.

29. Erich Bridges, "Of 'Jesus Mosques' and 'Muslim Christians,'" *Mission Frontiers Bulletin* (July 1997): 19–22. For reasons of security, specific details remain shrouded in secrecy. Reports are word of mouth, and verification rests with the credibility of the reporter.

30. For a brief history and critique of the positive use of the Qur'an (and Qur'anic style Bible translations) in Christian apologetics, see Schlorff, "Translational Model," 306–11.

"Hindu Christians" and "Buddhist Christians" face similar issues. Consider Hindus. Ralph Winter, founder of the U.S. Center for World Mission, wrote in *Mission Frontiers* (1994), "The Hindu world is the most perverted, most monstrous, most implacable, demonic-invaded part of this planet. . . . The perversion of Satan in this part of the world is absolutely legendary."[31] Hindu web sites picked this up, and a great outcry resulted. Subsequently, Winter and his publisher retracted what he had written. Winter says now:

> I have heard reports in the last five years that there are probably more de-vout followers of Christ in India who still consider themselves Hindus than the total number of equally devout followers of Christ who call themselves Christians.[32]

In the same vein, Joseph D'Souza, director of Operation Mobiliza-tion of India, observes:

> "Hindu" is a cultural as well as a religious term. Hindu culture has great things going for it, even as it has elements that need to be redeemed by the gospel. What Christians have traditionally attacked represents large elements of classical Hinduism and Brahminism—such as God being im-personal, the caste system, etcetera. However there are other systems that allow for a personalized, incarnated God . . . which allows for *bhakti* (worship). This has become a great bridge builder to millions of people who are favorable and responsive to the gospel.[33]

As for the "Muslim-Christian" question, Samuel Schlorff and Dean Gilliland debated this issue in a pair of articles in the July 2000 issue of *Missiology,* the official journal of the American Society of Missiology.[34] Each spokesman represents a host of active practitioners and a great body of discussion. Each debater has contributed decades of excellent practice and theory. Yet neither's position is fully satisfactory, in the view of this writer. Schlorff's perceptive observations have enriched this chapter at numerous points. Regrettably, however, his overall po-sition seems unduly anti-creational, anti-cultural, and anti-incarna-tional. Gilliland, on the other hand, leans too much on pragmatic and mystical arguments. God does indeed work in all sorts of contexts, as

31. Ralph Winter, quoted by Stan Guthrie, "Sticks and Stones: Christians Examine Role of Rhetoric in India Violence," *World Pulse* (21 January 2000): 2.
32. Ibid.
33. Joseph D'Souza, quoted in ibid.
34. Schlorff, "Translational Model"; and Dean Gilliland, "Modeling the Incarnation for Muslim People: A Response to Sam Schlorff," *Missiology* 28, no. 3 (July 2000): 329–40.

Gilliland demonstrates. Yet Gilliland limits his positive examples to conversions, rather than going on to show mature disciples or churches. If making disciples is part of the core of Christian faith and life, Gilliland's position falls short.

It is disappointment with the level of this debate—and the larger discussion it represents—that has generated some of the emphases in this chapter, including the focus on discipling. As long as evangelicals remain fixated on the question of whether someone can be "saved" through another religion, our theology of religions will remain superficial. After all, who knows what God's Spirit does or does not do in human hearts? But if we enlarge the question to whether someone can grow up to maturity in Christ in another religious context, whether someone can become a full-fledged disciple of Christ while worshiping in another faith, then the limitation of other religions and the value of missionary work become clearer.

Does Islam facilitate discipleship? I suggest that Islam impedes discipleship in doctrinal, communal, and sacramental areas.

### Doctrines

In Islam, God's grace extends only as far as creation and revelation, never stretching to incarnation nor crucifixion. As a prophet, Jesus is subordinate to Muhammad, "the seal of the prophets." As Scripture, the Bible is subordinate to the Qur'an, the final and unadulterated message. The suffering servant motif is absent altogether.[35] Nor is that motif necessary, since the human condition is not sin but ignorance and lack of training in righteousness. At their best, Muslims are like Saul of Tarsus, a "Pharisee of the Pharisees," rich in religion but naked in the presence of grace. The very excellence of Islam's theology and moral standards gives rise to an alternate object of loyalty, a religious system that stands against Christ as Lord.

Thus, while Jesus and the Bible are honored in Islam, the context is not conducive to growth as a disciple. A follower of Jesus continually must struggle with twisted doctrines. Schlorff, John Wilder, and Charles Kraft have suggested heterodoxies likely to occur in "Muslim churches." Wilder states:

> As to doctrine, the movement's Muslim orientation might lead it, among the more likely possibilities, to some form of retreat from the doctrine of the Trinity; a deemphasizing or "explaining" of Christ's Sonship, perhaps

35. Although the suffering servant motif is absent among Sunnis, the largest body of Muslims, it is present among Shiites when they commemorate the "passion of Hussein." This Muslim leader was the Prophet Muhammad's grandson. He died in battle and is seen as one who gave his life for the faith and the faithful.

through a device such as Adoptionism; a denial of Christ's true death; an acceptance of the inspiration of only those parts of Scripture they found most acceptable, such as the Pentateuch, the Psalms and the Gospels; and the discarding of one or both sacraments, retaining circumcision, possibly as a substitute for baptism.[36]

"Probably a more distant concept of God than we are familiar with in the West would tend to be fatalistic and legalistic."[37]

Even without doctrinal skewing, the isolated believer or home group would have little opportunity for theological education, for digging deep into the great themes of the faith, such as God, creation, community, stewardship, Christ, incarnation, atonement, redemption, resurrection, reconciliation, regeneration, the Holy Spirit, and heaven.

### Community

If doctrines matter, so does community. Disciples are not lone rangers. Relationship is at the heart of the doctrine of God. A call to unity is at the heart of Christ's teaching. A call to fellowship is at the heart of the doctrine of the church. A corporate life also is at the heart of the Muslim concept of the ummah, the believing community. Muslims do not pray in a closet but practice the precepts in the public square. Daily corporate prayers; an annual month-long fast (with feasting at night); recitation of the creed in unison in the mosque on Fridays; a once-in-a-lifetime pilgrimage to the holy city of Mecca if one is healthy enough and wealthy enough; religious and social celebrations commemorating Abraham's offering of his son, the prophet Muhammad's birthday, the end of the fast, and the return from pilgrimage; a religious tax for the poor; and the conviction that church and state should not be separate, that law should be based on theology, all make faith a social experience. Acting out the faith together satisfies one of the deepest human needs, according to the Muslim—the need to be trained, formed, shaped in righteous patterns.

How profoundly Muslim-background believers yearn for inclusion in the people of Christ! They long for brothers and sisters. They ache to be members of that great company of faith that has stretched down through the ages. Aisha came to Christ twelve years ago and has been an active evangelical. Now she is considering becoming a nun. The sisterhood's *community* attracts her, as well as its order, zeal, and intelli-

36. John W. Wilder, "Some Reflections on Possibilities for People Movements among Muslims," *Missiology* (July 1977): 311–12.

37. Schlorff, "Translational Model," 310, summarizing Charles Kraft, "Psychological Stress Factors among Muslims," *Media in Islamic Culture*, ed. C. R. Shumaker (Clearwater, Fla.: International Christian Broadcasters, 1974), 142.

gent service. Christians dare not bring a gospel of individualism. They must bring a gospel of kingdom community.

Admittedly, some Muslim-background believers must fellowship discreetly, given laws against apostasy and their particular stations in life. Fellowship may involve two or three believers gathering together at irregular junctures. The apostle Paul's words apply here. "Are you a slave? Don't let that worry you—but of course, if you get a chance to be free, take it" (1 Cor. 7:21 TLB).

In fact, a slight break with historic Christianity may be warranted. It is not only Muslim treatment of apostates that limits believers' fellowship with other Christians. It is also the history of the Western Christian Church. This, after all, was the source of the Crusades. Western Christians continue to be the source of much Zionist, anti-Palestinian rhetoric. Therefore, some Muslim-background believers cannot bear to be known as "Christians." They call themselves followers of Jesus.

Certainly, Muslim-background believers' discipleship will not look precisely like its Western counterpart. Western theology and mission practice reflect Western values. "Managerial missiology," for example, causes concern to non-Western believers. Quantification, speed, efficiency, and goal achievement sometimes trample worship, relationships, willingness to suffer, mystery, and beauty. Poverty, political oppression, and ethnic tensions tend to be overlooked by Western theologians. Muslim-background believers must enter into these realities carefully.

Yet whatever form it takes, discipleship will need community. It is true that the Muslim world is salted with lone believers, Nicodemuses and Esthers who read Bible portions quietly by themselves or, if they lack those, simply sit regularly in the presence of the Lord. But religion is more than what happens within oneself. Religion requires relationships. To pass the faith to the next generation requires a vital community.[38] And Islam itself clearly cannot provide a Christian the community she needs.

38. While recognizing that God may save people in all sorts of religious contexts, Norman Anderson nevertheless recommends solid proclamation of the gospel. "If we ask ourselves what enabled us to give up trying to save ourselves and to throw ourselves on God for salvation, the answer will almost certainly be the message of the gospel. So it is imperative that we should give others the same opportunity. Yet again, those who find forgiveness (without solid gospel teaching) may sadly lack assurance, and will almost certainly lack a message they can pass on to others or the joy and victory that a knowledge of the risen Christ alone can give. How, then, can we withhold from them the full truth as it is in Jesus?" ("Christianity and the World's Religions," in *The Expositor's Bible Commentary*, ed. Frank Gaebelein [Grand Rapids: Zondervan, 1979], 156).

*Sacraments*

Doctrinally and communally, Islam impedes Muslim-background believers' growth as Christ's disciples. Even more, Islam resists the Christian sacraments. Baptism, in particular, marks a watershed. It may be possible for a Muslim to tolerate a family member's worship of Jesus, who is, after all, one of the greatest of the Muslim prophets. In a religion that advocates making pilgrimages to saints' tombs, Jesus may be seen as one more saint. But baptism is not tolerable. Baptism marks departure from Islam to Christendom. Baptism waves the red flag of apostasy.

Yet believers yearn for it. When I was in the Muslim region of the Philippines several years ago, a woman evangelist asked me, "Ma'am, should women baptize?" Half-Muslim by birth, Yasmin had spoken widely of her faith in Christ. Now she cared for small congregations in four rural Muslim communities. Where she worked, foreign missionaries rarely were permitted. Few Filipino pastors had the connections, sustained interest, time, money, and courage to come. Year after year, therefore, believers went unbaptized. Their need echoed poignantly when Yasmin stared at me with fiery black eyes that had flashed through many an apologetic debate and, like Jacob wrestling, would not let me go. "Ma'am, should women baptize?"

Half a world away, Saulati, who grew up in a strong Muslim family in East Africa, came to Christ as a graduate student at the University of British Columbia. After she believed, she grew as Christ's disciple. Several of us who knew her asked each other, "Should she be baptized?" But none of us broached the subject. She took the initiative two months before she went home. In a semiprivate ceremony in a church, she was baptized, tears running down her face. Six months after she went home, she was dead. I believe that when she went to her baptism, she was preparing for her death. She hoped it would be many years in the future. Whenever it came, however, she wanted to die as a baptized believer. And she did. Baptism matters.

## Sulayman's Way

Is Islam a nurturing context for discipling Muslim-background believers, the discipling that the gospel requires? No. In doctrine, in community, and in sacrament, it is difficult to grow as Christ's disciple while remaining within Islam. Positively, Islam does contain God-given patterns of wisdom, beauty, and caring. In these we take joy. Sadly, Islam also contains creedal and social structures that systematically turn people from Christ, that defraud people from a relationship with their Lord.

There is, however, at least one more thing to say. As a Western theologian, I have a responsibility to articulate the entire gospel clearly, courteously, and contextually. Yet my grasp of the gospel is provisional. Western theology is not neutral but is influenced by specific philosophical and political histories and contexts. Thus, I must learn from Muslim-background believers.

While working in Mali several years ago, I met Pastor Abdul Maiga. His region is over 99 percent Muslim. In the year before we met, Pastor Maiga's congregation of sixty had shared the gospel with two thousand local Muslims who had received the message without animosity. Pastor Maiga models a teachable spirit. He counsels his people, "Each person has different needs. So consider the individual's context and listen to him. It is not a waste of time to spend one hour listening to a Muslim leader. If necessary, you listen for one month, two months, three, four, five, maybe six months. Finally, everybody runs dry. Then you can talk."

This kind of teacher will nurture disciples.

In Zamboanga one Sunday, I picked my way over arching split-bamboo walkways to worship with thirty Muslim-background Samals who had been baptized the year before. As we sang, boats glided past our bamboo house church perched over the water. Babies toddled on the unfenced, gaping walkways. Fresh-caught tropical fish were fanned out on narrow wooden slat sidewalk markets. Men squatted along platforms, rattling dice. In the wealthier houses, hardwood floors and intricately carved furniture gleamed. And, yes, TVs chattered. Not far away, the civil war between the government and Muslim guerillas continued. Even though I wore contact lenses, I took my glasses to church, just in case I was kidnapped. Foreigners routinely were taken for ransom to finance the war.

In this setting, we worshiped. The sermon was in the Samal language. Our communion food was Coke and white bread. Well-rounded systematic teaching was weak but improving. Most members had experienced Christ's power, often through healing. Some might say, "I am Christian." Some might say, "I am Muslim." But all of them knew that Jesus is the way, the truth, and the life, and no one comes to the Father except through him.

# 4

# The Universality of the "Jesus-Story" and the "Incredulity toward Metanarratives"

## STANLEY J. GRENZ

Lieutenant Worf, officer on the starship *Enterprise*, was uncharacteristically late for duty on the bridge. When his concerned colleagues burst into his quarters, they found the Klingon seated on the floor engaging in an ancient religious ritual. During his subsequent visit to the delinquent crew member, Captain Jean-Luc Picard determined that Worf's behavior was tied to a recent incident in which Worf was reconnected with his cultural heritage, including the religious stories of his people. The wise captain then placed Worf on leave and ordered him to travel to a nearby planet with the instruction that he immerse himself in Klingon beliefs in order "to discover if they can hold any truth" for him.

Picard's response to Worf in this installment of *Star Trek: The Next Generation* (1993) reflects an important aspect of contemporary Western society, namely, a widespread commitment to a particular type of cultural pluralism. At the heart of this postmodern outlook is the assumption that the world consists of a variety of cultural communities, each of which has its own set of narratives that provides the basis for its unique understanding of the cosmos and of life within the cosmos.

85

The narratives and the corresponding outlook of any given society have validity within that community. At the same time, the belief structure of a specific society cannot claim universal applicability, nor can any particular community-based outlook expect to carry universal appeal.

Christians claim that God's action in Christ is intended for all people. According to Christian teaching, the purposes of the God of the Bible overflow the boundaries of nation, language, culture, and religion, and these purposes are uniquely revealed in Jesus of Nazareth, who is the Christ. Hence, Christians proclaim a faith that arises out of a "scandal of particularity," that is, the belief that the eternal reality of God (or eternal truth) is disclosed in one historical human life. As a consequence, Christianity is inherently a missionary religion.

Although all Christian traditions reflect the missionary impulse to some extent, evangelicals are the bearers of the Christian claim to universality-in-particularity in a special way. From its beginning, the evangelical movement has been characterized by a global-oriented evangelistic fervor, to the extent that David Bebbington cites the missionary spirit as one of evangelicalism's defining characteristics.[1] This missionary zeal is motivated in part by the convertive piety that lies at the heart of the evangelical conception of the faith.[2] Their emphasis on personal regeneration as constituting the heart of the gospel message imbues evangelicals with a commitment to the task of evangelizing the entire world. To this end, evangelicals proclaim to people everywhere the message of the new birth, the good news of a personal salvation that they believe God intends for all people. In short, evangelicals are convinced that the biblical narrative, which focuses on the life, death, resurrection, and ascension of Jesus of Nazareth together with the sending of the Holy Spirit, is not just one more local story intended for a particular (Christian) "tribe." Instead, they maintain that it embodies the story of all humankind and, as a result, that the Jesus-narrative is for all.

At first glance, it would appear that belief in the universality of the Jesus-story places evangelicals in inevitable conflict with the postmodern commitment to cultural pluralism. How, then, can evangelicals maintain the claim to universality that lies at the heart of their faith in the midst of a pluralistic world? In other words, how does the Jesus-

1. Bebbington describes the missionary spirit as "activism." See David Bebbington, *Evangelicalism in Modern Britain: A History from the 1730s to the 1980s* (Grand Rapids: Baker, 1989), 2–3, 10–12.

2. For an explication and defense of this conjecture, see Stanley J. Grenz, *Revisioning Evangelical Theology: A Fresh Agenda for the Twenty-first Century* (Downers Grove, Ill.: InterVarsity Press, 1993), 21–35.

story fit—if at all—within a context characterized by "incredulity toward metanarratives"?

This essay attempts to respond to this question by proposing that the
Jesus-story embodies a particular vision of God's goal for all humankind and, hence, a particular understanding of the fullness of community, the quest for which Christians find embedded in other religious
narratives as well. The theocentric character of the Jesus-story provides the key to affirming its universality in the midst of the contemporary incredulity toward metanarratives. To set forth this thesis, the
essay looks first at the contemporary intellectual shift away from an
all-encompassing historical narrative. The second section engages with
the central characteristics of the metanarrative that Christians tell.
This leads finally to a constructive proposal for a Christian theology of
the religions and, hence, for an articulation of the universality of the
Jesus-story that seeks to take seriously the postmodern suspicion of
metanarratives.

## The Rise and Demise of the Metanarrative

In a context imbued with the pluralist spirit, any attempt to articulate an overarching or global "story" is greeted with suspicion. But
what exactly do postmodern thinkers mean when they speak of "incredulity toward metanarratives"? The answer to this question requires a
cursory look at the advent of history in Israel followed by the secularization of the concept of history that paved the way for the postmodern
rejection of the metanarrative.

### Israel and the Theocentric Narrative of History

Life within ancient societies was oriented around narrative.[3] The
most readily evident of these narratives are the mythical stories that
speak about primordial origins or about the intrigues of the gods. Initially, the mythical approach to sacred narrative was connected to a cyclical understanding of time, as is evident in the religious stories and
practices of the ancient Near Eastern societies from Egypt to Greece.[4]
According to this cyclical conception, life follows a rhythmic pattern, a
circle of a finite number of events that occur repeatedly and with ob-
servable regularity. Canaanite worship rituals, which focused on two
gods who were associated with the major seasons of the year, offer a

3. For a fuller treatment of Israel and the theocentric narrative of history, see
Stanley J. Grenz and John R. Franke, *Beyond Foundationalism: Shaping Theology in a
Postmodern Context* (Louisville: Westminster John Knox Press, 2001), 252–58.
4. For a comparison of the Greek outlook with that of the biblical communities, see
Karl Loiwith, *Meaning in History* (Chicago: University of Chicago Press, 1950), 4–10.

prime example. As the coming drought began to dry out the vegetation in early summer, religious rituals lamented the death of the fertility god Baal and the triumph of Mot, the god of death. Then as the winter rains brought the promise of good crops, the Canaanites celebrated Baal's rebirth.[5]

Israel, however, broke with the particular mythical approach that dominated the neighboring cultures.[6] The Hebrews recast the religious narrative in the form of a linear historical span,[7] a trajectory, running from beginning to consummation. In this way, Israel gave birth to the historical narrative or to narrative as history. In short, the Hebrews "invented" history.

*The narrative of God acting.* This historical consciousness did not arise out of philosophical speculation[8] but was an outworking of Israel's theological understanding. The idea of the linearity of time emerged from the sense that Yahweh had acted savingly in the experiences of the patriarchs and later of the nation itself. These experiences formed a sequence of events, a whole that was greater than simply the sum of its parts. Israel concluded that Yahweh had a definite plan for the nation and that the God who journeys with his people[9] had been traveling with them since the days of the patriarchs. This journey, in turn, marked their identity as a nation.[10] Consequently, Israel's conception of the linear, historical nature of time was dependent on the God who acts in time. Gerhard von Rad offers this explanation:

> Thus, Israel's history existed only in so far as God accompanied her, and it is only this time-span which can properly be described as her history. It was God who established the continuity between the various separate events and who ordained their direction as they followed one another in time.[11]

As a result, time became a narrative, the story of God at work in Israel's experiences.

The prophets added a crucial perspective to this theological understanding. They retold the stories of former days as pointers foreshad-

5. Hans-Joachim Kraus, *Worship in Israel: A Cultic History of the Old Testament*, trans. G. Bushwell (Richmond: John Knox Press, 1966), 38–43.

6. Gerhard von Rad, *Old Testament Theology*, vol. 2, trans. D. M. G. Stalker (New York: Harper & Row, 1965), 110.

7. Loiwith, *Meaning in History*, 19.

8. von Rad, *Old Testament Theology*, 106.

9. Werner H. Schmidt, *The Faith of the Old Testament: A History*, trans. John Sturdy (Philadelphia: Westminster, 1983), 52.

10. von Rad, *Old Testament Theology*, 106.

11. Ibid.

owing the future. The prophets engaged in this "eschatological reading" of the historical narratives[12] because they were convinced that Yahweh was bringing about a new era for his people,[13] and this new era was connected to a final display of divine justice. Central to the prophetic message was the belief in a God who was just and therefore desired justice. When neither the exodus nor the monarchy established justice in Israel, the prophets increasingly directed their hopes away from the present and toward a future that stood as a contradiction to the injustice of the present.[14] The prophets declared that God would vindicate himself by sending a righteous king who would come in the name and power of Yahweh. Moreover, they concluded that God's act of self-vindication could not be an isolated, national event. The future demonstration of the divine glory had to be universal in scope; it had to occur in the presence of all nations.

*The narrative of the one true God.* The linearity of the historical narrative arose from another crucial theological innovation as well. Israel came to the conclusion that their God was the sole divine reality (in other words, they embraced monotheism).[15] Prophets such as Ezekiel and Isaiah declared that Yahweh—and not the deities worshiped by Israel's neighbors—is the only God, and as the only God, Yahweh is not merely a tribal deity but the God of all humankind. On this basis, the prophets came to see history as the activity of the one God asserting rulership over all the nations. They believed that this divine work, which constitutes the linearity of time, had begun in the past and would continue until the day when "the earth will be filled with the knowledge of the glory of the LORD, as the waters cover the sea" (Hab. 2:14 NIV; see also, Ps. 102:15; Isa. 66:18–19).

Monotheism in Israel led to an understanding of the universal scope of the historical narrative. The One whom Israel worshiped was not only the God of the nations but also the God of all creation. As the only God, Yahweh was the Creator—the *sole* Creator—of the world. For Israel, Yahweh's creative work was not limited to some initial act in the primordial past. Rather, it was ongoing and ultimately still future, for the Creator was actively bringing creation to its divinely intended goal. Consequently, as Werner Schmidt notes, belief in God as Creator meant that "creation is not only the remembered past, but also the ex-

---

12. Ibid., 113; John H. Sailhamer, *Introduction to Old Testament Theology: A Canonical Approach* (Grand Rapids: Zondervan, 1995), 212.

13. von Rad, *Old Testament Theology,* 112–13.

14. Schmidt, *Faith of the Old Testament,* 216.

15. Wolfhart Pannenberg, *Systematic Theology,* vol. 1, trans. Geoffrey W. Bromiley (Grand Rapids: Eerdmans, 1991), 246.

pected future."[16] In Israel, then, creation became eschatology,[17] and history was the narrative of God bringing creation to the eschatological new creation. In this manner the idea of God as Creator led to an all-encompassing understanding of history as traversing the whole of time from the primordial past to the future consummation. This universal scope gave the historical narrative its ultimate meaning: It is the story of God actively bringing to pass the divine purpose for creation.

### The Secularization of the Historical Narrative

Jesus and the disciples shared the linear understanding of time that developed in Israel. Israel's historical narrative likewise provided both the context and the categories for the earliest formulation of the gospel message. The New Testament, in turn, bequeathed to the church and consequently to "ecclesiastical" or "church-dominated" culture the biblical narrative of God at work bringing creation to its divinely intended goal. Yet this theocentric narrative of history did not retain its place as the driving conception of Western society.

The ground was laid for the loss of the constitutive role of the biblical narrative already in the late patristic era. As the church settled into the world, the idea of the narrative of history as a cosmic story was eclipsed by the story of journey of the soul, as both the church and history came to be viewed in relationship to eternal, unchangeable realities. By the Middle Ages, church theologians had replaced the idea of history as the movement of God in bringing creation to new creation with the image of the people of God seeking a destination beyond history. The historical epoch since Christ's advent, in turn, became simply the space between the two grand events of history, the incarnation and the last judgment.

The historical consciousness was not completely lost, however. It churned beneath the surface, seeping into the Renaissance well and then gushing forth in the Enlightenment. Yet the narrative was transformed in the process. What had begun as a theocentric understanding of history became "the story of man."

*History as progress.* The secularization of historical narrative has its roots in the innovative Renaissance idea that human life in the present has a dignity of its own and is not just the prelude to the life everlasting. Francis Bacon added that the goal of knowledge is not merely to advance believers along the *via contemplativa* but that it has utility for life in the here and now. Yet it was during the Enlightenment that the key

16. Schmidt, *Faith of the Old Testament*, 177.
17. Ibid.

element necessary for the emergence of the new understanding of history emerged: progress.

Although the chief interest of the Age of Reason was the discovery of the timeless, universal laws that govern the universe, Enlightenment thinkers were not totally ahistorical in their thinking. On the contrary, they were imbued with a sense of optimism as to what the new empirical method of inquiry could accomplish. Because the universe was thought to be both orderly and knowable, "human omniscience" now loomed as an attainable goal.[18] Not only was the progress of knowledge a hoped-for anticipation, it came to be seen as a necessary and certain expectation. The harbingers of the Enlightenment believed that the advancement of knowledge was destined to continue indefinitely into the future.[19] Once discovered, nature's laws could be applied to personal and social life so as to make humans happy, rational, and free.

Enlightenment thinkers, therefore, were not content to affirm that the method of empirical science *could* change the world; they saw signs that this change was already occurring. Historians in the Age of Reason painted the Middle Ages as an era of superstition and barbarism out of which humankind was now emerging. The progress they noted in their own time gave devotees of the Enlightenment a confidence about the future. Despite the ebb and flow of history, they were convinced that the human story was moving unmistakably upward and forward. Imbued with the conviction that moral and social progress was inevitable,[20] proponents of the Enlightenment looked to the future with hope. Carl Becker offers this characterization of the attitude prevalent during the Age of Reason:

> Mankind has at last emerged, or is emerging, from the dark wilderness of the past into the bright, ordered world of the eighteenth century. From this high point of the eighteenth century the Philosophers survey the past and the future. They recall the miseries and errors of the past, as mature men recall the difficulties and follies of youth, with bitter memories it may be, yet with a tolerant smile after all, with a sigh of satisfaction and a complacent feeling of assurance: the present is so much better than the past. But the future, what of that? Since the present is so much better than the past, will not the future be much better than the present? To the future the Philosophers look, as to a promised land, a new millennium.[21]

18. Isaiah Berlin, *The Age of Enlightenment* (New York: Mentor Books, 1956), 14.

19. J. B. Bury credits Bernard Le Bovier de Fontenelle with being "the first to formulate the idea of the progress of knowledge as a complete doctrine" (J. B. Bury, *The Idea of Progress: An Inquiry into Its Origin and Growth* [New York: Macmillan, 1932], 110).

20. According to Bury, among the first to reach this conclusion was the Abbé de Saint-Pierre (Bury, *Idea of Progress*, 128).

21. Carl L. Becker, *The Heavenly City of the Eighteenth-Century Philosophers* (New Haven: Yale University Press, 1932), 118.

As Isaiah Berlin rightly concluded, this era "was one of the most hopeful episodes in the life of mankind."[22]

*History as development.* With the advent of Romanticism, a new perspective on the historical narrative came to the fore. Thinkers such as G. W. F. Hegel viewed history as the illustration of a pattern bound up with the very nature of reason and ultimately with the ground of all being itself. Consequently, Hegel and others spoke about the present as the unfolding of what was latent in the past.

This assumption gave historians a new tool for practicing their trade: the concept of development. The rubric of development provided the plotline in accordance with which they could determine what from among the raw materials of the past was truly significant and through which they could tell the story of the past. The "discovery" of historical development not only fostered research into every aspect of human experience, it also made it difficult for anyone to offer any narration that did not follow the story line of progressive development from primitive beginnings to the fullness characteristic of the present.

Hegel viewed history as the narrative of the Absolute Spirit coming to self-consciousness through the cultural activities of humankind. In so doing, he introduced the idea of development into the very life of God. Some who followed in his wake, however, replaced the main character of the historical narrative, the Absolute Spirit, with a more mundane acting subject: humanity. This idea was propagated by the so-called left-wing Hegelians, such as Ludwig Feuerbach and Karl Marx. But perhaps the thinker in whose work the idea of development reached its initial apex was Auguste Comte. Comte divided history into three epochs, the "theological" (which ended in the Renaissance), the "metaphysical" (which was now ending), and the "positive" (which was already being inaugurated). In the third stage of human history, Comte theorized, God would be eliminated, and the object of worship would be humanity itself. Hence, Comte's system, according to John Baillie's appraisal, "is pure secularism in the strict and only true sense of the term, and the task he sets himself is the apparently self-contradictory one of inventing a secularist religion."[23]

### The End of the Linear Narrative

Western culture inherited the Hebrew legacy of linear history. Yet in the wake of the Renaissance, the Enlightenment, and Romanticism, Western thinkers separated the idea of linear history from its moorage in the biblical narrative. By exchanging the God-centeredness of the

22. Berlin, *Age of Enlightenment*, 29.
23. John Baillie, *The Belief in Progress* (New York: Charles Scribner's Sons, 1951), 138.

biblical vision for a human-centered understanding, modern historians traded the theocentric biblical story of God for an anthropocentric narrative, the story of man. Although the hero of this new secular narrative purported to be the universal human, its actual hero was Western man under the guise of the universal human, and what was packaged as the story of civilization was in fact the story of Western civilization. The postmodern condition entails the recognition and rejection of this pretense.

*Incredulity toward metanarratives.* In 1979 the Conseil des Universités of the government of Quebec requested a report on "knowledge in the most highly developed societies." For this task, they turned to Jean-François Lyotard, a French philosopher from the Institute Polytechnique de Philosophie of the Université de Paris in Vincennes, France. His response came in the form of a short piece bearing the unpretentious title *The Postmodern Condition: A Report on Knowledge.*[24]

In this work, Lyotard spelled out in an accessible manner the revolution in outlook that lay beneath the cultural phenomenon occurring throughout the Western world. Moreover, he articulated the theoretical and philosophical footing for the postmodern rejection of the modernist *hubris.*[25] Lying behind the modern view was a sharp contrast between premodern interpretations of the world that appeal to myths and stories and the modern program of discovery that is supposedly purely objective and therefore allows humans to see the world as it really is.

Postmodern thinkers such as Lyotard point out that in the name of science the Enlightenment outlook claimed to dispel from the realm of knowledge the "prescientific" beliefs, myths, and stories that primitive peoples use to speak about the world. But unbeknown to the architects of modernity, this outlook was itself dependent on an often unacknowledged appeal to variations on the metanarrative of progress,[26] or the progress of science, which served to unite the smaller stories of the sciences into one, unified history.[27] According to Lyotard, the grand nar-

---

24. Jean-François Lyotard, *The Postmodern Condition: A Report on Knowledge,* trans. Geoff Bennington and Brian Massumi (Minneapolis: University of Minnesota Press, 1984).

25. One commentator explains: "Most notably, it articulated the links between French poststructuralist philosophy and postmodern cultural practices ('culture' being understood to include science and everyday life as well as the arts), so that the latter could be seen—at least in the ideal sketched by Lyotard—as an instantiation of the former" (Susan Rubin Suleiman, "Feminism and Postmodernism: A Question of Politics," excerpted and reprinted in *The Post-Modern Reader,* ed. Charles Jencks [New York: St. Martin's Press, 1992], 318).

26. Lyotard, *Postmodern Condition,* 29, 31–36.

27. Ibid., xxiii–xxiv.

ratives of scientific progress that have legitimated modern society are losing their credibility and power.[28]

Lyotard took the matter one step further, however. History has repeatedly known times when the older narratives waned, only to be replaced by newer myths. The postmodern condition is not merely marked by the loss of that particular myth of modernity. Rather, the postmodern ethos entails the end of the appeal to any central legitimating myth whatsoever. Not only have all the reigning metanarratives lost their credibility, Lyotard postulates, but the idea of a grand narrative is itself no longer credible. Not only are people aware of a plurality of conflicting legitimating stories,[29] but everything is "delegitimized." Consequently, the postmodern outlook demands an attack on any claimant to universality; it has declared "war on totality."[30]

In his review of Lyotard's *Le Postmoderne expliqué aux enfants*, Terry Eagleton offers the following description of the postmodern mood:

> Post-modernism signals the death of such "meta-narratives" whose secretly terroristic function is to ground and legitimate the illusion of a "universal" human history. We are now in the process of awakening from the nightmare of modernity, with its manipulative reason and fetish of the totality, into the laid-back pluralism of the post-modern, that heterogeneous range of life-styles and language games which has renounced the nostalgic urge to totalize and legitimate itself. . . . Science and philosophy must jettison their grandiose metaphysical claims and view themselves more modestly as just another set of narratives.[31]

*The socially constructed world of the local story.* The rejection of the metanarrative has been accompanied by another postmodern innovation, the sociological idea of social construction. The insight that humans live in socially constructed worlds emerged from both the demise of Enlightenment realism, with its assumptions of the objectivity of the world together with the epistemological prowess of human reason, and the advent of globalization.

28. Ibid., 37.
29. Walter Truett Anderson finds six stories that are vying for loyalty in the postmodern world. To the three cited above, he adds the Islamic fundamentalist story, about a return to a society governed on the basis of Islamic values and koranic belief; the Green story, about rejecting the myth of progress and governing societies according to ecological values; and the new paradigm story, about a sudden leap forward to a new way of being and a new way of understanding the world (Walter Truett Anderson, *Reality Isn't What It Used to Be* [San Francisco: Harper, 1990], 243–44).
30. Lyotard, *Postmodern Condition*, 82.
31. Terry Eagleton, "Awakening from Modernity," *Times Literary Supplement* 4377 (20 February 1987): 194.

Social constructionists argue that humans do not enjoy an Archimedean vantage point from which to gain a purely objective view of reality "out there." Instead, humans structure their world through the concepts they bring to it, and these linguistic tools are human social conventions that map the world in a variety of ways depending on the context of the speaker. Globalization, in turn, has led postmodern thinkers to give up the modern dream of discovering the one, universal symbolic world that unites all humankind. They acknowledge that humans inhabit a globe that is home to "multiple realities." As different groups of people construct different "stories" about the world they encounter, these different languages facilitate a multiplicity of ways of experiencing life. As a result, social constructionists argue, people do not merely espouse different political opinions and religious beliefs; they live in different "worlds."[32]

The demise of the grand narrative means that postmoderns no longer search for the one system of "truth"—the one metanarrative—that can unite humans into one people or the globe into one "world." Narratives still function in the postmodern world. But the narratives postmoderns tell are local rather than universal. Postmoderns continue to construct models (or paradigms) to illumine their experience. Because they perceive life itself as a drama lived out within a socially constructed world, they engage in the process of fabricating stories that can define personal identity and give purpose and shape to social existence.[33] In this process, however, postmoderns remain dispossessed of the modernist illusion. They realize that rather than representing reality, all such models are "useful fictions."

## The Christian Claim to Universality

The postmodern turn has cleared the deck of the modern, secular metanarrative. But in the wake of the rejection of the story of man, all metanarratives have become suspect. Contemporary cultural pluralism has room only for the local story. In this intellectual context, every religion is viewed as merely one such local story among others. This poses a crucial difficulty for evangelicals, insofar as they are convinced that the gospel is for all. Must the Christian community be content with viewing the Jesus-narrative as nothing more than one local story

32. Hilary Lawson explains, "Through language, theory, and text, we close the openness that is the world. The closures we make provide our world. . . . We do not have different accounts of the same 'thing,' but different closures and different things" (Hilary Lawson, *Reflexivity: The Post-Modern Predicament* [London: Hutchinson, 1985], 128–29).

33. Anderson, *Reality Isn't What It Used to Be*, 108.

among others? Finding an answer to this question necessitates a return
to the specific metanarrative that Christians espouse.

### The Story of God Establishing Community

The Hebrews invented history and bequeathed to the New Testament church the narrative of the Creator actively bringing creation to
its divinely intended goal in the new creation. Christians, however,
have not always been in agreement regarding the focus of this divine
work. In the modern era, many theologians, captivated by the spell of
radical individualism, were convinced that the central plot of the biblical narrative was personal salvation. They believed that the goal of the
divine activity was to transport saved individuals to a heavenly home
somewhere "beyond the blue." The postmodern context, however, has
offered a vantage point from which to consider again the question as
to what comprises the central theme of the biblical narrative. The result of this rethinking has been a rediscovery of the crucial concept of
community, a rediscovery that provides a perspective from which to
understand the universality of the Jesus-story.

*Community as God with humankind.* From the creation of the heavens and the earth, with which the biblical drama begins, to the vision
of the new earth, which forms the drama's climax, the plot of the biblical narrative is God at work creating community. The theme of the
Bible is the establishment of community in the highest sense of the
word—a redeemed people, living within a redeemed creation, enjoying the presence of the Triune God. The divine intent is evident already in God's declaration, "It is not good for the man to be alone"
(Gen. 2:18 NIV). Yet the central dimension of community as depicted
throughout the biblical narrative is the quest for the presence of God
among humans.

The quest for the divine presence within the community is evident
in the early narratives of the Old Testament. Before the fall, God com-
muned with the first humans in the Garden. Then at various times and
in various locations the patriarchs experienced God's presence and
built landmarks, altars, and memorials to commemorate these encounters (e.g., Gen. 28:13–18). Later, God delivered Israel from Egypt and
constituted them as his covenant people (Exod. 20:2–3) in whose presence he would come to dwell. During the wilderness sojourn, Yahweh
made his abode among them in the tabernacle; like theirs, his house
would be a tent. When Israel established fixed dwellings in the Promised Land, God also put the divine glory within a house, the temple in
Jerusalem.

The theme is evident not only at the beginning of the biblical narrative but at its culmination as well. The idea that community consists of

God dwelling with humankind is clearly manifested in the grand vision of the new heaven and new earth. In the future new order, the peoples of the new earth will live together in peace. Nature will again fulfill its purpose of providing nourishment for all earthly inhabitants (Rev. 22:1–3). All creation will experience harmony (Isa. 65:25). But most glorious of all, God will dwell with humans, thereby bringing to completion the divine design for creation. The seer of the Book of Revelation offers this glorious vision of God's presence in the eternal community: "And I heard a loud voice from the throne saying, 'Now the dwelling of God is with human beings, and he will live with them. They will be his people, and God himself will be with them and be their God'" (Rev. 21:3 NIV ILE). In this new order, "The throne of God and of the Lamb will be in the city, and his servants will serve him. They will see his face, and his name will be on their foreheads" (Rev. 22:3b–4 NIV ILE).

*Community as the Spirit within the church.* At the center of the biblical narrative of God at work establishing community stands the story of Jesus, who is Immanuel—God with us (Matt. 1:22–23). In Jesus, the divine "Word became flesh and made his dwelling among us" (John 1:14 NIV). In him, God is present with humankind.

Before his death, Jesus promised that he and his Father would take up their dwelling with his disciples (John 14:23). Thereby he pointed toward the subsequent sending of the Holy Spirit (John 14:26). Since his outpouring at Pentecost, the Spirit has facilitated the fulfillment of Jesus' assurance of his continual presence with his followers. As the one who now constitutes the presence of God, the Spirit effects the divine goal of establishing community. Consequently, the eschatological fellowship that arrives in its fullness only at the consummation of human history is already present in a partial yet genuine manner. Although community comes to expression in the present era in a variety of forms, its focal point is the fellowship of the followers of Christ, the "one new humankind" composed of Jews and Gentiles reconciled to each other (Eph. 2:11–22). Christ's community is formed by the Spirit, who is bringing together a people that transcends every human division—a people from every nation and every socioeconomic status and consisting of both male and female (Gal. 3:28). The Spirit inhabits believers individually (1 Cor. 6:19) and corporately (1 Peter 2:4–5) as the temple of God. Because of the finished work of Christ and the continuing work of the Spirit, therefore, God is truly among humans.

### The Universality of the Story of God

God is present in the church through the indwelling Spirit. Evangelicals are not content to end the narrative here, however. In their estimation, the story of God at work establishing community is not merely a tale told by and for one particular tribe. It is not merely the story of the fellowship of Jesus' followers. Rather, evangelicals claim that the biblical narrative is for everyone and encompasses all humankind. In expanding the story of the community of Jesus to encompass humankind, evangelicals appeal to the Bible, which provides evidence of an expansive notion of the narrative of God.

*The universality of the divine intent.* The biblical story is expansive indeed insofar as it is the narrative of the God whose saving intentions encompass all humankind (cf. 1 Tim. 2:3–4).

The curtain on the biblical drama opens with God's act in bringing the world into existence and in forming humankind. This overarching context of creation gives a theocentric cast to the human reality. In the primordial garden, God speaks to the first humans and calls them to respond to the divine address. Beginning with the fall, however, the creature who was designed to be accountable to God turned away from the Creator. Nevertheless, the Creator's purpose for humankind is not thereby annulled, for God remains resolute in his desire to bring the divine design, set forth in the beginning, to completion in the new creation.

Its context in the drama of creation-fall-new creation gives a universal cast to the biblical salvation narrative. God's saving purposes overflow the boundaries of any one people to encompass all. The early narratives of Genesis present this idea clearly. In the wake of the fall, God promises that the offspring of Eve—whose name means "the mother of all the living" (Gen. 3:20)—will eventually crush the serpent (Gen. 3:15). After the flood, God enters into another covenant with all humankind through Noah (Gen. 9:1–17). Of greatest significance, however, is God's covenant with Abraham, through whom God promises to bless "all peoples on earth" (Gen. 12:3).

In the Genesis narratives, God's universal promises form the backdrop for the particular covenant with Israel. From the beginning, God's election of Israel had a universal intent. God chose this nation for the sake of all peoples. Through Israel the electing God desires to bless humankind. Although the divine election is universal in intent, therefore, it is particular in content.[34]

Jesus came primarily as Israel's Messiah, and his ministry was primarily set in the context of the elected people of God. Nevertheless, his mission was not limited to Israel, as is evidenced, for example, in his healing of Gentiles (e.g., Mark 7:24–30). In Luke's birth narrative, Simeon underlines the universal salvific purpose of Jesus' mission and its

---

34. George Lindbeck, "The Gospel's Uniqueness: Election and Untranslatability," *Modern Theology* 13, no. 4 (October 1997): 445.

link to Israel's election. Upon encountering the Christ child, he declares, "For my eyes have seen your salvation, which you have prepared
in the sight of all people, a light for revelation to the Gentiles and for
glory to your people Israel" (Luke 2:30–32 NIV). In keeping with this insight, the early community spoke of Jesus as "the Savior of the world"
(e.g., 1 John 4:14). And the early Christian leaders were convinced that
in Christ God had acted for the reconciliation of all humankind (2 Cor.
5:19; 1 John 2:2).

The biblical authors repeatedly sound the theme of a universal intent for particular election. As Joseph Ratzinger declares summarily,
"Election is always, at bottom, election for others."[35] This principle
emerges as well in the New Testament understanding of the church.
Similar to Israel in the Old Testament, the church is elected by God for
the sake of the world. Election for the sake of others provides an important motivation for the Christian missionary impulse. Rather than
huddling together as the "chosen few" who live unto themselves, Christians desire to proclaim the gospel to "the many" so that "the many"
might participate in what has been God's eschatological goal for humankind from the beginning.

As this statement suggests, the biblical narrative forges a crucial link
between creation and new creation. Although God's intention is not derived completely from creation, it nevertheless is closely connected
with original creation, because it marks the completion of creation.
The same universe that God called into existence "in the beginning"
God will transform into the eschatological new creation. In the same
way, the very people who now exist in this world God will make perfect
through the resurrection after the pattern of the risen Lord Jesus
Christ, for through faith they are united to Christ. Insofar as this is
God's intention from the beginning, the eschatological new creation is
present in embryonic form in creation. Moreover, the renewed community of those who will dwell eternally in the new creation is present
in embryonic form in the divine intent for humankind as given "in the
beginning," a design or purpose that all humans share. This universal
divine purpose for humankind means that, because it arises from an
understanding of God's intent for humankind, the biblical narrative encompasses all and is for all.

*The universality of the divine activity.* Not only does God's intent encompass the nations, but God is active savingly among all peoples. Perhaps the most radical Old Testament articulation of this idea came
through the prophet Amos. In warning the haughty Hebrews of im-

35. Joseph Ratzinger, *The Meaning of Christian Brotherhood*, trans. W. A. Glen-Doepel
(New York: Sheed and Ward, 1966), 79.

pending judgment, God declared, "Are not you Israelites the same to me as the Cushites? . . . Did I not bring Israel up from Egypt, the Philistines from Caphtor and the Arameans from Kir?" (Amos 9:7 NIV). Hence, in the face of Israel's tendency toward self-righteousness, God reminded the covenant nation that other peoples have also been the recipients of providential guidance.

The universal activity of God suggests that some type of knowledge of the true God may be found among people who stand outside the boundaries of the line of election. Jesus reserved the highest praise for the faith he found in a Roman centurion, a Gentile (Luke 7:9). The conversion of Cornelius convinced Peter that "God does not show favoritism but accepts men from every nation who fear him and do what is right" (Acts 10:34–35 NIV).

Not only does God intend that all nations join together in worship of the only true God (e.g., Zech. 14:16; Matt. 8:11; Rev. 21:24–25), but the Bible presents such worship as already happening. The narratives of the early patriarchs suggest that in worshiping the Canaanite-Mesopotamian high god, El, the early patriarchs were in fact paying homage to Yahweh, the God of Israel. During Moses' confrontation with Pharaoh, God provides the theological background: "I appeared to Abraham, to Isaac and to Jacob as God Almighty [El-Shaddai], but by my name the Lord [Yahweh] I did not make myself known to them" (Exod. 6:3 NIV). Christopher Wright concludes:

> What we have here, then, is a situation where the living God is known, worshipped, believed and obeyed, but under divine titles which were common to the rest of contemporary semitic culture, and some of which at least, according to some scholars, may originally have belonged to separate deities or localizations of El.[36]

A similar phenomenon is evident elsewhere in Israel's early history. Certain individuals stood in positive relationship to the one God, even acting as his mouthpieces, although they were not directly members of Israel. Prominent examples include Melchizedek (Gen. 14:18–19; cf. Heb. 7:1–10), Jethro (Exod. 18:1, 9–12, 27), and Balaam (Numbers 22). Moreover, although Elisha's healing of Naaman (2 Kings 5:1–19; cf. Luke 4:25–27) led the Syrian military officer to join in the worship of Yahweh (2 Kings 5:17), such worship neither required that he attach himself to the nation of Israel nor precluded his participation in

36. Christopher J. H. Wright, "The Christian and Other Religions: The Biblical Evidence," *Themelios* 9, no. 2 (1984): 6.

the pagan religious rituals that his position required (e.g., 2 Kings 5:18–19).

A similar understanding of the worship of God is evident in the New Testament as well. Cornelius is the most obvious example, for his prayers and acts of charity were accepted by God before he heard the message about Christ (Acts 10:4). The same idea lies behind Paul's astounding connection between the unknown deity worshiped by the Athenians and the true God whom the apostle desired to declare to them (Acts 17:22–23). In short, the biblical writers extend the sphere of God's presence in the world beyond the ranks of those who attach themselves to Israel or to Jesus' followers.

*The universality of the Jesus-story.* The touchstone of the universality of the biblical narrative is the Jesus-story that stands at its center. The New Testament writers present the Jesus-narrative as having a universal significance.

The universality of Jesus is evident in the portrait given him by the biblical writers. According to the New Testament portrayal, Jesus is the exemplary human being. He is the revelation of who all humans are to be. The design for humans that Jesus reveals focuses on living in relationship with God and being rightly related to others. Further, Jesus' universality is evident in his vocation as Israel's Messiah. Not only is he the fulfillment of the hopes and aspirations of the Hebrew people, he is, by extension, the Savior of all humankind (Luke 2:29–32). The New Testament presents Jesus as the obedient one, the divine Son who was obedient to the will of his Father in order to reconcile sinful humans to God. In his death he took upon himself the sins of all, and he rose from the grave to bring eternal life to all who live in union with him.

The New Testament writers take the universality of Jesus a step further, however, placing the saving narrative of Jesus within a wider, cosmic context. The highly developed Christology of the early church links Jesus with the divine act of creation. Thus, the apostolic writers boldly assert that God created the world through Christ (Col. 1:15–16), who is the divine Word (John 1:1). As the Christ, Jesus' role in creation is cosmic in extent, for he is the one in whom all things find their center (Col. 1:17). He is also, of course, the one through whom God reconciled the world (2 Cor. 5:18–19). Consequently, through connection with Jesus, humans—and the entire cosmos—come to participate in God's new creation.[37] This eschatological reality is not a new divine act of creation

37. See Helmut Thielicke, *Theological Ethics*, vol. 1, trans. John W. Doberstein, ed. William H. Lazareth (Philadelphia: Fortress Press, 1966), 383–451; and Dietrich Bonhoeffer, *Ethics*, trans. Neville Horton Smith (New York: Macmillan, 1965), 120–213.

*ex nihilo*, however, but the transformation of *this* universe, which God called into existence out of nothing "in the beginning."

The universal christological impulse evident throughout the New Testament is vividly portrayed in Paul's typology of the First Adam and the Second Adam (Rom. 5:12–21; 1 Cor. 15:21, 45). By means of this linguistic device, the apostle asserts that God's purpose for humankind is eschatological transformation after the pattern of the resurrected Christ. To this end, all humans must meet at the foot of the cross and at the empty tomb. Through his death and resurrection Christ is the "life-giving spirit" (1 Cor. 15:45) who opens the way for the transformation of what was begun in the creation of the First Adam.[38]

The ultimate basis for the Christian claim to universality, therefore, rests on the fact that the goal it announces is in reality nothing else than the goal of all creation.[39] The narrative Christians announce and embody is the story of God bringing all creation to new creation. Because God desires that all humankind participate in the coming eschatological transformation, this narrative is the story of all and its embodiment in the Christian community is on behalf of all. The task of the Christian community is to articulate the transcendent vision of God's eschatological new creation and to embody that transcendent vision, which they believe is nothing less than God's intention for all humankind.

## Christian Universality and the Religions

The postmodern condition is characterized by the loss of the metanarrative that emerged in Western culture in response to the secularization of history and in the wake of globalization. In this context, evangelicals proclaim the Jesus-narrative, which they claim is not merely one local story among others but lies at the heart of the grand story of God acting salvifically for all humankind, indeed, for all creation. At first glance, the postmodern incredulity toward metanarratives and the evangelical missiological impulse appear to be so incommensurate and antithetical so as to preclude any kind of fruitful engagement. A consideration that has been implicit throughout the preceding pages, however, provides a suggestion for a way forward, namely, the thoroughly theocentric—or religious—character of the Christian narrative.

38. For a similar attempt to connect believers and nonbelievers together through the Adam-Christ typology, see Paul L. Lehmann, *Ethics in a Christian Context* (New York: Harper & Row, 1963), 154–55.

39. For a similar conclusion, see Brian Hebblethwaite, *Christian Ethics in the Modern Age* (Philadelphia: Westminster, 1982), 136.

Sociologist Peter Berger, whose pioneering work in the theory of social construction continues to be influential,[40] points out that religion plays a key role in the world-construction task. Religion legitimates the socially constructed world that participants in any society inhabit by locating a society and its institutions within a sacred and cosmic frame of reference, by bestowing on participants in a society a sense of being connected to ultimate reality, and by giving cosmic status to the *nomoi* (or common orders of interpretation) of that society.[41] To use Berger's descriptive metaphor, religion is "the human enterprise by which a sacred cosmos is established."[42] Religion, therefore, provides a "sacred canopy" for a society.

Berger's point, therefore, is that every construal of the world is ultimately religious in form. The Christian faith offers one particular constructed world. Christians invite others to view the world through the lens of the Jesus-story. In this manner, the question of the universality of the Christian narrative becomes the question of the universality of one particular religious construal of the world among many such constructions. Moreover, if all socially constructed worlds are ultimately religious, as Berger suggests, then the question of the universality of the Jesus-story may be recast as the question of the role of other religions within this particular religious narrative: Do other religious narratives have a place within the narrative that Christians recite? Does the particular Christian story function as a metanarrative that encompasses the religions? In short, their commitment to the universality of the Jesus-story in the context of a cultural pluralism that makes all metanarratives suspect demands that evangelicals think through their theology of the religions.[43]

## Toward an Evangelical Theology of the Religions

Evangelicals, it seems, invariably focus their discussion of the religions on the topic of the eternal destiny of individual persons who stand outside the church or who live beyond the pale of the gospel proclamation. This question ought not to be minimized, of course. Nevertheless, it does not comprise the central consideration for a theology of the religions in the context of the incredulity toward metanar-

40. For a summary and appraisal of Berger's contribution, see Robert Wuthnow, *Rediscovering the Sacred: Perspectives on Religion in Contemporary Society* (Grand Rapids: Eerdmans, 1992), 9–35.

41. Peter L. Berger, *The Sacred Canopy: Elements of a Sociological Theory of Religion* (Garden City, N.Y.: Doubleday, 1969), 32–36.

42. Ibid., 25.

43. For the author's own construction of a theology of the religions within the context of a broader evangelical apologetic theology, see Stanley J. Grenz, *Renewing the Center: Evangelical Theology in a Post-theological Era* (Grand Rapids: Baker, 2000), 249–86.

ratives. In fact, it may actually point the discussion in the wrong direction.[44] A more fruitful beginning point for an evangelical theology of the religions in this particular context is the question as to whether the religions play what J. A. DiNoia calls a "providential role" in the divine economy. Do the religions of the world participate in any way in God's purposes in this penultimate age?[45]

Although some evangelicals deny any positive significance for all other religions,[46] the biblical narrative suggests otherwise. As was noted earlier in this essay, several of the biblical writers leave open the possibility of either faith or true worship beyond the central salvation-historical trajectory of Israel and the church. The universalizing tendency of the biblical narrative opens the door to the conclusion that human religious traditions may indeed participate in some meaningful manner in the divine program for creation in this penultimate age.

The suggestion that the religions may have a providential role in the work of God in history en route to the culmination of the divine program leads once again to a consideration of God's overarching intent for creation in general and humankind in particular, which in this essay was summarized by "community." The biblical visionaries anticipate the establishment of the eternal community of a reconciled humankind dwelling within the renewed creation and enjoying the presence of the redeeming God. Although the fullness of community comes only as God's gift at the culmination of history, the biblical writers also assert that foretastes of the future reality can be found in the present. The providential place of human religious traditions, therefore, may lie in their role of fostering community.

*Community and human existence.* Although the concept of community arises immediately from the biblical vision, certain contemporary sociologists offer insight into its significance. These thinkers speak about the importance of the "social web" or the experience of community to human existence. The stage for such an understanding was set in part by the French sociologist Emile Durkheim, who theorized that social cohesion is facilitated by "collective representations," the group-based symbols with which individuals identify. In his estimation, a "conscious collective," a pre-given solidarity of shared meanings and values, is a prerequisite to social diversification.[47] George Herbert

44. Klaas Runia, "The Gospel and Religious Pluralism," *Evangelical Review of Theology* 14, no. 4 (October 1990): 362.

45. See, for example, Per Lonning, *Creation—An Ecumenical Challenge* (Macon, Ga.: Mercer University Press, 1989), 58.

46. For an example of this approach, see David F. Wells, *God the Evangelist* (Grand Rapids: Eerdmans, 1987), 24.

47. Emile Durkheim, *The Division of Labor in Society*, trans. George Simpson (New York: Macmillan, 1964), 277.

Mead, in turn, showed the importance of community for identity formation. According to Mead, meaning is no individual matter but is interpersonal or relational. The mind, therefore, is not only individual but also a social phenomenon,[48] and the self—the maturing personality or one's personal identity—is socially produced.[49] Building on the work of these pioneers, certain contemporary thinkers assert that a sense of personal identity develops through the telling of a personal narrative,[50] which is always embedded in the narrative of the communities in which the person participates.[51] The transcending story that gives meaning to a personal narrative is mediated to the individual by the community, which transmits traditions of virtue, common good, and ultimate meaning.[52]

Religion, in turn, plays a significant role in this process. As sociologists since Durkheim have noted, religion creates and maintains social solidarity insofar as it provides the symbols by means of which people understand their world. By providing the foundation for the social community in which we live, religion provides the framework for group and personal identity formation. As contributors to the worldview of their devotees, religions are not merely systems of beliefs. Rather, they are integrally related to the entire socioeconomic and political structures of the life of their adherents.[53]

*Community and the religions.* The seemingly universal quest for community and the social role of religion in human life lead to the conclusion that the human religious phenomenon carries a positive intent. Whatever their ultimate vision of reality may be, all religious traditions contribute to identity formation and social cohesion. Their immediate goal is to assist their adherents in the task of gaining a sense of identity as persons standing in relationship to something "larger" than the individual, however that encompassing reality may be understood. In this sense, religions fulfill a divinely sanctioned function. Because God's ultimate purpose is the establishment of community, evangelicals ought to affirm each religious tradition in its intent to promote so-

48. George Herbert Mead, *Mind, Self, and Society*, ed. Charles W. Morris (1934; reprint, Chicago: University of Chicago Press, 1967), 133, 164, 186–92.

49. For Mead's argument, see ibid., 135–226. In part 3 of the volume, entitled "The Self," Mead builds a cumulative case for the social theory of the self.

50. Robert N. Bellah et al., *Habits of the Heart: Individualism and Commitment in American Life* (Berkeley: University of California Press, 1985), 81.

51. See, for example, Alisdair MacIntyre, *After Virtue*, 2d ed. (Notre Dame: University of Notre Dame Press, 1984), 221.

52. For example, George A. Lindbeck, "Confession and Community: An Israel-like View of the Church," *Christian Century* 107 (9 May 1990): 495.

53. Wright, "The Christian and Other Religions," 8.

cial cohesion among human beings, for in this manner each contributes to the present experience of community,[54] albeit always in a broken form. As DiNoia notes, "Other religions are to be valued by Christians, not because they are channels of grace or means of salvation for their adherents, but because they play a real but as yet perhaps not fully specifiable role in the divine plan to which the Christian community bears witness."[55]

This basically positive appraisal must be balanced by a cautionary attitude, however. Although directed toward a divinely sanctioned purpose, religion readily becomes an expression of human fallenness, even falling prey to the demonic. The Roman Catholic ecumenist Eugene Hillman articulates this two-sided Christian appraisal of all religions: "The fallibility and peccability of fallen humankind are reflected in religions no less than in all the other human systems and institutions which can also, in various surprising ways, serve God's purposes."[56] The potential for evil is bound up with the specificity of religion. Religion never occurs in the abstract. Instead, the human response to God always takes a specific form. Because humans are by nature social beings, rather than responding to God in isolation, the human response always has a social character,[57] coming to expression as a specific religion characterized by certain beliefs, practices, and structures. And as Reinhold Niebuhr pointed out, every social form or particular community carries within itself tendencies toward arrogance, self-centeredness, and ruthlessness in the pursuit of its ends[58] that make it susceptible to an "unrestrained egoism."[59]

As was noted earlier, religion plays a role in personal identity formation and provides the sanction for specific societal forms. Further, the social structures that a particular religion sanctions and the type of personal identity a religion fosters are closely connected to the understanding of the world—to the fundamental convictions about the world and the divine— the religion propounds. This connection means that any religion can be

54. A biblical parallel to this positive appraisal of religion lies in Paul's affirmation of government as God's agent in promoting good and punishing evil (Rom. 13:1–6).

55. J. A. DiNoia, *The Diversity of Religions: A Christian Perspective* (Washington, D.C.: Catholic University of America Press, 1992), 91.

56. Eugene Hillman, *Many Paths: A Catholic Approach to Religious Pluralism* (Maryknoll, N.Y.: Orbis, 1989), 51.

57. Arnulf Camps, *Partners in Dialogue*, trans. John Drury (Maryknoll, N.Y.: Orbis, 1983), 47.

58. Reinhold Niebuhr, *The Nature and Destiny of Man*, vol. 1 (New York: Charles Scribner's Sons, 1964), 208.

59. Reinhold Niebuhr, *Moral Man and Immoral Society* (New York: Charles Scribner's Sons, 1932), xi.

assessed according to both the personal identity/social structures it fosters and the underlying belief system that sanctions the social order. The primary question in appraising a specific religion, therefore, concerns the extent to which the beliefs it espouses and the practices it enjoins lead to the construction of a sense of personal identity and social structures that cohere with God's intent for human life. Indeed, just as in the Old Testament setting, to choose the true God is to opt for the truly human as well, whereas the worship of false gods leads to injustice.[60]

In the postmodern context, however, the difficulty inherent in the process of critical appraisal is compounded. The postmodern condition has brought to light that the various religious traditions propagate differing conceptions about the nature of ultimate reality and about the final purpose or goal of existence. Despite what some modernists suggest, the world's religions are not simply the guise that the one, hidden religion wears. Also suspect is the modern notion that all the so-called religions are in the end seeking the same goal. The world's religions may be attempting to provide answers to the human predicament, but they understand that predicament—and hence its solution—quite differently.[61] Grace Jantzen therefore rightly cautions theologians to avoid the assumption that "all religions have a concept of salvation at all, let alone that they all mean the same thing by it or offer the same way to obtain it: it is misleading to assume that there is some one thing that is obtained when salvation is obtained."[62]

Despite their common quest for social cohesion (or community), the various communities articulate differing visions and embody differing understandings as to what actually constitutes true community. This, in turn, leads to the crucial question, Why give primacy to the world-constructing language of the Christian community?

### The Jesus-Narrative and the Religions

The postmodern incredulity toward metanarratives does not consist merely of the refusal to "privilege" any one particular narrative. It also entails the rejection of the possibility of establishing any supra-communal, neutral perspective from which to adjudicate among the competing religious construals of the world.

This situation does not shut down public discourse about the nature of community, however. Nor does it necessarily demand a pluralism that limits the truth-value of any religious vision, including the Chris-

60. Wright, "The Christian and Other Religions," 8.
61. S. Mark Heim, *Is Christ the Only Way?* (Valley Forge, Pa.: Judson, 1985), 138.
62. Grace M. Jantzen, "Human Diversity and Salvation in Christ," *Religious Studies* 20 (1984): 579–80.

tian, to the particular religious community that embodies it. On the contrary, by their very nature, religious convictions carry with them an implicit claim to universality. As Pamela Dickey Young notes:

> If religious traditions make no claims to truth beyond themselves they become trivial. As merely innocuous expressions of one point of view alongside another, they would carry no power or depth to invite or command participation. Reasons for adhering to a religious tradition would not include that it told the truth about the way the world and its inhabitants are.[63]

The postmodern condition is not averse to the concept of truth, therefore. What it does is alter the way in which the conversation about truth must be pursued. Mark Heim encapsulates the new conversational style as it affects dialogue regarding alternative religious visions: "The discussion of religious differences shifts then from a sole focus on flat issues of truth and falsehood, or degrees of these, to include consideration of alternatives: not 'Which religion alone is true?' but 'What end is most ultimate, even if many are real?'"[64]

The communitarian reminder that the goal of all social traditions is to construct a well-ordered society even though the various communities differ regarding what that society entails offers a perspective from which to recast the truth question. The beginning point of any such conversation is the issue as to which theologizing community articulates an interpretive framework that is able to provide the transcendent vision for the construction of the kind of world that the particular community itself is in fact seeking. Although this question of internal coherence is crucial, the matter cannot rest here. Rather, it must advance to tackle the question, Which religious vision carries within itself the ground for community in the truest sense? Even here, however, recourse cannot be made to some vague, universal concept of community. Instead, the dialogue partners—including Christians—can engage in this conversation only on the basis of their embeddedness within particular religious traditions. At the same time, because it brings into play voices representing a variety of traditions and outlooks, the discussion can occasion the context for viewing one's own tradition through a new, even genuinely self-critical, perspective.

63. Pamela Dickey Young, *Christ in a Post-Christian World: How Can We Believe in Jesus Christ When Those around Us Believe Differently—Or Not at All?* (Minneapolis: Fortress Press, 1995), 68.

64. S. Mark Heim, *Salvations: Truth and Difference in Religion* (Maryknoll, N.Y.: Orbis, 1995), 160.

Like other community-based visions, a central goal of the Christian message of salvation is the advancement of social cohesion, and it speaks of this goal as community (or fellowship). At the heart of the Christian message is the declaration that the goal of life is community—fellowship with God, with others, with creation, and in this manner with oneself. Taken as a whole, the biblical narrative speaks of God at work establishing community. God's *telos* is nothing less than gathering a reconciled people, nurtured in a renewed creation and enjoying fellowship with the eternal God (Rev. 21:1–5).

Of course, all human religious traditions contribute to social cohesion and hence to the building of a particular society. Consequently, all offer some semblance of community, even when viewed from a specifically Christian perspective. But the Christian message does not stop with the quest for community in general. Evangelicals firmly believe that the Christian vision sets forth more completely the nature of community that all human religious traditions seek to foster. Christians humbly conclude that no other religious vision encapsulates the final purpose of God as they have come to understand it. Other religious visions cannot provide community in its ultimate sense, because they are *theologically* insufficient. They do not embody the fullest possible understanding of who God actually is.

At the heart of the specifically Christian theological vision is the acknowledgment of God as the Triune one. Christians declare that the only true God is none other than the Triune God, the eternal community of the three trinitarian persons. The Christian vision speaks of humankind, in turn, as created in God's image. The divine design is that humans mirror within creation what God is like in God's own eternal reality. Moreover, Christians declare that the goal of human existence has been revealed most completely in Jesus Christ, the Son, who in his life, death, and resurrection modeled the divine principle of life, namely, life in intimate fellowship with his heavenly Father by the Holy Spirit who indwelt him, and consequently life in fellowship with and for the sake of others and indeed with and for all creation.

Viewed from this perspective, evangelical adherence to the finality of Christ means that Jesus is the vehicle through whom humans come to the fullest understanding of who God is and what God is like. The incarnate life of Jesus reveals the truest vision of the nature of God, namely, that God is the Triune one and hence inherently social. When coupled with the biblical teaching of humankind created in the divine image, the Christian vision of God as Triune provides the transcendent basis for human life-in-community, which all belief systems in their own way and according to their own understanding seek to foster. This vision looks to the divine life or, more particularly, to the narrative of the Triune God at work in the world as the basis for understanding what it means to be human persons-in-community. Just as God is a plurality-in-unity, so also to be human means to be persons-in-community. This theocentric perspective leads to a vision of human society as the forging of the multiplicity of individuals into a higher unity (as is reflected so well in the motto of the United States: *e pluribus unum*, "one out of many").

In short, the biblical vision of God at work establishing community is not merely a great idea that God devised in all eternity. It is an outworking of God's own eternal reality. As a result, the human quest for community is not misguided. At its heart it is nothing less than the quest to mirror in the midst of all creation the eternal reality of God and thereby to be the *imago Dei*. In this manner, the Christian vision stands as the fulfillment of the human religious impulse as the early church fathers recognized and J. N. Farquhar[65] reintroduced into the contemporary discussion.[66]

### Conclusion: The Gospel and the Religions

Christians comprise the fellowship of persons who have come to see that the salvation God is effecting is the establishment of community in the highest sense. Although Christians readily acknowledge that other religions can contribute to the divine program, they are convinced that the vision of community with its focus on fellowship with the Triune God that is theirs through relationship to Christ constitutes a more complete appraisal of the human situation and a more definitive disclosure of the divine intention. It is, therefore, the touchstone for understanding the character of the community God intends for all humankind.

The Christian witness in the world is based on the universal intention of God's activity in human history. Inherent in the Christian vision is a claim to universality. Christians declare that the particular vision of God's purposes embodied in the Jesus-story is not intended merely for one particular tribe. Rather, it constitutes the divine goal for all humankind. Furthermore, this divinely given *telos* is the unity of humankind in fellowship with the Father through the Son by the Spirit (Eph. 4:4–6), which is the fulfillment of the quest for fullness of community found within particular religious narratives and actualized to varying degrees within particular religious traditions. Commitment to the vision of an eschatologically oriented, universally directed program of

65. J. N. Farquhar, *The Crown of Hinduism* (London: Oxford University Press, 1913).
66. DiNoia, *Diversity of Religions*, 75.

the God of the Bible leads Christians to see themselves as elect for the sake of the world. Ultimately, therefore, the universality of the Jesus-story comes into view as the believing community bears witness to the gospel as an act of worship offered to God on behalf of, and for the sake of, all humankind.

# Part 3
# Critical Concerns

# 5

# No God's-Eye View

*Tradition, Christian Hermeneutics,*
*and Other Faiths*

GERALD J. PILLAY

Christians live in a world peopled by adherents of several faiths, and in spite of seemingly insuperable methodological difficulties, they have to make sense of their faith in the context of this pluralism. The tendency is to make sense of these religions in the context of Christian faith—that is, to explain religions (Christianity included) from the vantage point of Christian faith and theology. This serves an important purpose within the Christian fold, and, perhaps, the question of the fate of those outside this fold is an irrepressible question that demands an answer. Invariably, though, Christianity is explained as the crowning glory and the fulfillment of all human religious quests. As a believer, of course, that is indeed how one understands it. But adherents of other religions claim the same for their religion as well, and there is no independent or cosmic vantage point from which we human beings can adjudicate the matter. For us there is no God's-eye view.

We need to establish, then, a theology of religions that allows not only an explanation of the certainty that comes with faith in Christ but that also explains why proclamation and mission are not only acceptable but a necessary consequence. Merely to explain religions from a Christian perspective does not escape the charge of exclusivism. A Christian theology of religions has to go beyond a theology of mission to a public declaration of the universality of Christian truth claims, the grounds for proclamation. A case understandable only "within the fold" will by its very nature be self-justifying.

In attempting to probe further this challenge, we need first to examine some recent reflections on the phenomenon of religious pluralism that have advocated ways to explain the relationship of Christianity to other religions. Do they really offer useful strategies for the task?

## Christian Faith and Other Faiths

A theology of religions may follow different routes. It could, for instance, attempt a form of meta-theory by systematizing into a rationally apprehended scheme the origins and development of the different theologies with the goal of establishing a common theological frame of reference.

Another approach is to develop a universal theology, a theology that transcends individual theologies of religions. It is based on an agreement about what the different religions reveal about the divine. A. K. Gangadean, an advocate of this approach, describes universal theology as "the inevitable outgrowth of interreligious theology and indeed of theology in general. It is essentially the articulation of the universal Divine Form that must live at the heart of any and every form of life."[1] Gangadean rejects what he calls the "paradox of self-reference" and the "pathology of Absolutism"[2] and pursues a "dialogical," "holistic" unity between religions.[3]

Religious studies scholars have tended to steer away from such an approach. They share, in general, the view that the comparative study of religion must be disinterested and neutral. Unbiased scholarship demands a method whereby each religion is examined on its own terms: The task is to understand the texts, history, and key ideas of each religious phenomenon. Religions may be compared and contrasted, even analyzed in great depth, but analysis stops short of theological evalua-

1. A. K. Gangadean, "Universal Theology: Beyond Absolutism and Relativism," in *Religious Issues and Interreligious Dialogues: An Analysis and Sourcebook of Development Since 1945*, ed. Charles Wei-hsun Fu and Gerhard Spiegler (New York: Greenwood Press, 1989), 47.

2. Ibid., 60, 69.

3. Ibid., 123.

tion. Especially important for this approach is that scholars suspend their own beliefs in order to be true to their task. Against the monism of universal theology, the phenomenological approach accepts more readily the pluralism of religions but methodologically is restricted to analysis and description of religious worldviews.

The debate about the differences between theology and religious studies cannot be explored fully here. Francis Schüssler Fiorenza has, quite rightly, described the contrasts in this debate between "subjective faith" and "objective knowledge," "epistemic privilege" and "scientific neutrality," and "committed advocacy" and "disinterested impartiality" as constituting the main challenges facing "an adequate self-understanding" for both theology and religious studies as disciplines.[4]

Yet another variant of this position is the view that world religions themselves have no future. In their present form they are, according to Abe Masao, "coming to an end and reaching their limit" largely because of "recent radical changes in world conditions and the human situation." They no longer "genuinely deserve to be called 'world religions.'"[5] A "genuine form of 'world religion' must now be sought and actualized . . . in order to cope with the present and future world situation and human predicament."[6]

There is a theological variant of the phenomenological understanding of religions in contemporary theology that seeks to be more relevant to post-religious culture. This theology rejects the notion that each religion has its own importance and that each perspective is equally valid since it disallows belief in God in any real sense and certainly in any traditional religious sense. It holds, though, to the necessity of religion, but its radical post-religious position goes well beyond even traditional nontheists. The role of religion is reduced to supporting the ethical life. Don Cupitt exemplifies this view in his *After God*, in which he argues that "we should now be uninhibited and eclectic in creating new religious meanings, practices, and narratives out of the materials available to us."[7] Religions are all declining and are "all available to be looted of whatever they possess that may be useful to us in the future."[8]

Traditional religions are undermined by the jettisoning of God. "The coming" and "the departure of the gods" is explained in purely psycho-

4. Francis Schüssler Fiorenza, "Theological and Religious Studies: The Contest of the Faculties," in *Shifting Boundaries: Contextual Approaches to the Structure of Theological Education*, ed. Barbara Wheeler and Edward Farley (Louisville: John Knox Press, 1991), 126.

5. Abe Masao, "The End of World Religions," *The Eastern Buddhist* 13 (spring 1980): 34.

6. Ibid.

7. Don Cupitt, *After God: The Future of Religion* (New York: Basic Books, 1997), 120.

8. Ibid.

sociological terms. Yet every religious proclivity is allowed ("Let a hundred flowers bloom")[9] while a new world religion must be fashioned. "One may be tempted to conclude," he says:

> that no entirely new . . . conceptualisation of religion can hope to be understood until the decay of the old faiths has gone much further than it has yet. . . . I don't agree. I think that we must hurry. Unless something new is launched quickly, I fear that the process of post-modernization will have gone so far, and will have become so destructive, that it will be too late.[10]

These sentiments are inherently contradictory and confusing, but they take an uncompromising line toward traditional or established religion.

There is no gainsaying that in a world of increasing globalization, urbanization, mass media, materialism, speed, and change that the conditions that made for easy belief and attachment to a tradition have been eroded. The breach with history, tradition, and community is palpable, which is why many have concluded that the insights of traditional religions were left behind when the conditions and heritage that sustained them were superceded by the postmodern world. Postmodernist writings, therefore, must be heeded because they articulate this general sense of rootlessness.

However, the quest for a universal theology, or an "end of world religion" view, or a Cupittian approach betrays a lack of appreciation of the mysterium (for want of a better word) of religious beginnings and the historicity of religion—the web of interconnections between belief, cosmology, memory, history, traditions, identity, and self-understanding. But even this stops at a phenomenological or sociological way of speaking of religion. As insightful as these approaches might be, the nature of faith is existential and personal at the same time as it is social and public. The approaches to theology touched on here are scholarly abstractions with no real connection with believing or worshiping communities. This is not to say that those who share similar ideas do not meet for mutual support and intellectual stimulation. But worshiping communities are more than merely the meeting of people of like minds.

The origins of several of the great religions of the world are lost in antiquity, and the processes whereby they became cultural and global faiths are not accessible in their totality to the academic in his or her study. Each great religion uniquely articulates the meaning and purpose of life and cannot be understood piecemeal or in a partial way

9. Ibid., 123.
10. Ibid., 128.

without sacrificing the coherency, comprehensiveness, and authenticity of its expression. For all the criticisms leveled against the old religions because of their absolutism and self-righteousness, the new orthodoxy seems to presume too much. The question to be asked yet again is whether the offerings of contemporary academics, anxious to save the world from anachronistic religion, come from any better or higher vantage point.[11]

There is no intellectually transcendent position from which judgments about the different religions can be made without relativizing the truth claims of each religious tradition. Moreover, the attempt to capture the ultimate divine form that would satisfy everybody, by the arbitrary "looting" of every religion, would necessarily be highly speculative and too general to have any real meaning. In the end, the attempt is bound to yield yet another religion.[12] The Baha'i religion, which seeks to foster religious unity, is a case in point. The well-intentioned bringing together of elements of different religions has led to the creation of another religion.

Those who are convinced that a post-religious position is inevitable in our times ignore the lack of relevance their intellectual excursions have for the majority of people who believe they encounter God as adherents of these religions. The unspoken premise of the "intellectually sophisticated," from their post-religious standpoint, is that believers are premodern, still on their way to attaining real enlightenment. Those who see "their light" are at the cutting edge of religious insight.

A theology of religions could also begin by trying to explain the Christian position vis-à-vis the other established religions. After all, several of the established religions predated it. Christian theologians have had to confront the rich heritage of texts and religious cultures that existed long before the coming of Christ.

But the "history of religion" way of placing Christian theology in the context of world religions is itself not free of problems. For example, Christianity and Islam could be described in the context of Middle East-

11. These positions not only undermine the basis of Christian theology but also disallow the position of a Hindu scholar such as Pratima Bowes, who writes, "As a Hindu I believe that all religious traditions . . . provide a way for man to integrate himself into the divine or ultimate reality and that their beliefs and practices exist to provide a path to this reality by way of linking it with the ordinary living process. . . . Yet these traditions differ from one another in important ways, both in belief and practice" (Bowes, "Religious Traditions," *Religious Traditions* 3 [April–May 1980]: 1).

12. In the end this is religious reductionism. For Cupitt, "What survives of the old religions, then, is a small number of tricks and techniques of religious existence: ways of being a self and of relating oneself to the whole of which one is a part. These tricks can help us to love life and live well; that now is religion" (*After God*, 104).

ern, Semitic faith and alongside Judaism—their commonalities and theological differences could thus be elicited. From the perspective of global religions, the Semitic religions and their variations can be described by comparing and contrasting the commonalities and differences of entire families of religion. There is a great deal of historical value in this enterprise, but the very general nature of this approach is like an exercise in cartography: A map of the universe has less detail than a world map, which has much less detail than a country map, which, in turn, cannot capture the vibrancy of a bustling street or the coziness of a family around the dinner table. Yet it is at the latter levels that the existential meaning of religion is best understood and what theology has to take account of.

The interreligious dialogue approach also seeks to understand Christian theology alongside other faiths. This approach has produced important insights into other world religions and deeper self-understanding about one's own religion. While in the West the call for interreligious dialogue is relatively recent, Christians in non-Western cultures, with their own heritage of religious texts and spirituality, have had to make sense of the Bible vis-à-vis these other religions and cultural heritages. These cultures have been molded and given life by these religions for centuries. While early Jewish Christians explained the significance of the Christ from the vantage point of the Old Testament, Christians in other cultures have been involved in the same process in relation to their former religions, some for almost two thousand years. The fact that it was not necessary for a Greek to first become a Hebrew before becoming a Christian was one of the earliest insights of the Christian church.

Dialogue is the means whereby religions break out of their self-imposed confines and encounter other religious truth claims. There are many ways that religions can mutually enrich each other through intellectual challenges, sharing of elements of spirituality (Tagore's beautiful and spiritually insightful verses in *Gitangali* could enrich the prayers of a devout Christian, for example), and even new stimulation for joint public action.[13]

13. Examples of key proponents, from quite different approaches, who advocate dialogue are John B. Cobb, Jr., *Beyond Dialogue: Toward a Mutual Transformation of Christianity and Buddhism* (Philadelphia: Fortress Press, 1982); John Hick, ed., *Truth and Dialogue in World Religions: Conflicting Truth Claims* (Philadelphia: Westminster, 1974); Raimundo Panikkar, *The Intrareligious Dialogue* (New York: Paulist Press, 1978); Konrad Raiser, "Beyond Tradition and Context: In Search of an Ecumenical Framework," *International Review of Mission* 71 (January 1982): 347–54; Leonard Swidler, "Religious Pluralism and Ecumenism from a Christian Perspective," in *Religious Issues and Interreligious Dialogues;* Mark Taylor, "Celebrating Difference, Resisting Domination: The Need for Synchronic Strategies in Theological Education," in *Shifting Boundaries*, 259–94.

The religious dialogue approach prompts openness and erodes attitudes of superiority and arrogance that insularity promotes—it certainly helps to remove stereotypes and caricatures. The attempt to achieve enlightened coexistence for the sake of racial and global harmony is plausible since religion has often exacerbated human conflict. However, in this connection the following point has to be made. Religious rhetoric in the middle of war has led to the general assumption that religions cause war. There are undoubtedly numerous examples of how religion aids the fanaticized consciousness.[14] Concepts of just war and jihad in principle allow for the use of violence in extreme cases (after all else has been tried) in order to achieve justice. But it is a justification for violence nonetheless. The very sophisticated rationalization of violence in the world today has often been aided and abetted by religious talk. However, as David Martin recently pointed out, the link between war and Christianity (or religion in general) may not be as direct as many assume.[15] When the overt religious motif for war, as in the case of the Crusades, is missing, it is more difficult to tease out the myriad ways in which enemies describe each other—religious difference is only one such way.

Yet every religion has a powerful impulse to peace. Religions have frequently aided the process of creating and supporting peaceful coexistence between peoples and cultures. In order to encourage this peace-making drive in the various religions for the sake of global coexistence, however, there has developed a tendency to emphasize the commonalities among the world religions. This urge, as can be expected, is strongest in the area of theological and social ethics. It is less well sustained in the theological mainstream or in the core doctrine of God. For example, one of the great religions of the world, Buddhism, is nontheistic. It provides an attractive and thought-provoking morality with many parallels to Christianity but without a clearly articulated doctrine of God.

The ecumenical movement within the family of Christian denominations included two distinct approaches toward attaining unity between the churches: the faith and order, and the life and work movements. The former sought to establish a basis of Christian unity through doctrine and polity—the approach of affirming a common faith and practice. The latter, conceding the diversity of theology and expressions of ministries, sought unity in the social and public witness of the gospel.

14. G. J. Pillay, "Theology and the Fanaticised Consciousness" (Pretoria: University of South Africa, 1991).

15. David Martin, *Does Christianity Cause War?* (Oxford: Oxford University Press, 1997).

After all, must there be total agreement on the fine points of doctrine before Christians can join together in caring for the poor? Life and work put that question to the churches during the last century. Within the context of interreligious discussion, this approach would perhaps have greater support and success in terms of religions joining together in public and global witness for social justice and peace.

Peaceful coexistence is a task and a responsibility for human beings everywhere, and religions have a special contribution to make in achieving it. All the world religions can and must be open to learn from each other the ways of peace, how to counter the arrogance that believers lapse into, how to change the stereotypes about "other believers," and, especially, how to enter real relationships with others based on mutual respect and trust. Religious coexistence is part and parcel of multicultural coexistence in an international global society.

Mahatma Gandhi came to a similar conclusion when he pondered the issue. Although Gandhi was attracted to several things in Christianity and came to revere the Sermon on the Mount, he expressed the opinion that there was no need for anyone to convert to other religions, for all religions are valid pathways to God. Believers of the different religions have the duty to be faithful in the path in which they find themselves. After all, he maintained, the goal at the end is the same.

The validity of each religion was emphasized consciously by Gandhi, Swami Vivekananda, and others as an antidote to religious imperialism. At the Parliament of Religions, which met in Chicago in 1893, Vivekananda cited the oft quoted Hindu hymn: "As the different streams having their sources in different places all mingle their water in the sea, so, O Lord, the different paths which men take through different tendencies, various though they appear, crooked or straight, all lead to Thee." He went on to quote the well-known text from the Gita, "Whosoever comes to Me, through whatsoever form, I reach him; all men are struggling through paths which in the end lead to me."[16]

Interestingly, several decades before the religious dialogue movement, spearheaded mainly by Christians, Vivekananda, a Hindu, made this call for a concord between the world's religions and urged all to seek peaceful coexistence together, ruling out the necessity for conversion from one religion to another.[17] Vivekananda found the resolution, however, in a possible universal religion. "If there is ever to be a universal religion," he said:

16. "Response to Welcome" at the World's Parliament of Religions, 11 September 1893, in *The Complete Works of Swami Vivekananda*, vol. 1 (Calcutta: Advaita Ashrama, 1991), 4.
17. Ibid., 24.

it must be one which will have no location in place or time: which will be infinite like the God it will preach, . . . which will not be Brahminic or Buddhist, Christian or Mohammedan, but the sum total of all these, and still have infinite space for development . . . which will recognise divinity in every man and woman, and whose whole scope . . . will be created in aiding humanity to realise its own true, divine nature. . . . Offer such a religion, and all the nations will follow you.[18]

But does the affirmation of a religion's right to exist and express itself a priori rule out conversion? Whatever the sensitivities of each religious grouping toward losing members to other religions, there surely cannot be a contrived armistice preventing people from questioning their inherited positions, seeking new paths, and converting to different beliefs. There would have been no Buddhism, Christianity, or Islam if this opinion had been held consistently. Conversion happens all the time—from changing one's political opinions to more radical and upsetting changes of heart and life. It is a form of intellectual fascism to think that change can be controlled or disallowed. Nor can one circumscribe the ways in which people account for why they convert. Many indeed explain their commitment to Christ as the goal of their journey of faith. Converts often speak of Christ as the fulfillment of their quest. But I have also heard a former Christian missionary, now a scholar of Sikhism, explain why he became an agnostic. He spoke with all the zeal of a convert, which he indeed is, and is an articulate proselytizer to boot. These are personal stories of faith (or in his case, "unfaith"). There is no way neutrally to adjudicate these claims. A wise old Indian guru once said that each of us is on the playing field; not one of us is sitting in the pavilion.

J. N. Farquhar, the well-known scholar of Hinduism, argued in his *Crown of Hinduism* that Christ is the fulfillment of Hinduism's "highest aspirations and aims"[19] (Swami Vivekananda himself spoke of Buddhism as the fulfillment of Hinduism).[20] A. G. Hogg of Madras, among others, immediately pointed out how this assessment inadvertently belittles Hinduism, for Hindus not only "seek" but also "find" within their tradition.

18. Ibid., 19.
19. J. N. Farquhar, *Crown of Hinduism* (London: H. Milford, 1913).
20. "Response to Welcome," 21–23. He spoke of their total dependency on each other. Concerning Buddhism, he wrote, "On the philosophic side the disciples of the Great Master dashed themselves against the eternal rocks of the Vedas and could not crush them, and on the other side they took away from the nation that eternal God to which every one, man and woman, clings so fondly. The result was that Buddhism had to die a natural death in India . . . the land of its birth" (22).

Karl Rahner, a Catholic theologian, also tried to cope respectfully with other religions from the standpoint of Christian faith through his idea of the "anonymous Christian." According to Rahner, there are many who may not be part of the church but who are still Christians by virtue of their closeness to God, even if they are not aware of it.[21] This is not a new view. Some early apologists claimed that the Christian faith is prefigured in ancient Greek texts and even that Socrates was a Christian before Christ.

People of other faiths might appreciate the attempt to treat their religious sincerity with respect, but surely they cannot be expected to accept a viewpoint that returns to them an eviscerated religion. In other words, even Rahner's attempt "colonizes" the good and holy achievements of other religions.

## Tradition and Understanding

The commonalities among the various religions cannot obscure irreducible differences. A tendency to wish them away variously afflicts theologians, scholars of comparative religious studies, phenomenologists, and religious activists alike. The differences among the world religions, which remain stubbornly irreconcilable, are the distinguishing characteristics of each religion, even though they remain intransigent stumbling blocks in religious dialogue and obstacles to the rationalizing process. Their value exists precisely in their ability to defy easy rationalization. Bracketing the characteristic markers that embody the unique beginning, history, and tradition of each religion risks altering the nature of the belief system itself. There is, therefore, a theological responsibility to bear the burden of these intractable conundrums sim-

21. Karl Rahner argues that "if it be true that the man who is the objective of the Church's missionary endeavour is or can be already prior to it a man who is on the way towards his salvation and finds it in certain circumstances without being reached by the Church's preaching, and if it be true that at the same time that the salvation which he achieves is the salvation of Christ, because there is no other, then it must be possible to be not only an anonymous 'theist,' but also an anonymous *Christian*" (*Theological Investigations*, vol. 6 [London: Darton, Longman, and Todd, 1969], 391–92). To the question that perplexes some, namely, how is this to be conceived outside the traditional understanding of admission to the community of faith through baptism, he answers, "The attempt to account for the grace of redemption and nearness to God in such a way would merely negate it *as* grace. . . . No matter what a man states in his conceptual, theoretical and religious reflection, anyone who does not say in his heart, 'there is no God' (like the 'fool' in the psalm) but testifies to him by the radical acceptance of his being, is a believer. . . . Anyone who has let himself be taken hold of by this grace can be called with every right an 'anonymous Christian'" (395). For a response to Rahner's view (and there are many), see William Danker, "The Anonymous Christian and Christology: A Response," *Missiology: An International Review* 6, no. 2 (1978): 235–41.

ply because there is no other way to do justice to the truths embedded in them. They remain impediments to the organizing, systematizing, and rationalizing schemes of scholarship.

Since the specific task here is to make sense of Christian thought and history in the context of other world religions, the point has to be made that several cardinal, distinguishing truths of the Christian religion have been "bowdlerized" (to borrow an observation of Ernst Gellner) by Christian theologians themselves. The paradox of incarnation; redemptive, vicarious suffering in the context of human solidarity; resurrection in the context of hope in history; and the trinitarian view of God in the context of human freedom are some of the difficulties too hastily ditched for the sake of a rational theology and harmonious religious coexistence. In the absence of more evidence, historical or archaeological, to support counterclaims or unconventional interpretations, Christian scholarship becomes iconoclastic, rendering Christian truth-claims innocuous. Indeed, the liberalism of the nineteenth century was an attempt to transform Christianity into a sublime ethical monotheism—an option that has now been tried for almost two hundred years by many Christian theologians.

How can the meaning of Christianity be rediscovered and held for each time and each place? Perhaps one should begin with a trite observation: Its ground texts have to be taken seriously. This may appear obvious, but it is an ongoing challenge for both conservative and liberal theology. Those who rely on "the Bible says," as if the Bible's interpretation is self-evident, have long been dismissed as uncritical literalists. But neither is truth uncovered merely by analyzing biblical texts in minute detail, dissecting their numerous parts, uncovering not just meaning but meanings hidden between, betwixt, and behind as well. The text is now so dissected and fragmented that there is no coherent way to read it. In addition, much of this fragmentation through scholarship happens outside the context of worship. These texts were endorsed by the early church because they had supported the church in its life and worship.

Literalism reduces the Scriptures to a collection of proof texts applied piecemeal. Protestants who adhere to literalism usually read the Scriptures within one or other denominational tradition, often having its genesis in the sixteenth century. The piecemeal way in which the texts are read often betray a selective reading of church history itself.

The liberal option is usually guilty of arbitrary and selective readings of the text. It makes its own concerns the only basis to understand the text. The historical context of the text and its interpretative history is relativized against the present context, which remains unchallenged. In other words, while our modern predicament raises challenges to the content and context of the text and the inherited interpretive tradition, no challenge is posed to the context of the contemporary interpreter. The interpretive process, or the interrogation of the text, is all one way—tautological and self-justifying. It is a reading that self-consciously cuts itself adrift of any interpretive tradition.

Neither approach preserves the fullness of textual meaning, nor do these approaches keep open the possibilities for each age to encounter the text and its informing tradition. In each new context the hermeneutical challenge has to be taken up anew and rediscovered in and against the weight of historical interpretation. The meaning of the gospel cannot be mediated any other way, except historically.

## Living Tradition

Critical reflection within the Christian Tradition[22] has never stopped, even in the face of corruption, relentless persecution, harassment, bloodshed, and censorship. Christian Tradition is founded on the tension between petrifying historical forms of theological reflection that were once revolutionary and eruptions of radical inspiration. Tradition is never simply *traditum*—what we have received or what is handed down. Tradition is living and expanding *(tradendum)*. All of Christian history is, as G. Ebeling points out, the history of interpretation of Scripture, the reflection on the texts in every context in which the gospel incarnates itself.[23] *Tradendum* as living tradition results from borrowing, accumulating, adapting, and responding to the questions of each context. If this interpretive process (contextualization) were not dynamic, proclamation of the living Word would not be possible. Hence, there is no finality for theology.

An evangelical view is characterized by a commitment to the *euangelion*—the good news of Christ, the Word made flesh. The basis for this extraordinary historical claim is the faith of the earliest Christians, preserved for us in the New Testament (Scripture) and the witness of

22. Tradition with a capital "T" is used to refer to the informing rationale of Christian reflection, that which historically informs Christian thinking. It is based on the written tradition (Scripture) but has expanded as each age has reflected on Scripture. It is the "collective consciousness" that informs Christian reflection and facilitates each new attempt to articulate the gospel. Tradition in lower case is best prefixed by an adjective such as "interpretive" and refers to traditions in the plural.

23. G. Ebeling, *The Problem of Historicity in the Church and Its Proclamation* (Philadelphia: Fortress Press, 1967); also his *Word of God and Tradition* (London: Collins, 1968), 11f.

the apostles (apostolic tradition).[24] The Scriptures are the written tradition, a fact easily overlooked in the polarization of Scripture and tradition. The apostolic reading is a distinctive reading of the Old Testament and the Hebrew tradition, in the same way that the Qur'an is a distinctive reading of its tradition as well.

For all their commonalities and common origin, Islam and Christianity represent quite different readings of the same sources. The different traditions are each built on different claims that resist any well-intentioned Marcion-like excising. Nor can the differences between these traditions be harmonized away without removing the riddles they pose to cultures now and in the future. It is these conundrums that force each age to transcend its immediate preoccupations.

Within the context of religious pluralism, respect for the authority of the text and the informing tradition are crucial starting points. Christian truth emerges from both the written text (Scripture) with its distinctive message (gospel) and the tradition that nurtures these texts (the apostolic witness). There is no more direct route to the text. Rudolph Bultmann, despite some telling criticisms of his theology, appreciated that Christian Tradition begins with the early Christian community, behind whom it is impossible to get. Perhaps in the overreactions to his theology, this insight into the importance of this early Christian consciousness and the faith of Jesus himself went unappreciated.

Where there is a lack of confidence in the authority of Scripture and where there is a breach with the informing tradition, there is also a crisis in Christian self-understanding, since there is no other way to work out what constitutes an authentic Christian position. Raimundo Panikkar, who encouraged dialogue between Christianity and Hinduism and who insisted that there can be fruitful and mutual enrichment of each other in what he called a "dialogical conversation," also believes that the relationship between Christianity and other religions can be discovered only when at least the following three conditions are fulfilled:

> We must remain loyal to the Christian tradition. This is the theological problem. We must not isolate other traditions; they must be interpreted according to their own self-understanding. This is the hermeneutic problem. We cannot leave aside the critical scrutiny of contemporary culture. This is the philosophical problem.[25]

24. As Jaroslav Pelikan stated it, "Tradition is the living faith of the dead; traditionalism is the dead faith of the living. It is traditionalism that gives tradition such a bad name" (Jaroslav Pelikan, *The Vindication of Tradition* [New Haven: Yale University Press, 1984], 65).

25. Raimundo Panikkar, "In Christ There Is Neither Hindu nor Christian: Perspectives on Hindu-Christian Dialogue," in *Religious Issues and Interreligious Dialogues*, 479.

Panikkar's reference to the hermeneutical problem is a call to adopt a self-critical stance. Similarly, Hans Küng, in his *Theology for the Third Millennium*, while urging Christian interpretation to be more sensitive to the context of religious pluralism, characterizes a fully ecumenical theology as one that is responsible before history.[26]

Panikkar, however, goes even further when he writes, "We could sum up the hermeneutical problem with the following affirmation: the correct interpretation of another religion demands that interpreters be convinced of the truth of that religion (from which the believer lives) and, therefore, that they undergo a certain conversion."[27] How this is possible in any sense (for either believers or theologians) is difficult to see unless one can be both Christian *and* Hindu. To understand Christianity one has to begin with its truth claims—"according to its own self-understanding," as indeed this must be allowed to every other religion as well. The point at issue is not the question of loyalty to one's own tradition but whether it is possible to adopt a faith relation to every religion.

Historical responsibility is the only appropriate attitude for Christian theology since Christian claims are made within the context of human struggle and religious devotion. Revelation, as Wolfhart Pannenberg was at pains to show, is historical in nature, occurring within the arena of human life and finding expression in language.[28]

Notwithstanding post-structural and postmodern arguments against foundationalism, it is an enduring truth that what constitutes Christian faith for the Christian is faithfulness to Christ, of whom we can know nothing without the apostolic witness. Anti-foundationalist positions—sometimes adopted uncritically—sever interpretation from its source. If the tradition of textual interpretation loses its status (i.e., if scholars believe that meaningful theological reflection can be done by ignoring the influences of Tradition on our thinking and in-

26. Hans Küng, *Theology for the Third Millennium: An Ecumenical View* (New York: Doubleday, 1988), 204f.

27. Ibid., 484.

28. Wolfhart Pannenberg, ed., *Revelation as History* (New York: Macmillan, 1968), 125–28. Scholars such as Paul Knitter have called for a revisionist method of theology whereby it is "recognised explicitly that 'tradition' cannot be understood only as Christian tradition. By itself, Christian tradition is both incomplete and inaccessible for the work of theology" (Paul Knitter, "Beyond a Mono-religious Theological Education," in *Shifting Boundaries*, 163). But we must be careful not to be methodologically immodest, since whatever is required of a scholar of Christianity is also required of scholars of every other religious tradition. Each has to interrogate his or her own texts (with all the special skills, languages, and knowledge of the culture that task requires) as well as texts of other traditions if this view is to have any meaning. Hindu and Muslim theologians don't function that way. This seems, therefore, a very Western, Christian approach to theology.

stitutions), then possibilities for religious knowledge and truth are compromised.

How is the authenticity of Christian reflection to be judged? Understanding is not possible in the abstract or in a mere citation of the text or creed. Neither is the whole truth about God to be found at the end of an interpretive project. Scholars often repeat the hubris of Babel.

Nicholas Wolterstorff makes the case for the centrality of the Bible for Christian existence when he writes:

> The Bible is truly indispensable for Christian existence, in part because you and I have no other access to God's speech in Jesus Christ than by way of the Bible, in part because, over and over, on the occasion of someone being confronted with some passage from the Bible, God convicts that person of the reality of his revelation in Jesus Christ.[29]

This is what Christian theology means by grace, the working of the Spirit, and revelation at work in the hermeneutical experience of the text. Wolterstorff further argues that

> there is a streak of radical Protestantism that holds that we are not to bring any of our beliefs about God to our interpretation of Scripture but are instead to get all of them *from* our interpretation of Scriptures. It cannot work; interpretation of someone's discourse can only occur in the context of already knowing something about that person.

He places interpretation at the heart of the encounter with God. "Interpretation of Scriptures must go hand in hand with cultivation of devotional practices for knowing God."[30]

Interpretation of the text never begins from nothing. It is part of a longer process of Christian understanding that began with the apostles themselves, who explained their encounter with Christ. The Word lives every time it is articulated (proclaimed) and Christ is heard again. Each context draws out the text and plumbs its depths in a new way.

There is a sense in which the informing tradition, narrowly defined, can be distorting and even oppressive. For example, a patriarchal tradition can, as we have repeatedly seen, exclude women. Race, class, and ethnic prejudice have also existed alongside this gender oppression. However, liberationist and feminist readings of the Scriptures have altered in fundamental ways our understanding of the Tradition

29. Nicholas Wolterstorff, "The Importance of Hermeneutics for a Christian Worldview," in *Disciplining Hermeneutics,* ed. Roger Lundin (Grand Rapids: Eerdmans, 1997), 32.

30. Ibid., 46.

and by doing so extend the informing Tradition. Tradition is renewed by the critical moments within it, and the insights that are uncovered become part of that Tradition.

This is the creative nature of *tradendum*—freedom to interpret and reinterpret based on a responsibility to the founding Tradition. In this connection, Pelikan writes, "From Origen in the third century and Augustine in the fifth, to Thomas Aquinas in the thirteenth century and Martin Luther in the sixteenth, . . . all [have] recognized . . . that it [the freedom to interpret] did not imply the elimination of the letter in favour of an exclusive concentration on the spirit."[31]

Understanding, insight, or a meaningful basis for judgment is quite impossible except within an interpretative and expanding Tradition.[32] It is a false dichotomy to place the quest for truth in juxtaposition to Tradition. Tradition is built on the apostolic witness and the ongoing faith encounter of Christians from all the cultures of the world. "For much of our history," writes Pelikan, "insight has often come through the recitation and arrangement of the materials from tradition."[33] He adds:

> A "leap of progress" is not a standing broad jump which begins at the line of where we are now; it is a running broad jump through where we have been to where we go next. The growth of insight—in science, in the arts, in philosophy and theology—has not come through progressively sloughing off more and more of tradition, as though insight would be purest and deepest when it has finally freed itself of the dead past.[34]

A tradition-bound Christianity is inward-looking and repetitive, lacking both spirit and creativity. A tradition-less Christianity ceases to be Christian at all. This naturally won't bother relativists or those who adopt a nonrealist or antirealist position, since they would take every claim to truth to be valid. According to Cupitt, "All of us are entirely free to build our worlds in ways that seem best to us, we have no basis for calling other people's worlds irrational."[35] Elsewhere he declares, "We no longer actually need roots, identity, stability, or a provenance. We can live without those things. Me, I don't want them anymore. I'd prefer to be without identity. I'd like to belong to no ethnic group, and

31. Pelikan, *Vindication of Tradition*, 71.

32. Hans-Georg Gadamar's discussion of the "historically effected consciousness" and his analysis of the "historicity of understanding" make these points incisively (Hans-Georg Gadamar, *Truth and Method* [New York: Crossroad, 1992], 314–79, 265–85).

33. Pelikan, *Vindication of Tradition*, 73.

34. Ibid., 81.

35. Cupitt, *After God*, 173.

to have no Other. They call me a nihilist: but I'm beginning to feel at ease, at home in nihilism."[36]

Cupitt's nihilism is entirely contrived, founded on wishes. Only disembodied reason—"stripped of roots, identity and provenance"—is free of Tradition and history. Christianity is antithetical to nihilism. The Word became suffering flesh in history, and its truths are accessible only as the Word in culture.

> The living Tradition is "Christian" by virtue of the two-way process of judgment and affirmation that takes place between Christian communities and the Scriptures. Pelikan ends his monograph *The Vindication of Tradition* with these lines from Goethe, What you have as heritage, Take now as task; For thus you will make it your own.[37]

John Hick's categorization of possible Christian responses to other religions helps in summarizing the case made here. He suggests three categories of approaches: exclusivism, inclusivism, and pluralism.[38] The exclusivist position, he says, "relates salvation/liberation exclusively to one particular tradition" or to one group. The inclusivist position holds that "while salvation is only possible through Christ . . . the benefits are not confined to those who respond to it."[39] In this group would fall any discussion of the "unknown Christ of Hinduism" or Karl Rahner's "anonymous Christian." The exclusivist stance, he argues, is not renounced but universalized through this inclusivism. "Is it not a somewhat empty gesture to insist upon affixing a Christian label to them?" he asks.[40]

Third, the position that Hicks himself argues for is the pluralist view, which he thinks accepts the implication of a true inclusiveness, namely, that "there is a plurality of saving human responses to the ultimate divine reality. There is not merely one but a plurality of ways of salvation or liberation." If salvation is understood to be "the actual transformation of human life from self-centredness to Reality-centredness," then it cannot be confined to any one religious tradition.

In his view, what prevents Christians from moving from an inclusivist to a pluralist view is their belief in incarnation and the doctrine of the Trinity, which was defined at the Councils of Nicaea and Chalcedon (an "all or nothing Christology"[41]). However, if this Christology of "sub-

36. Ibid., 99.
37. Pelikan, *Vindication of Tradition*, 82.
38. Frank Whaling, ed., *The World's Religious Traditions* (Edinburgh: T & T Clark, 1984), 152ff.
39. Ibid., 152.
40. Ibid., 153.
41. Ibid., 154.

stance" was replaced with a "degree Christology" in which "incarnations applied to the activity of God's spirit or God's grace in human lives, so that the divine will is done on earth,"[42] then any claim to exclusivism would be invalid. God would be perceived as working through all religions as he does through Christ.

Hick concedes that there is no special vantage point for one who holds the pluralist position. "The answer," he writes:

> is that he does not know this, if by knowledge we mean infallible cognition. . . . The pluralist position is arrived at inductively. . . . If we look for the transcendence of egoism and a re-centering in the transcendent Real, then I venture the proposition that as far as human observation and historical memory can tell, this occurs to about the same extent in the great world traditions [43]

He therefore advocates that we "avoid the particular names used within particular traditions and use a term which is consistent with the faith of each of them—Ultimate Reality or the Real."[44] Relating to other traditions, in this view, has the benefits of informing us and making us aware "of other aspects or dimensions of the Real, and of other possibilities of response to the Real."[45]

What I have been describing as an attempt at universalizing could also be included in the category inclusivist, since this too attempts to draw all possibilities into a whole—often achieved by relativizing any claim to distinctiveness. Hick's plea for a full awareness of the implications of living in a religiously plural society has to be taken seriously simply because it is true that all religions do exist in a globally connected world. Cultures no longer live in relative isolation from each other; they cannot.

However, the fact of a religiously plural society or the fact that theology can be enriched by contact with other cultures and religions does not necessarily make the case for a pluralist position. All religions have survived because their adherents believe that their religion supports their experience of God. There is no scope here to go into the question of Christology to any great extent except to say that Hick's argument for a Christology of degree based on D. M. Baillie's Christology is not self-evident, as John Baillie showed in responding to Hick. He writes, "I think my brother would have said that all enabling grace that has ever in any age been given to men has proceeded from the Son as well

42. Ibid., 134.
43. Ibid., 158.
44. Ibid., 159.
45. Ibid., 164.

as from the Father and the Holy Spirit."[46] There appears to be no easy way to jettison the early Christian faith in Jesus as God made flesh and what the early church came to understand as the trinitarian view of God.

But there is a further requirement: An authentic Christian reflection can no longer ignore other cultures and other religions. It has to be articulated *in the context of the whole of life,* its sociopolitical crises and the ideological battleground of public life. The Christian faith can be fully grasped only in its universality, that is, insofar as its significance for the whole of life and history can be expressed. Lesslie Newbigin, in his discussion of the relation of Christianity to other religions (and how Christians may meaningfully speak of the finality of Christ), placed the Christian tradition within the history of human beings, not within the history of religions. Hence, for Newbigin, "The Gospel is 'a secular announcement.'" It is not merely a religious announcement. He explains, "To speak of the finality of Christ is to express such a conviction and such a commitment concerning the point of the human story as a whole. It is not a point of vantage above all sectional viewpoints. It is vulnerable. But without accepting the risks which it involves, there can be no universal history."[47] This option to articulate the universal meaning of Christ is part and parcel of the nature of the Christian faith. A Christian theology of religions ultimately is part of a theology of history—the Christian view of the meaning and purpose of history, time, and eschatology.

Christian theologies of religions have often floundered because this universal perspective is lost or ignored. They explain the status of Christianity relative to other faiths. Farquhar, for example, sees Christianity as the crown of Hinduism. The Catholic model has traditionally placed the church at the center with other Christians and then placed other devout people in ever-widening concentric circles around it. In this perception, the religions are like planets, and a theology of religions describes the universe in which these planets exist. Christianity is the "sun" in the center of that universe. In this regard, Hick's categorization of Christians as exclusive or inclusive is quite accurate.

Rudolph Otto spoke of each religion moving around its own axis. Each great religion of the world, without laboring this metaphor, in a

46. John Baillie, "Some Comments on Professor Hick's Article on the 'Christology of D. M. Baillie,'" *Scottish Journal of Theology* 11 (1958): 268; refer also to Douglas Mc-Cready, "The Disintegration of John Hick's Christology," *Journal of Evangelical Theological Society* 39, no. 2 (June 1996): 256–70.

47. Lesslie Newbigin, *The Finality of Christ* (London: SCM Press, 1969), 72.

sense functions with its own "universe of meaning," its own point of reference and "plausibility structures." Christianity certainly does. This does not mean that there are no similarities between the religions of the world. There may even be intersections between religions like intersecting circles, but theological self-understanding exists in a coherent "universe of meaning." A religion cannot be grasped piecemeal or on the basis of having a special vantage point above all these universes of meaning: a God's-eye view.[48]

Early Christians quickly became aware that faith in Christ unsettled their natural, familial, social, and cultural worlds. They had to encounter as individuals the life and teachings of Christ. Peter had to learn how this new community transcended ethnic, tribal, and national allegiances, even his Jewish pride. The new community of Jesus shared a solidarity across nations, races, gender, and classes (even between slaves and masters) from the beginning.

Christian faith is catholic because it is contextualized everywhere. It is for this reason that reflection within Tradition must preserve the creative tension between contextualization and catholicity, for not all interpretation is necessarily authentic. It is a process of critical theological discourse and exchange that establishes its catholicity and thereby its authenticity.

Cultural meaning and apostolicity are part of the authentic articulation of Christian faith. It is the way a worshiping community not only explains its encounter with the living Christ but also locates itself within the body of Christ. Christian reflection is committed to articulating its universal significance in the best way it can, interrogating its sacred heritage as it discovers anew the meaning of the gospel. It is not pluralist but must remain an open witness in the context of pluralism.

---

48. David Pailin claimed that "the limitation imposed upon the Christian theologian by having to start from the Christian tradition is not, however, very great. It may in some ways be compared to the limitations which the interpreter of a poem, a musical script or a character in a play feels imposed upon him by the text" (David Pailin, "Authenticity in the Interpretation of Christianity," in *The Cardinal Meaning: Essays in Comparative Hermeneutics: Buddhism and Christianity*, ed. Michael Pye and Robert Morgan [The Hague: Mouton, 1973], 158).

Robert Morgan points out that "wherever the reference of the Christian tradition to Jesus has been abandoned, as it was for example by D. F. Strauss, Christians have rejected the innovation" (Robert Morgan, "Expansion and Criticism of the Christian Tradition," in *The Cardinal Meaning*, 71). He writes, "Christians' conviction about Jesus is summarised by saying that he is Gospel! The crucial question to ask about the historical Jesus would therefore seem to be whether he is experienced as Gospel by those who accepted him in his lifetime. If Christian response to Jesus has nothing in common with the response made by those who accepted him in his lifetime, then it is not truly Jesus who is introduced in Christian proclamation" (71–72).

Other religions have the responsibility to explain their claim to universality as well. Christian theology is not required to pass judgment; it
cannot. It is called only to be faithful to the task of bringing the Word
to speech so that *all* may hear the gospel.

# 6

# Evangelical Illusions

*Postmodern Christianity and the Growth of Muslim Communities in Europe and North America*

IRVING HEXHAM

It is a fundamental principle with us that to renounce reason is to renounce religion; that religion and reason go hand in hand; and that all irrational religion is false religion.

John Wesley[1]

The concept of an "unbiased and objective" science, aimed at "absolute
truth" based on pure reason that arose during the nineteenth century has
today entirely lost its reason and justification. We have now come to understand that in reality science is always based upon a personal contem-

---

1. John Wesley to Dr. Thomas Rutherforth, 28 March 1768, in Albert C. Outler, ed.,
*The Works of John Wesley*, vol. 12 (Grand Rapids: Zondervan, n.d.), 354. Note the same
volume contains Wesley's *A Compendium of Logic*.

porary-historical premise. . . . Community, which until now was regarded only as a political concept, has now become a basic scientific principle.

Hans Löher[2]

Faced with the growth of Muslim and other religious communities in traditionally Christian countries, many evangelical theologians are adopting philosophical views shaped by postmodernism as a solution to the challenges of religious pluralism. For example, the well-known New Testament scholar N. T. Wright, in his book *The Challenge of Jesus*, says, "We must take on board the full weight of the postmodern critique of Enlightenment theories of knowledge."[3] Exactly what the "postmodern critique" means he never spells out, but he makes it clear that it is the growth of religious pluralism that causes him to take the postmodern critique seriously.[4] Therefore, he warns other Christians against denying "the presence of postmodernity."[5]

When we turn to other evangelicals, we find a growing number embracing a postmodern approach to religious pluralism. Thus, Gerald McDermott can confidently proclaim, "One of the boons of postmodernism is that now evangelicals are on a level playing field."[6] Other writers who advocate this type of thinking include Stanley Grenz,[7] Nancey Murphy,[8] Richard Middleton, and Brian Walsh.[9] None of them embrace secular postmodernism in its pure form. Nevertheless, they all seem to believe that the essential critique of modern thought and rational argument offered by postmodern thinkers is correct. Therefore, they attempt to create an evangelical form of postmodernism that allows them to retain some Christian truth claims while accepting many of the basic presuppositions of the postmodern critique of rationality.

2. Hans Löher, *Über die Stellung und Bedeutung der Heilkunde im nationalsozialistischen Staate* (Berlin: Nornen-Verlag, 1935), 22; cited in George L. Mosse, *Nazi Culture* (New York: Schocken Books, 1981), 230. The translation I have given is slightly different from that of Mosse. Cf. Alan Sokal and Jean Bricmont, *Fashionable Nonsense: Postmodern Intellectuals' Abuse of Science* (New York: Picador, 1998).

3. N. T. Wright, *The Challenge of Jesus: Rediscovering Who Jesus Was and Is* (Downers Grove, Ill.: InterVarsity Press, 1999), 194.

4. Ibid., 152.

5. Ibid., 154.

6. Gerald R. McDermott, *Can Evangelicals Learn from World Religions? Jesus, Revelation, and Religious Traditions* (Downers Grove, Ill.: InterVarsity Press, 2000), 21.

7. Stanley J. Grenz, *A Primer on Postmodernism* (Grand Rapids: Eerdmans, 1996).

8. Nancey Murphy, *Anglo-American Postmodernity: Philosophical Perspectives on Science, Religion, and Ethics* (Boulder, Colo.: Westview, 1997).

9. J. Richard Middleton and Brian J. Walsh, *Truth Is Stranger Than It Used to Be* (Downers Grove, Ill.: InterVarsity Press, 1995); and *The Transforming Vision: Shaping a Christian World View* (Downers Grove, Ill.: InterVarsity Press, 1984).

Postmodernism proper derives its name from Jean-François Lyotard's 1979 essay *The Postmodern Condition: A Report on Knowledge.*[10] Lyotard defines the postmodern as "incredulity towards metanarratives."[11] What exactly this means is difficult to say. Throughout his work, Lyotard makes it clear that the source of postmodern philosophies lies in the works of Friedrich Nietzsche[12] before concluding that

> the postmodern would be that which, in the modern, puts forward the unpresentable in presentation itself. . . . A postmodern artist or writer is in the position of a philosopher: the text he writes, the work he produces are not in principle governed by preestablished rules. . . . The artist and the writer then, are working without rules in order to formulate the rules of what *will have been done*. Hence the fact that the work and text have the characteristics of an *event.*[13]

This observation leads Lyotard to end his essay with this call: "Let us wage war on totality; let us witness to the unpresentable; let us activate the differences and save the honor of the name."[14]

This attack on conventional knowledge reminds me of a passage in Peter Drucker's classic work *The End of Economic Man,* in which he writes, "The Nazi agitator whom, many years ago, I heard proclaim to a wildly cheering peasants' meeting: '*We don't want lower bread prices, we don't want higher bread prices, we don't want unchanged bread prices, we want National Socialist bread prices,*' came as near to explaining fascism as anyone I have heard since."[15] So too the postmodernist doesn't want conventional truth, rational truth, or any other form of truth—the postmodernist wants postmodern truth.

The incoherence of Lyotard and other postmodern writers who totally disregard empirical evidence is noted by Ernest Gellner, who wryly observes, "It is almost impossible to give a coherent definition or account of postmodernism."[16] Then he cites Paul Rabinow, who says, "All one can say is that it is a kind of hysteria of subjectivity."[17] Gellner agrees with this judgment, observing that

10. Jean-François Lyotard, *The Postmodern Condition: A Report on Knowledge* (Minneapolis: University of Minnesota Press, 1979).

11. Ibid., xxiv.

12. Ibid., xii, 39, 81.

13. Ibid., 81.

14. Ibid., 82.

15. Peter Drucker, *The End of Economic Man* (New York: John Day Company, 1939), 13–14.

16. Ernest Gellner, *Postmodernism, Reason, and Religions* (London: Routledge, 1992), 29.

17. Ibid.

the operational meaning of postmodernism in anthropology seems to be something like this: a refusal (in practice, rather selective) to countenance any objective facts, any independent social structures, and their replacement by a pursuit of "meanings," both those of the objects of inquiry and of the inquirer. Thus there is a double stress on subjectivity: the world-creation by the person studied, and the text creation by the investigator.[18]

This negative appraisal of the role of postmodernism in anthropology is reinforced by Karla Poewe's essay "Writing Culture—Writing Fieldwork: The Proliferation of Experimental and Experiential Ethnographies,"[19] in which she shows what a dead end this approach actually is. The significance of both Gellner's and Poewe's judgments is important because evangelical theologians are turning to postmodern theories precisely because they believe these theories bring them closer to real life and the experience of contemporary people in a religiously plural society. Yet they and many other writers, including advocates of secular postmodern theories, such as Lyotard, admit that postmodernism is actually a theoretical construct that continually re-creates its own world, completely disregarding traditional empirical approaches to reality. Thus, although most evangelical writers reject certain aspects of postmodernism, they agree that we need to abandon foundationalist claims to knowledge in favor of some form of communal or relational knowledge and admit that these theories are inspired by the teaching of Friedrich Nietzsche and Martin Heidegger on the Continent, and Alasdair MacIntyre, Richard Rorty, and Thomas Kuhn in North America.[20]

Building on the work of these secular scholars, advocates of evangelical postmodernism say that we must abandon concepts of truth that have been polluted by Enlightenment rationality in favor of a more thor-

18. Ibid., 29–30.

19. Karla Poewe, "Writing Culture—Writing Fieldwork: The Proliferation of Experimental and Experiential Ethnographies," *Ethonos* 61, no. 3–4 (1996): 177–206.

20. The groundwork for evangelical acceptance of postmodern ideas was laid by Cornelius van Til in *A Christian Theory of Knowledge* (Nutley, N.J.: Presbyterian and Reformed, 1969); and earlier *The Defense of the Faith* (Nutley, N.J.: Presbyterian and Reformed, 1963). His work was popularized by Rousas J. Rushdoony in books such as *Intellectual Schizophrenia: Culture, Crisis, and Education* (Philadelphia: Presbyterian and Reformed, 1961). Behind these writers, even though they may disagree on particular points, is Herman Dooyeweerd's *A New Critique of Theoretical Thought*, 4 vols. (Philadelphia: Presbyterian and Reformed, 1953). In South Africa similar ideas were developed by H. G. Stoker in *Oorsprong en Rigting*, 2 vols. (Kaapstad: Tafelerg, 1967); J. A. L. Taljaard; and others. See H. J. J. Bingle, ed., *Truth and Reality—Waarheid en Werklikheid* (Braamfontein: De Jong's Bookshop, 1971). These ideas are debated in E. R. Geehan, *Jerusalem and Athens: Critical Discussions on the Philosophy and Apologetics of Cornelius van Til* (Nutley, N.J.: Presbyterian and Reformed, 1971); and Ronald H. Nash, *The Philosophy of Gordon H. Clark: A Festschrift* (Philadelphia: Presbyterian and Reformed, 1968).

oughly biblical view. Why this is so and what exactly this "biblical view" involves is never really made clear, although some indications are given in various passages. For example, Grenz finds the locus of truth in Jesus Christ[21] and appears to say that certainty can be located in a Christian metanarrative grounded in our participation in community.[22] Nancey Murphy builds on the work of Alasdair MacIntyre to produce a similar notion of communal truth.[23] How Middleton and Walsh understand truth is unclear. What is certain is that they somehow link it to justice and the community of faith directed by biblical insights.[24]

Whatever their differences, advocates of a modified evangelical postmodernism in one way or another appeal to communal insights informed by the Christian tradition and the words of Scripture as key factors in arriving at truth. Thus, by selectively embracing those aspects of postmodernism that support his own views, N. T. Wright attempts to forge a theory of knowledge that he calls "critical realism."[25] Unfortunately, when he spells out the meaning of this approach, it varies little from secular postmodern philosophy and relies on "the articulation of worldviews,"[26] a term he borrows from the work of Walsh and Middleton among others.[27]

Consequently, after a long and sometimes useful discussion of history and the scientific method, Wright states that "we cannot stand outside our worldviews, any more than we can see without our eyes."[28] This is because worldviews have to do with "the presuppositional, precognitive stage of a culture or society."[29] Consequently, a worldview "embraces all deep-level human perceptions."[30] "Worldviews," he claims, "are thus the basic stuff of human existence, the lens through which the world is seen, the blueprint for how one should live in it and above all the sense of identity and place which enables human beings to be what they are."[31] They are, he continues, "like the foundations of a house: vital but invisible."[32]

21. Grenz, *Primer on Postmodernism,* 164.

22. Ibid., 168–69.

23. Murphy, *Anglo-American Postmodernity,* 123–29, 210.

24. Cf. Middleton and Walsh, *Truth Is Stranger Than It Used to Be,* 169–76, 183–85.

25. N. T. Wright, *The New Testament and the People of God* (Minneapolis: Fortress Press, 1992).

26. Ibid., 65.

27. Ibid., 123.

28. Ibid., 121.

29. Ibid., 122.

30. Ibid., 123.

31. Ibid., 124.

32. Ibid., 125. Many of the problems created by this type of argument are discussed in Karl Mannheim, *Essays on the Sociology of Knowledge* (London: Routledge & Kegan Paul, 1952).

To be brutally frank, this is sophisticated gobbledygook[33] that comes straight out of the pages of Jakob Wilhelm Hauer's[34] *Deutscher Glaube*[35] and the writings of the Nazi psychologist Ludwig Klages.[36] Significantly, it is not the way "worldview" is used by Abraham Kuyper,[37] James Orr,[38] or Francis Schaeffer,[39] all of whom see a worldview as an intellectual construct, or system, based on principles that make sense of a particular religious commitment.[40]

## The Poverty of Postmodernism

Wright, Grenz, Murphy, Middleton, Walsh, and other evangelical theologians advocating postmodernism assure us that postmodern thinking is a fact of modern life and is unquestionable. Actually this is far from true. Anyone who reads contemporary conversion accounts,

33. In calling it gobbledygook, I do not deny the importance of understanding situational knowledge. Cf. Irving Hexham and Karla Poewe, *Understanding Cults and New Religions* (Grand Rapids: Eerdmans, 1996), 12–24, 163–66, which is useful in terms of understanding people's commitments and arguments. Rather, my position is close to that of Mary Douglas, who sees the importance of relational factors while affirming the importance of a real world and commonsense rationality. Cf. Mary Douglas, *Natural Symbols* (London: The Cressent Press, 1970).

34. For a long discussion of Hauer's work, see Horst Junginger, *Von der philologischen zur völkischen Religionswissenschaft: Das Fac Religionswissenschaft an der Universität Tübingen von der Mitte des 19. Jahrhunderts bis zum Ende des Dritten Reiches* (Stuttgart: Franz Steiner Verlag, 1999).

35. Jakob Wilhelm Hauer, *Deutscher Glaube: Monatsschrift der Deutschen Glaubensbewegung, 1934–1944* (Tübingen).

36. Ludwig Klages, *Der Geist als Widersacher der Seele*, 3 vols. (Leipzig: Ambrosius Barth, 1932). Cf. Anne Harrington, *Reenchanted Science: Holism in German Culture from Wilhelm II to Hitler* (Princeton: Princeton University Press, 1996), 211–12.

37. Abraham Kuyper, *Calvinism: Six Stone-lectures* (Amsterdam: Höveker & Wormser, 1898). A view somewhat different from my own is taken by Peter S. Heslam in *Creating a Christian Worldview: Abraham Kuyper's Lectures on Calvinism* (Grand Rapids: Eerdmans, 1998).

38. James Orr, *The Christian View of God and the World as Centering in the Incarnation: Being the First Series of Kerr Lectures*, 3d ed. (New York: Charles Scribner's Sons, 1897).

39. Francis A. Schaeffer, *The Complete Works of Francis A. Schaeffer*, vol. 1 (Westchester, Ill.: Crossway, 1983), 124.

40. Orr, *Christian View of God*, 365–70; Kuyper, *Calvinism*, 4–5. For a rather restricted discussion of the history of the term *worldview*, see David Keith Naugle, "A History and Theory of the Concept of 'Weltanschauung' (Worldview)" (Ph.D. diss., University of Texas at Arlington, 1998). The main problem with this work is that for his section on the German background to the term *Weltanschauung* he relies almost exclusively on Helmut G. Meier, "'Weltanschauung' Studien zu einer Geschichte und Theorie des Begiffs" (Ph.D. diss., Westfälischen Wilhelms-Universität zu Münster, 1967) and fails to discuss German primary sources.

especially conversion to Islam, soon discovers that people convert because they believe they are embracing the truth. It's easy to cite Hollywood scripts and TV soap operas in which postmodern attitudes are commonplace. It's much harder to come up with solid sociological evidence that the majority of people, or even a large minority, in modern society embrace postmodern relativism. They do not. Most people, except perhaps students of literature, still hold to some remarkably traditional views about truth, science, and personal behavior.[41]

Despite the assurances of Wright and other advocates of postmodernism, the postmodern world they claim exists outside the church is an illusion of their own making. When Wright writes, "Let me spell out the context within which we find ourselves and the Western world today"[42] and then sketches a vision of a relativistic postmodern society, he totally misinterprets the true situation. So too do Grenz, Murphy, Middleton, Walsh, and a host of other evangelical advocates of postmodern analysis as the new cure-all for youth ministry and evangelism.

The simple fact is that *Star Trek* is not the world in which most people live, nor are other TV shows, novels, or films. Therefore, if we want to know what type of world we live in and how our contemporaries think, we need to take a close look at reliable social survey evidence, not popular entertainment. When this is done, the picture is very different from that presented by the advocates of postmodernism. There is no longitudinal empirical evidence of a fundamental change of values in North American or European society in this century let alone the last thirty years of postmodern rhetoric. Nor can it be argued that people are less rational or less influenced by rational considerations than in the past. If anything people are more rational today due to the advent of computer technology rather than less rational. Finally, in general, individualism is on the increase, not decrease. For better or worse, modernity is alive and well, and we would do well to adapt our message to it rather than embrace an intellectual illusion promoted by a small sector of the intellectual elite who are out of touch with ordinary people. Social surveys such as those conducted by Reginald Bibby in Canada and by Rodney Stark in the United States simply do not support the claims of postmodern theorists.[43]

41. When I started work at the North Western Gas Board in Stockport, England, at the age of fifteen in 1958, there were thirteen apprentices. By the time I was eighteen, with the exception of myself, all but one, who was already married, felt compelled to get married because they got their girlfriends pregnant. Recognizing that this is not a scientific survey, it still seems to me to say a great deal about the supposed morality of modern times.

42. Wright, *Challenge of Jesus*, 154.

43. Conversation with Reginald Bibby, 5 October 2000, Lethbridge Lodge, Lethbridge.

Of course, ordinary people are not philosophers. But to be frank, I find it difficult to find professional philosophers who are enthusiastic about postmodernism either, and few are prepared to throw out foundationalism.[44] Most admit serious problems in the realm of epistemology. But then they point out that problems are not new and express confidence that a solution will appear in time. Others, such as Hugo Meynell, have launched devastating attacks on the postmodern enterprise by pointing out the inconsistencies and philosophical weaknesses of both Continental and American postmodern thinkers.[45] Similarly, the fact that a thinker of the stature of Jürgen Habermas can still embrace "the Enlightenment Project" despite doubts about foundationalism shows that the triumphalism of much postmodern rhetoric is misplaced.[46]

Finally, the close connection between Continental postmodernists and national socialism ought to give pause to anyone advocating deconstruction or similar theories. To raise the specter of national socialism may sound like an ad hominem argument, but in this context it is relevant and therefore permissible. If Paul de Man was the only postmodern thinker to have been a Nazi, one could easily argue that this proves nothing.[47] But far too many of the seminal figures in the postmodern movement appear to have their intellectual roots in national socialism to dismiss their involvement as a mere coincidence.[48]

For example, the accusations against Martin Heidegger, who is one of the acknowledged sources of postmodern thought,[49] are devastating. At first the defenders of Heidegger tried to argue that he was a Nazi for a short period until he recognized the evils of the party and withdrew from political life. This sounded convincing until Hugo Ott's biography proved beyond all doubt that Heidegger was and remained a Nazi until

44. For example, as early as 1994 the postmodern attack on foundationalism was coming under strong attack from philosophers. See Horace L. Fairlamb, *Critical Conditions: Postmodernity and the Question of Foundations* (Cambridge: Cambridge University Press, 1994).

45. Hugo A. Meynell, *Redirection Philosophy* (Toronto: University of Toronto Press, 1998).

46. Jürgen Habermas, *The Philosophical Discourse of Modernity* (Cambridge, Mass.: MIT Press, 1995).

47. On the de Man affair see David Lehman, *Signs of the Times: Deconstruction and the Fall of Paul de Man* (New York: Poseidon Press, 1991).

48. Here I am deliberately not discussing the work of Hans-Georg Gadamer. His own autobiographical writings and the recent biography by his acolyte Jean Grondin, *Hans-Georg Gadamer eine Biographie* (Tübingen: Mohr Siebeck, 1999), raise far too many questions that go beyond the scope of this chapter.

49. Grenz, *Primer on Postmodernism*, 86, 103–8.

at least the end of World War II.[50] Once there was no way to avoid this fact, Heidegger's admirers switched their line of argument, insisting that whatever his political convictions may have been, his philosophy stands by itself and must be judged as a major philosophical contribution to twentieth-century thought.[51] The confidence of his defenders was punctured by the publication of Reinhard May's revelation that the master "appropriated" without acknowledgment key sections for his classic *Being and Time*[52] from long-forgotten German translations of Chinese and Japanese texts.[53] Put more crudely, the man was a plagiarist. Even more damaging was Johannes Fritsche's demonstration that key passages in *Being and Time* share a common structure with Adolf Hitler's *Mein Kampf* and that the entire argument is rooted in national socialist ideology.[54]

It is also significant to note that while thinkers such as Michel Foucault, Georges Batailles, and Jean-François Lyotard were personally to the left of the political spectrum, their books and ideas have been taken up and propagated by the new right in Germany and elsewhere.[55] Equally worrisome is the fact that postmodern politics in Germany are clearly rooted in national socialism and the transformation of the postwar left into a new right.[56] If nothing else, these connections show the inherent instability of such ideas and serve as a warning against their adoption by Christians.

50. Hugo Ott, *Martin Heidegger: A Political Life,* trans. Allan Blunden (London: Fontana, 1994).

51. Tom Rockmore in *Heidegger and French Philosophy: Humanism, Antihumanism, and Being* (London: Routledge, 1995) shows how Heidegger actively rehabilitated himself through his contacts with former students in France following World War II and the way he distorted his own earlier arguments to make himself appear respectable.

52. The English edition of *Being and Time* was translated by John Macquarrie and Edward Robinson in 1962 and published by Harper & Row in London. Johannes Fritsche shows that significant portions were mistranslated, thus obscuring Heidegger's affinity to Nazism (*Historical Destiny and National Socialism in Heidegger's Being and Time* [Berkeley: University of California Press, 1999], 2, 19–21, 51–52, 62, 198). An examination of the German edition, *Sein und Zeit* (Tübingen: Max Niemeyer Verlag, 1979), supports Fritsche's claims.

53. Reinhard May, *Heidegger's Hidden Sources,* trans. Graham Parks (London: Routledge, 1996).

54. See Fritsche, *Historical Destiny.*

55. Richard J. Goslan, *Fascism's Return: Scandal, Revision, and Ideology since 1980* (Lincoln: University of Nebraska Press, 1998), 224–28.

56. Hans-Georg Betz, *Postmodern Politics in Germany: The Politics of Resentment* (New York: St. Martin's Press, 1991). See also Pierre Krebs, *Im Kampf um das Wesen* (Horn: Burkhart Weecke Verlag, 1996). With his Ph.D. from the Sorbonne, Krebs is one of the acknowledged leaders of neo-fascism in Germany.

Not all North American postmodern thinkers explicitly acknowledge the influence of Continental philosophy. Murphy in fact wants to develop an "American postmodernism" freed from the burden of European scandals.[57] To do this she relies extensively on the works of W. V. O. Quine, Alasdair MacIntyre, and Thomas Kuhn among others.[58] Space does not permit a discussion of all these writers. Therefore, I will concentrate on the work of Thomas Kuhn, who has inspired many evangelical writers.[59]

Kuhn's writings[60] enabled many people to take up the cause of cultural relativism and later postmodernism.[61] In doing so they proudly rejected appeals to scientific objectivity and claimed that Kuhn had shown that the idea of objectivity is an illusion. Instead of objectivity in science we have paradigms or frameworks that inform the observers' observations and determine their theories.[62] Thus, all appeals to "the facts" are illusory because what we call facts are entirely determined by the way we see the world.

Before this argument against scientific method and the quest for objectivity is accepted, three points need to be made about Kuhn's work. First, the popular understanding that Kuhn rejects the scientific method and embraces relativism is completely false. In his later writings, Kuhn argues that he is talking about two kinds of science: "normal science" and "revolutionary science." In his view most science is "normal science," and even people who engage in "revolutionary science" must master the methods of normal science before they can begin to make progress. Such normal science depends on various objective factors such as accuracy in observation. Thus, Kuhn explicitly states, "It is emphatically *not* my view that 'adoption of a new scientific theory is an intuitive or mystical affair, a matter for psychological description rather than logical or methodological codification.' On the contrary, [there are] good reasons for theory choice . . . exactly the kind

57. Murphy, *Anglo-American Postmodernity*, 1.

58. Ibid., 2–3.

59. Cf. Middleton and Walsh, *Transforming Vision*, 169–73; Murphy, *Anglo-American Postmodernity*, 51–52; and Grenz, *Primer on Postmodernism*, 54–56.

60. Thomas S. Kuhn, *The Structure of Scientific Revolutions* (Chicago: University of Chicago Press, 1962).

61. Although the appeal is usually made to the work of Kuhn, writers such as Paul Feyerabend and N. R. Hanson would be better representatives of relativism. Feyerabend is strongly criticized in Derek Gjertsen, *Science and Philosophy: Past and Present* (New York: Penguin, 1989), 153–64.

62. For a strong criticism of this position, see Karl R. Popper, *The Myth of the Framework*, ed. M. A. Notturno (London: Routledge, 1994).

of standard in philosophy of science: accuracy, scope, simplicity, fruit-fulness and the like."[63]

Second, even if Kuhn's early work did support cultural relativism, both the historical and conceptual basis of his theorizing have been devastated by Bernard Cohen, Israel Scheffler, and others. In a pains-taking study of the historical circumstances surrounding changing scientific theories, Cohen[64] has shown that science has advanced as the result of slow progress and the accumulation of knowledge based on increasingly accurate observations, not sudden paradigm shifts.[65] Further, the internal logic and self-contradictions in Kuhn's views were clearly exposed by Scheffler as early as 1967.[66] After a detailed study of Kuhn's argument, Scheffler concluded that Kuhn's position was self-contradictory and that in the end he saved his arguments from total ridicule by circularity and appeals to ideas that he himself earlier rejected.[67]

The idea of a paradigm shift, or changing frameworks, is useful shorthand for real changes in perception. But the mechanism by which such changes occur and the significance of those changes in terms of objectivity have been greatly misunderstood by the public and many academics. Apart from the humanities, education faculties, and some schools of theology, there is in general a return to hard science and a strong sense of objectivity in many branches of science.[68]

63. Thomas Kuhn, "Logic of Discovery or Psychology of Research," in *Criticism and the Growth of Knowledge*, ed. Imre Lakatos and Alan Musgrave (Cambridge: Cambridge University Press, 1970), 261. See also Thomas S. Kuhn, *The Essential Tension: Selected Studies in Scientific Tradition and Change* (Chicago: University of Chicago Press, 1977).

64. J. Bernard Cohen, *Revolution in Science* (Cambridge: Harvard University Press, 1985). For further criticisms of Kuhn's work, see also Gjertsen, *Science and Philosophy;* and Keith Dixon, *Sociological Theory: Pretence and Possibility* (London: Routledge & Kegan Paul, 1973). A more sympathetic yet critical approach is found in Alan Ryan, *The Philosophy of the Social Sciences* (London: Macmillan, 1976).

65. Other scathing criticisms of Kuhn's work include Stephen Toulmin, *Human Understanding* (Princeton: Princeton University Press, 1972); and Stanley L. Jaki, *The Road of Science and the Ways to God* (Chicago: University of Chicago Press, 1978). For a book that deals with the general problem of irrationalism, although it does not directly confront Kuhn, see John C. Burnham, *How Superstition Won and Science Lost* (New Brunswick, N.J.: Rutgers University Press, 1987).

66. Israel Scheffler, *Science and Subjectivity* (Indianapolis: Bobbs-Merrill, 1967), 74–89.

67. Ibid., 88–89.

68. Cf. Ronald N. Giere, *Explaining Science: A Cognitive Approach* (Chicago: University of Chicago Press, 1988); and Jaki, *Road of Science*. For a popular account of contemporary physics, see John Gribbin, *In Search of Schrödinger's Cat* (New York: Bantam Books, 1984).

One problem that plagues talk about "objectivity" is the straw man erected by relativists who assert old problems as though they are new discoveries.[69] Thus, the observation that all researchers have their own biases is not new, nor does it preclude the attempt by social scientists to minimize bias. In other words, objectivity in science is a goal that, although it can never be achieved, should be continually aimed at, for to abandon the quest for objectivity is to abandon science altogether.[70]

Finally, it needs to be pointed out that Kuhn's ideas are not very original despite the impact he made in the English-speaking world. Although Kuhn presents his views as his own discovery, they are essentially those of Oswald Spengler, who even more systematically than Kuhn argued that scientific thought is essentially relative to particular societies and groups of thinkers.[71] They are also remarkably similar to the ideas of the Jewish writer Ludwik Fleck, whose work, despite his racial origins, was well received by national socialist academics.[72] These ideas were picked up by numerous other Continental thinkers in a sustained attack on modern science that initially caused British and North American observers to recoil in horror.[73] Later, in the 1960s they were popularized alongside the rise of neo-Marxism by people such as Kuhn and eventually entered evangelical Christian thinking through the work of scholars influenced by Herman Dooyeweerd and the Institute for Christian Studies in Toronto.

The problem with the approach taken by the followers of Dooyeweerd and later by evangelical postmodernists is that their arguments are framed within a flawed framework that works only to the extent that those people who enter into the discussion are in communication

69. Anyone who doubts this ought to read Herbert Spencer's classic work *The Study of Sociology* (London: Henry S. King, 1874), in which Spencer spends over four hundred pages discussing the problem of academic objectivity and ways to avoid prejudice and biases that may distort one's findings.

70. Most critics of objectivity fail to recognize that they are propagating arguments popularized by European fascism in the 1930s. See Aurel Kolnai, *The War against the West* (London: Victor Gollancz, 1938), which is very sobering reading for anyone who rejects objectivity as a goal of science. A more recent work in this vein is Jeffrey Herf, *Reactionary Modernism: Technology, Culture, and Politics in Weimar and the Third Reich* (Cambridge: Cambridge University Press, 1984), 2–17, 218–55.

71. Oswald Spengler, *Der Untergand des Abendlandes* (1923; reprint, München: Deutscher Taschnebuch Verlag, 1977), 67ff.

72. Robert S. Cohen and Thomas Schnelle, *Cognition and Fact: Materials on Ludwik Fleck* (Dordrecht, the Netherlands: Reidel, 1986).

73. Robert A. Brady, *The Spirit and Structure of German Fascism* (1937; reprint, New York: Howard Fertig, 1969), 34–46.

with other people sharing common assumptions.[74] That is, evangelicals can talk to liberal Christians, Marxists, and former Marxists who have also embraced postmodern philosophy.[75] But this approach fails miserably when it confronts any worldview that retains a traditional concept of truth such as that found in Islam. Therefore, it is worth considering the spectacular rise of Islam in Europe and what this important social development tells us about the truth of the claim that we live in a postmodern world in which traditional forms of rationality are no longer acceptable.

## The Rise of Muslim Europe

Anyone visiting Western Europe today encounters secular societies in which the nominal religion of most people is still Christianity. Therefore, it is easy to assume that Europeans are essentially Christian, even though many churches are empty and real faith is rarely encountered. The truth is that many people in Western Europe are rapidly turning away from Christianity to Islam. Thus, there are more practicing Muslims in England today than practicing Christians, if attendance at weekly prayers or church services is used to measure religious commitment. Equally startling is the fact that official German statistics show that if present trends continue there will be Muslim majorities in all major German cities within fifty years.[76]

The growth of European Islam needs to be seen as a long-term trend. In 1900, after centuries of Muslim rule, one-third of the population of Turkey was Christian. By 1970, however, 99 percent of Turkey's population was Muslim while today that figure is 99.8 percent.[77] In 1900 there were next to no Muslims in Germany. By 1970, .7 percent of the German population was Muslim. This figure rose to 2.4 percent by 1980 and is roughly 3 or 4 percent today.[78] The situation in the United Kingdom is similar. In 1900 there were no Muslims in Britain. By 1970 roughly 635,000 people, or 1.1 percent of the population, were Mus-

---

74. For sustained critiques of Dooyeweerd by writers who note the inability of his approach to sustain real dialogue between differing intellectual positions, see Vincent Brümmer, *Transcendental Criticism and Christian Philosophy* (Frankner: T. Wever, 1961); and A. L. Conradie, *The Neo-Calvinist Concept of Philosophy* (Pietermaritzburg: Natal University Press, 1960).

75. Here it is important to note that postmodernism arose out of and is closely connected to intellectual Marxism in the West. See Jonathan Arac, ed., *Postmodernism in Politics* (Minneapolis: University of Minnesota Press, 1986), ix–xxxviii.

76. *Idea Spectrum* 69, 2 June 2000, 3.

77. David Barrett, *Encyclopedia of World Christianity* (Oxford: Oxford University Press, 1982), 680.

78. Ibid., 314.

lim.[79] Today figures range from 1.8 to 3 percent of the population, depending on one's source.[80] The growth rate of Islam in America follows a similar pattern. There were approximately 10,000 Muslims in the United States in 1900. The number had risen to 1,000,000, or .5 percent of the population, by 1970 and increased to 1,883,000 people, 1.8 percent, by the mid-1980s.[81] Today it stands at roughly 6,000,000, or 2.3 percent.[82]

Most American and European Muslims were born into immigrant families who converted to Islam centuries ago. There are, however, growing signs that an increasing number of Europeans from Christian and secular homes are converting to Islam. In England it is estimated that this figure is around twenty-five hundred per year. This seems insignificant. In fact, however, it is a remarkably high rate of conversion given the short amount of time Islam has actively sought converts in Britain. Rodney Stark and Lynne Roberts have convincingly demonstrated the ease with which significant growth rates can be mistakenly dismissed as "insignificant" in their article "The Arithmetic of Social Movements: Theoretical Implications."[83] They argue, "A lack of awareness of the arithmetic of growth rates often has obscured the vision not only of social scientists studying social movements, but, more importantly, the vision of the movement founders and their first generation of followers."[84]

To demonstrate their point they provide the example of someone who starts a new religion and after twenty years of hard labor has just under four thousand converts. At that point the founder and his or her early converts may lose hope and give up. This is because they project the past growth in terms of numbers onto the future and falsely assume that in another twenty years they will have only eight thousand members. Actually, if the early growth continued at its previous rate, which was around 30 percent, the true membership in twenty more years would be over seventy thousand.[85] When we examine the growth of Islam in Europe and North America, we find a situation that replicates Stark and Roberts's theoretical model, suggesting that in the next decade we will see a surge in conversions and the number of people

79. Ibid., 699.

80. A variety of different sources for the membership of various religious communities can be found at http://www.adherents.com.

81. Barrett, *Encyclopedia of World Christianity*, 711.

82. Carla Power, "The New Islam," *Newsweek*, 16 March 1998, 35.

83. Rodney Stark and Lynne Roberts, "The Arithmetic of Social Movements: Theoretical Implications," *Sociological Analysis* 43, no. 1 (1982): 53–67.

84. Ibid., 53.

85. Ibid., 54.

claiming to be Muslim, making possible the conversion of the majority of people in Europe by 2050.

Equally important as the rate of conversion is the dedication of new converts. Probably the best-known English convert is the former pop singer Cat Stevens,[86] who, after a long course of training in Iran, became an outspoken British Muslim leader.[87] Stevens is not alone in his religious quest or willingness to take a lead in creating a truly British Islam.[88] Nor are British converts milk-and-water Muslims, corrupted by liberalism and the secular society into which they were born. Rather, they are as devout as any Muslims anywhere. They have resisted the teaching of religious studies courses to Muslim children in state schools,[89] they have demanded and received sexually segregated classes for teenagers,[90] and they have successfully fought for the right to run their own Muslim state schools.[91]

British Muslims have actively raised large amounts of money to support the liberation of Palestine,[92] many have embraced the teachings of the Taliban,[93] and others are busy recruiting volunteers to fight for Muslim rights throughout the world.[94] More recently, British Muslim leaders declared a holy war against Russia because of Russian involvement in Chechnya.[95] Of course, many of the people doing these things are the children of Muslim immigrants to Britain. The parents were once very Westernized liberals, while their children are devoted tradi-

86. Lilly Irani, "Former Folk Singer Talks about His Conversion to Islam," *The Stanford Daily*, 3 June 1999.

87. James Landale, "Former Pop Star Joins in Fight for Gay Curb," *The Times*, 22 March 2000.

88. Another convert is Dr. Ahmed Andrews, who teaches the sociology of religion at the University of Derby. See Jonathan Petre, "Catholics Turn to Islam as Faith Conversions Rise," *The Daily Telegraph*, 3 September 2000; and Ali Köse, *Conversion to Islam: A Study of British Natives* (London: Kegan Paul, 1996).

89. Victoria Combe, "Muslims Win Fight for Exclusive RE Classes," *The Daily Telegraph*, 5 February 1996.

90. Victoria Combe, "Muslims Claim Victory on Segregated Classes," *The Daily Telegraph*, 23 February 1996.

91. Jonathan Petre, "Britain to Get Its First Muslim State School," *The Daily Telegraph*, 22 December 1966.

92. "Britain—Center of Terrorist Fund-raising?" *The Sunday Telegraph*, 11 March 1996.

93. Julian West and Jo Knowsley, "British Muslims Learn Taliban Teachings," *The Sunday Telegraph*, 27 July 1997. The article estimates that 20 percent of British Muslims have embraced Taliban teachings.

94. Sebastien Berger and Jon Hjibbs, "British Muslims Sent to Islamic Training Camps," *The Daily Telegraph*, 12 January 1999.

95. Jessica Berry and Julian Coman, "British Muslims Declare Holy War on Russia," *The Daily Telegraph*, 12 December 1999.

tionalists.[96] But a significant number of their leaders, such as Abu Ibrahim, who is leading the crusade against Russia, are British-born converts who have abandoned Christianity for Islam.[97]

The swelling tide of Muslim society is reflected in the sympathy expressed by Prince Charles for Islam. He wants the British monarch to be called "Defender of the Faiths," not "Defender of the Faith."[98] No wonder British Prime Minister Tony Blair felt it necessary to assure British Muslims that he has "read the Koran three times" and is said to have "impressed" leaders of the Muslim community with his knowledge of Islam.[99]

Although I have concentrated on the growth of Islam in Britain, similar stories could be told about Islam in Germany and many other Western European countries where immigrant communities are transforming themselves into communities of faith that are converting local people.[100] Similarly, Muslim communities are growing at an impressive rate throughout the United States.[101]

The growing Muslim communities in Europe and North America are creating the first real alternative society in the history of the West since the Enlightenment. Part of the reason for the "otherness" of Muslim society is the misleading and often insulting way Western newspapers, television, and radio treat Muslims and Muslim countries. Muslims are rarely identified as successful businesspeople or serious intellectuals. Rather, they are customarily "terrorists" and "extremists." Soldiers of Islam are described as "fanatics" and "rebels," not defenders of their homeland, patriots, or freedom fighters. Political leaders such as Saddam Hussein and Colonel Gadaffi are not mere opponents of Britain and America but "madmen." Respected scholars such as the Imam Khomeini are called "religious extremists" and "fundamentalists."[102] No wonder most Muslims and Muslim converts do not trust the Western media, which, as Edward Said has pointed out,

96. The turn from liberalism to tradition is noted throughout the Islamic world by V. S. Naipaul in *Among the Believers: An Islamic Journey* (New York: Penguin, 1981).

97. Ibid.

98. "Prince Praises Islam in 'Godless Britain,'" *The Times*, 11 May 2000.

99. Alexandra Frean, "Blair Studies Koran in Multifaith Campaign," *The Times*, 10 March 2000.

100. Cf. *Pressemitteilungen: Für friedliches Miteinander von Gläubigen unterschiedlicher Religionen*, http://www.ekd.de/presse/pm2382.html, 11 September 2000.

101. Cf. "Muslims in the United States," http://www.geocities.com/~itmr/world_AmericanMuslims.htm; "The Muslim Mainstream," *Christianity Today Online*, http://www.usnews.com/issue/980720/20isla.htm, 20 July 1998; Power, "The New Islam," 35–37; and Yvonne Yazveck Haddad, *The Muslims of America* (Oxford: Oxford University Press, 1991).

102. Cf. Imam Khomeini, *Islam and Revolution: Writings and Declarations*, trans. Hmid Algar (Berkeley: Mizan Press, 1981).

systematically distorts the image of Islam.[103] Consequently, to live in Western society as a Muslim is to live as a member of a misunderstood and misinterpreted minority community that is a truly alternative society.

## The Great Reversal

The rise of European Islam comes as a surprise to anyone aware of modern religious history. Until very recently most books on Islam described this enormously powerful world religion as a dying tradition incapable of adaptation to the modern world. Thus, at the World Missionary Conference held in London in 1888, numerous speakers argued that, while holding its own in terms of population growth, Islam was actually losing ground in the world generally.[104] It was also argued that Islam encouraged depopulation and actually destroyed wealth by creating a downward economic trend leading to increased poverty.[105] Later, in 1905 Allan Menzies could write, "The weakness of Islam is that it is not progressive."[106] Similarly, almost forty years later Laurence E. Browne confidently declared that

> Islam is lacking in the spiritual aspiration, the spiritual urge, and even the sense of the indwelling Spirit Himself, which alone can make a religion raise men to higher things. There seem to be two possibilities, either for Islam to remain as it is with no prospects of raising its followers to a higher level, or for Islam as a religion to cease to exist. One can see no prospect of Islam becoming a vital spiritual force in the world.[107]

Consequently, he believed Islam could not survive in the modern world.

J. N. D. Anderson echoed this view when he wrote, "Today, however, Islam is facing one of the greatest crises of its history. This crisis arises from the very nature of Islam when exposed to the conflicting currents of modern life." In his view, Islam was a "dominant creed" incapable of coexisting with other belief systems unless Muslims were the rulers and others the ruled.[108] Anderson continued his analysis by arguing

103. Edward W. Said, *Covering Islam: How the Media and the Experts Determine How We See the Rest of the World* (New York: Pantheon Books, 1981).

104. James Johnson, ed., *Report of the Centenary Conference on the Protestant Missions of the World Held in Exeter Hall London, June 9–19, 1888* (London: James Nisbet, 1889), 15–16, 21, 29–30.

105. Ibid., 26–27.

106. Allan Menzies, *History of Religion* (London: John Murray, 1905), 238.

107. Laurence E. Browne, *The Prospect for Islam* (London: SCM Press, 1944), 116.

108. J. N. D. Anderson, "Islam," in *The World's Religions*, ed. J. N. D. Anderson (London: Inter-Varsity Press, 1950); the quote is taken from the 1957 North American reprint (Grand Rapids: Eerdmans, 1957), 92.

that "there can be little doubt that it is the Muslim's instinctive feeling that the practice of his religion cannot properly be reconciled with living under the sovereignty of a non-Muslim Government. . . . In Islam, as we have seen, Church and State are one."[109] All of this led him to conclude that while "prophecy is notoriously dangerous" Islam was probably doomed and that in all likelihood Muslims would convert to Christianity on a massive scale.[110] Yet today passages such as this sound like a sick joke. How could so many scholars be so wrong?

When looking at the amazing growth of Islam in Europe, three things stand out. First, part of the explanation for Muslim growth lies in the response of the Islamic world to the establishment of the State of Israel and the defeat of Arab armies in the Six Day War of 1967. As Sigvard von Sicard has shown, the humiliating defeats of Arab forces by Israel led Muslim statesmen to search their souls for an answer as to why God had apparently deserted the Arab cause. This soul-searching led to widespread repentance for the ways in which they and their people had abandoned the teachings of Islam and a call for spiritual renewal. Consequently, starting in the 1970s various Muslim countries began reform programs and dedicated a proportion of their wealth to both the teaching and spread of Islam. The result was the present Islamic World Mission that we see today.[111]

Second, many converts are made through marriage. Faced with the reality of Muslim conversions many people respond by saying, "But most of them are through marriage," as though this fact somehow diminishes their significance. Actually, the fact that many are a result of marriage is highly significant and a sign that the conversion rate will continue to increase. This is because Muslim conversions follow an identifiable pattern of social ties in which the conversion of a friend or family member leads to further conversions[112] through the creation of "networks of faith."[113]

Third, Muslim scholars have developed convincing apologetics that present Islam in a favorable light when compared to Christianity. For

109. Ibid., 93.
110. Ibid., 97.
111. Sigvard von Sicard, "Contemporary Islam and Its World Mission," *Missiology: An International Review* (July 1976): 343–61.
112. Petre, "Catholics Turn to Islam." Cf. Lary Poston, *Islamic Da'wah in the West* (Oxford: Oxford University Press, 1992), 158–80.
113. Rodney Stark and William Sims Bainbridge, "Networks of Faith: Interpersonal Bonds and Recruitment to Cults and Sects," *American Journal of Sociology* 85 (1980): 1376–95. Cf. Roger Finke and Rodney Stark, *The Churching of America 1772–1990: Winners and Losers in Our Religious Economy* (New Brunswick, N.J.: Rutgers University Press, 1992).

the purposes of this chapter I will ignore the positive presentation of Islam itself and concentrate on Muslim criticisms of Christianity.[114] There are three main lines of argument. First, Muslims assail the reliability and trustworthiness of Christian Scriptures.[115] Second, they claim that in practice the adoption of Islam leads to a more ordered and humane society.[116] Finally, they argue that while Islam is compatible with modern science, Christianity is not.[117]

It is against the background of the rapid growth of Islam in Europe and the claims of Muslim apologists that I now want to examine evangelical response to the challenge of world religions found in the adoption of postmodernism.

## Loss of Nerve among Evangelicals

With these observations in mind, let us look again at the interaction between Christian preaching and other religious traditions, particularly Islam. When surveying the history of Christian missions in the nineteenth and early twentieth centuries, one sees a story of continued success and rapid growth that makes the present growth of European Islam seem all the more puzzling. Rarely in the history of the church has Christianity spread so quickly as during the nineteenth century. This expansion was far swifter and more effective than the earlier great Christian mission to evangelize Europe from the first to the tenth centuries.[118] By any standards the growth of the church in the nineteenth century until the mid-twentieth century was a remarkable achievement. Yet by the end of the nineteenth century many missionaries were dejected by what they saw as the failure of the missionary enterprise.

The Scottish missionary James Stewart (1831–1905) is typical of this new defeatist attitude. In his book *Dawn in the Dark Continent*,[119] he

114. For a scholarly discussion of this topic, see Kate Zebiri, *Muslims and Christians Face to Face* (Oxford: One World, 1997); and Poston, *Islamic Da'wah in the West*.

115. Ahmed Deedat, *Is the Bible God's Word?* (Durban: Islamic Propagation Center, 1986); idem, *50,000 Errors in the Bible* (Durban: Islamic Propagation Center, 1986); Zebiri, *Muslims and Christians Face to Face*, 50–67; and Maryam Jameelah, *Islam versus ahl al-Kitab Past and Present* (Lahore: Mohammad Yusuf Kahn, 1968), 254–59.

116. Zebiri, *Muslims and Christians Face to Face*, 157–61; and Jameelah, *Islam versus ahl al-Kitab*, 221–67.

117. Zebiri, *Muslims and Christians Face to Face*, 74–78; and Muhammad Qutb, *Islam and the Crisis of the Modern World* (London: Islamic Council of Europe, 1975), 1–3, 8–9.

118. Cf. Charles Henry Robinson, *The Conversion of Europe* (London: Longman, Green and Co., 1917), 348–436; and Richard Fletcher, *The Conversion of Europe* (London: Fontana, 1997).

119. James Stewart, *Dawn in the Dark Continent* (1903; reprint, Edinburgh: Oliphant Anderson & Ferrier, 1906).

devoted an entire chapter to what he calls the "Slow Progress of Missions," in which he bemoans the failure of Christian missions to make converts among various African groups.[120] More recently, numerous evangelical writers such as Vineyard founder John Wimber have agreed with this type of analysis, suggesting that missions lack power because of the corrosive effects of the Enlightenment on Christian thought.[121]

Like Stewart all of these writers commit the fallacy of treating growth in terms of static numbers, not growth rates calculated as a percentage of the total membership at any one time. Consequently, what many of them see as failure is actually success. Thus, missionaries and other Christians accepted the belief that they were failing, leading to a self-fulfilling prophecy. Yet, as observed in connection with the growth of European Islam, apparently small growth rates are often significant over the long term.[122] When these observations are applied to nineteenth-century mission, it becomes clear that contrary to what most people thought at the time, the missionaries were actually very successful indeed.[123] Nevertheless, the view that missions was a failure gained strength after the Edinburgh Mission Conference of 1910.

At the same time, the outbreak of World War I seemed to confirm the pessimistic diagnosis of Western society found in the writings of such disparate observers as Houston Steward Chamberlain,[124] Oswald Spengler, and Alfred Rosenberg.[125] The gloom was increased by the onset of the Great Depression followed by World War II, with the horrors of the Holocaust and all that it entailed. Western civilization indeed seemed bankrupt and beyond salvation. So too did the missionary enterprise, which was linked to colonialism and the supposed evils of modernity. Now instead of seeing science as something that brought untold benefits to humankind, the notion that modern science is evil and the cause of most of humanity's ills became widely accepted.[126] At the same time, the Enlightenment, which until the 1960s was held up

120. Ibid., 292–97, 307–28.

121. John Wimber, *Power Evangelism* (Toronto: Hodder and Stoughton, 1985), 50–56, 77–79.

122. For a discussion of this point, see Stark and Roberts, "Arithmetic of Social Movements."

123. Cf. Richard Elphick and Rodney Davenport, *Christianity in Southern Africa* (Cape Town: David Philip, 1997).

124. Houston Steward Chamberlain, *The Foundations of the Nineteenth Century* (London: John Lane, the Bodley Head, 1911).

125. Alfred Rosenberg, *Der Mythus des 20. Jahrhunderts* (München: Hoheneichen Verlag, 1935).

126. Arthur Herman, *The Idea of Decline in Western History* (New York: Free Press, 1997).

as one of the great milestones in human history by most educated people (including evangelical Christians), was increasingly disparaged.

Contrary to many Christians I do not believe that the Enlightenment was entirely a bad thing or necessarily anti-Christian. Of course, there were anti-Christian streams to Enlightenment thought, represented by philosophers such as Voltaire, who sought to destroy Christianity using the tools of reason. But in and of itself, the European, particularly British, Enlightenment was consistent with Christianity, as David Bebbington has ably argued, and in many ways grew out of the application of Christian thinking to everyday life.[127]

How then are we as Christians to face the "challenge of world religions"? My answer is simple: We must return to the ideals of the Christian Enlightenment project. We must affirm the values of science and reason that led to the greatest missionary movement in history during the nineteenth century.[128] We must proclaim our belief in Christianity because it is rational and accords with the evidence, and we must reject the idea that the philosophy of John Locke and other advocates of a rational social order were anti-Christian. As John Wesley recognized, they were not.[129] Nor did other Christian thinkers in Britain in the eighteenth century see Locke as anti-Christian.[130] This means evangelical Christians must begin to see through the "enormously seductive"[131] anti-Christian rhetoric of twentieth-century academics such as Carl Becker,[132] whose distortions of Locke and the European Enlightenment shape the understanding of many Christians.[133]

## Approaching Other Religious Traditions

One of the greatest problems that plagues the discussion of the relationship between Christianity and other religious traditions is the

127. David Bebbington, *Evangelicalism in Modern Britain: A History from the 1730s to the 1980s* (Grand Rapids: Baker, 1989), 50–74.

128. Kenneth Ingham, *Reformers in India* (1956; reprint, New York: Octagon Books, 1973).

129. Wesley, *Works of John Wesley*, vol. 13, 445–64.

130. Alan P. F. Sell, *John Locke and the Eighteenth-Century Divines* (Cardiff: University of Wales Press, 1977).

131. Gertrude Himmelfarb, *The New History and the Old* (Cambridge: Harvard University Press, 1987), 157.

132. Cf. Carl L. Becker, *The Heavenly City of the Eighteenth-Century Philosophers* (1932; reprint, New Haven: Yale University Press, 1968); and idem, *The Declaration of Independence* (1922; reprint, New York: Vintage Books, 1970).

133. Garry Amos, *Defending the Declaration: How the Bible and Christianity Influenced the Writing of the Declaration of Independence* (Charlottesville, Va.: Providence Foundation, 1989).

confusion of religions as social and intellectual systems with the people who belong to those traditions. Instead, we need to see the traditions and questions of religious truth separately from our relationship to believers.

As a graduate of the first religious studies program offered in England, I must acknowledge my debt to a group of outstanding professors including Ninian Smart, Edward Conze, and James Dickie (Jacob Zakki), all of whom served as academic mentors. Smart is a Christian philosopher from whom I learned the importance of empathy in understanding religious traditions other than my own. Conze was a Buddhist, and Dickie has become a leader in Britain's Muslim community. Both Conze and Dickie encouraged me to go on to graduate work despite the fact that they knew I was an evangelical Christian who held views very different from their own. They also taught me not to confuse Christianity with Buddhism or Islam but to view each religion on its own terms.[134] All three men, as well as the other faculty members at that time, encouraged debate, discussion, and disagreement and did not attempt to force their views on their students.

Since then I've met numerous people who hold faiths different from my own. Among these I must mention Ishmael Bavahasa, my Muslim neighbor in Winnipeg; Londa Shembe, the head of one group of the amaNazaretha in South Africa (who believed that his grandfather Isaiah Shembe was an incarnation of God); Tony Barber and Leslie Kawamura, both of whom are practicing Buddhists; and Henry Srebrnik, who is Jewish. All of these people became good friends and colleagues. Therefore, from the experience of friendship with people of other faiths I conclude that it is essential to separate religious systems from the individual. We may disagree about doctrine, but we can recognize our common humanity. Genuine friendship and respect cut across religious commitments.

On the other hand, recognizing differences is very important. None of the people I know who are members of other religious communities expects me to change my convictions simply because he or she is not a Christian. Nor would these people appreciate my telling them that at some deep "anonymous" level they are really Christians. What surprises me is that the people who seem to talk the most about pluralism, interreligious dialogue, and the need to abandon exclusive Christian

134. Conze makes this point in various books, for example, Edward Conze, *Buddhism: Its Essence and Development* (1951; reprint, London: B. Cassirer, 1957), 11–26. Dickie has written several books but did not address this topic, so I have to rely on his lecture notes. A similar point is made by Tucker Callaway in *Zen Way—Jesus Way* (Tokyo: Charles E. Tuttle, 1976).

claims to truth are usually the ones whose experience of other religions comes from books and formal interfaith gatherings, not through friendships with individual people.

The people I know who hold other religious beliefs take their religions very seriously and therefore do not believe that their beliefs are "really the same" as Christian beliefs or that Christians really believe the same as they do. Rather, they recognize differences that they respect. Talking to such people in postmodern terms is something they don't expect or respect. As sincere believers they seek truth and believe that they have embraced the truth. For Christians to abandon the debate about truth in religion is madness, particularly when there is a rich tradition of Christian works that over time have proven effective and can inspire our attempts to produce solid scholarship as we proclaim the gospel.[135] For me "understanding precedes criticism." But once we understand another religion it is our duty as both scholars and Christians to offer valid criticisms just as believers of other faiths have an obligation to tell us exactly what they think about our beliefs and the faith we profess.

Finally, the people I know who converted to Christianity did so for a variety of reasons. On the sociological level they met and established friendships with Christians. On the spiritual level they discovered a faith that worked in their lives and experience. On the intellectual level they raised questions that were eventually answered to their satisfaction. Yet until those questions were answered, all the other things, however important, were not enough to bring them to Christ.

For example, when I first met Bernd Ebel he was a professor at the University of Lethbridge in Alberta, Canada, and his wife had recently converted to Christianity to his great surprise. Educated in the former East Germany, he knew his Marx. Being born in a defeated country where a Russian occupying army did whatever it liked, he knew the horrors of life more than most. Therefore, for him to accept a God of love and justice was no easy thing. His grandfather was a believer, but his mother was not, and her sense of the injustice and cruelty of life deeply influenced him.

135. Many of the older missionaries were excellent scholars who produced superb works of scholarship that we ought to interact with whether or not we ultimately agree with their conclusions. For example, A. G. Hogg, *The Christian Message to the Hindu* (London: SCM Press, 1947); J. N. Farquhar, *The Crown of Hinduism* (London: Oxford University Press, 1913); C. G. Pfander, *The Mizan-ul-Haqq: Balance of Truth* (1835; reprint, Villach, Austria: Light of Life, 1986). Finally, although he is usually dismissed as "Barthian," as though that said everything, the detailed works of Hendrik Kraemer (such as *Religion and the Christian Faith* [London: Lutterworth, 1956]), deserve careful study yet today.

We had long talks, and he even borrowed C. E. M. Joad's *Recovery of Belief*,[136] which he admitted impressed him. More important, playing Bach and following the words in the German text brought Scripture alive in his life. Over several years his agnosticism gave way to a quiet but lively faith. At that point, in 1987, he had the good fortune to meet Rev. Alfred Maier, who ministered to his spiritual needs in a remarkable way. Early in October 2000 my friend died of cancer. Yet all who were present testified to his strong faith. Indeed, the family reported that shortly before his death, while in a semi-coma, he sang, "Jesus loves me this I know, for the Bible tells me so."

God worked a great miracle in Bernd Ebel's life. This man changed from an articulate agnostic to a professing Christian. But this was not something that happened easily, nor did it lack a rational component. Only after Bernd satisfied himself that the gospel was true did he commit his life to Christ. Of course, many other things factored in to his decision, but without the conviction of truth, the rest would have been meaningless. Therefore, with this example I conclude that we need to return to our roots and affirm our faith in Christ, his church, and the truth of the gospel.

136. C. E. M. Joad, *Recovery of Belief* (London: Faber and Faber, 1952).

# Part 4
# Responses

# 7

# An Evangelical Theology
# of Religions?

## PAUL J. GRIFFITHS

The declared topic of this book is evangelical thought about the question of a (Christian) theology of religions. The commission given to the book's six contributors was to write an essay on the one thing evangelicals most need to think about with respect to this topic. This is an important and challenging commission, and some of the essays speak to it very pointedly. A surprising absence in almost all of them, though, is attention to the territory to be mapped if a systematic theology of religions is to be developed. Perhaps the contributors think it obvious what this territory is, but the fact that they don't explain where their chosen questions belong on the map of topics that ought to be covered by a theology of religions (Gerald Pillay's essay provides a partial exception here) makes it difficult to assess (for an outside reader, at least) how evangelicals are thinking (or would like to think) about the theology of religions as a whole.

For example, Miriam Adeney's central question is whether Islam can nurture disciples of Jesus, and to this question she provides a nuanced and interesting negative answer. It's a good question and a good answer—one I largely endorse. But she says little about where in the territory of a theology of religions this question belongs. Similarly, Stanley Grenz wants to know what the providential role of the religions is in the divine economy. Another good and interesting question, but why this question, and where does it belong in the broader schema? And why does Irving Hexham think that addressing postmodernist attacks on truth is the most important question to raise in regard to a contemporary evangelical theology of religions? These questions are insufficiently contextualized, making it impossible to know where they belong and why the authors feel they belong where they do.

In the hope of drawing further comment from the contributors to this volume—and perhaps from other evangelicals who are thinking about these things—I'll begin this brief response by offering a map of the territory that (it seems to me) a theology of religions ought to cover. I'll then use this map to locate the contributions to this volume and to make some observations and recommendations about pressing questions not addressed.

## A Map of the Territory

First among the questions a theology of religions should address is, A theology of *what?* The very category "religion," whether used as a singular label for a type, or in the plural for various tokens of that type, raises some difficult questions for Christian theologians. The fact that the category itself raises questions should be especially obvious for evangelicals, since it is a term of almost no importance in Scripture. As far as the New Testament is concerned, there is no Greek word obviously rendered by *religion* in English (or, for that matter, *religio* in Latin). Jerome chose to use *religio* and derivatives only eight times in his Latin translation of the New Testament, and for four different Greek words. The King James Version New Testament uses *religion* and derivatives only seven times, choosing differently in three of the places where Jerome used *religio,* and using *religion* twice where Jerome chose differently.[1] The story is not much different if Old Testament evidence is included. *Religion,* then, is a term of almost no scriptural importance, and where it is used it bears few or no similarities to standard modern usage. This should raise questions, and I would very much like to hear more about why these questions were not addressed explicitly by any of the contributors to this volume.

The question of religion—what it is, how to think about it, whether Christians should think about it—is important because the topics we

---

1. Vulgate: Acts 2:5; 10:2; 13:50; 26:5; Col. 2:18; James 1:26–27. KJV: Acts 13:43; 26:5; Gal. 1:13–14; James 1:26–27.

late moderns (or early postmoderns) discuss under the label of religious diversity or religious pluralism were formulated by early modern philosophers who, for the most part, had no Christian interests and did not use a Christian vocabulary. For evangelicals to continue to discuss the questions thus bequeathed without raising or discussing the problems associated with them is to exhibit a curious thralldom to modernity. This thralldom is most strikingly evident in Hexham's essay, in which he makes the astonishing claim that John Locke's thought was Christian. It's true, of course, that Locke claimed this himself, but the claim can be defended only if trinitarian theism is unimportant to Christianity, since for Locke it was either false or irrelevant.[2] And such a view of Christianity is not lightly to be affirmed, I take it, by evangelicals or anyone else.

## The Question of Non-Christian Truth

I suggest, then, that evangelicals might consider more deeply than the contributors to this volume do what it is they're theologizing about when they theologize about religion or religions. One way of doing this would be to ask whether a more deeply and properly Christian language can be used for some of the questions considered in these essays. I have in mind here the traditional division of the world into Christians, pagans, heretics, and Jews. It's interesting to contemplate the fact that for a thousand years Christians understood Islam not as another religion but as a Christian heresy. There may well be reasons why this language and the judgments about the non-Christian world it implies cannot now be used, and it may be that some of these reasons require the use of the language of religion. But if the question is not raised, it is quite likely that commitments problematic for Christians will be smuggled into the discussion. It is, I think, possible to baptize the concept of religion and so make it available for properly Christian uses: A challenging twentieth-century attempt to do so was made by Karl Barth in *Church Dogmatics*.[3] But the contributions to this book show no sign of an awareness of the need to do this.

2. I wonder whether Hexham has read Locke's *Reasonableness of Christianity,* and, if he has, what he thinks is the relation between what is there defended as reasonable and orthodox Christianity.

3. Especially in §17 of the *Kirchliche Dogmatik,* vol. I/2, with the winsomely attractive part titled "Gottes Offenbarung als Aufhebung der Religion," usually misrendered into English as "God's Revelation as the Abolition of Religion" ("sublation" would be technically better for "Aufhebung"). The point, in any case, is that Barth offers a fully Christian engagement with the very idea of religion.

The fundamental question that underlies all the particular questions that are often discussed under the rubric of a theology of religions is, What should Christians think about those who are not Christians, those who are the aliens, the unbaptized? One aspect of this discussion is the question of salvation, what Christians should think and say about the eternal destiny of non-Christians. A kissing cousin is the missiological question: How much effort (and what kind of effort) should Christians expend on making the alien into kin, the unbaptized into the baptized? It has been a historic strength of evangelical thought to pay a good deal of attention to these questions (and of evangelical practice to act with passion and effectiveness on the conclusions of such thought).[4] Not much attention is paid to these topics in this volume, and that is fair enough given the extent and depth of the work already done on them by evangelical thinkers, an effort from which all Christians have benefited.

The fundamental question about non-Christians includes questions about the truth of what non-Christians claim and recommend. The contributors to this volume have more to say about these questions. Gerald McDermott, for example, argues that a Christian understanding of God as Triune entails the truth of the claim that God (as both Holy Spirit and Word) is active among non-Christians and that Christians should expect to find among their claims, recommendations, and patterns of action "scattered promises of God in Christ" and "revealed types." Amos Yong, too, offers a form of trinitarian theology that not only permits but requires empirical engagement with "the world's religions in a truly substantive manner." These are important suggestions, and ones I strongly endorse (though with some reservations about the particular details of Yong's program). If pushed only a little further, these approaches can yield the claim that Christians may have something to learn from the non-Christian that Christians do not yet know, something of importance, moreover, to their own understanding of the gospel.

Serious consideration of this possibility—the possibility that non-Christians may explicitly teach truths about (for instance) God that Christians do not yet know—is of the greatest importance to the future of evangelical theology, as also to Christian theology more generally,[5]

4. This is not to say, of course, that evangelicals are in substantive agreement about these matters. See, for example, the range of opinion in John Sanders, ed., *What about Those Who Have Never Heard? Three Views on the Destiny of the Unevangelized* (Downers Grove, Ill.: InterVarsity Press, 1995).

5. It is a possibility not yet fully affirmed by the Catholic magisterium, though one toward which various indications are now converging.

and there is nothing in Christian theology to rule it out. The importance of such consideration is that it provides the best avenue to serious engagement with the particulars of alien teachings, and this, in turn, is something in which evangelical theology has not yet shown much interest but which, nonetheless, holds great promise for the future of Christian thought. If the suggestions of McDermott's and Yong's papers are pushed in the direction I suggest, the result could be a flowering of evangelical scholarship on, for instance, the Qur'an or the philosophical riches of scholastic Tibetan Buddhism. Such scholarship would, if it remained evangelical, be always at the service of the gospel: It would be what the fathers of the church used to call (following Exod. 12:35–36) a despoiling of the Egyptians.[6] It would, inevitably, pay close attention to the particulars of what the Egyptians (the Buddhists, the Confucians, the Muslims) teach. Otherwise, dross could not be separated from gold. The greatest advances in Christian thinking have come when serious Christian thinkers have paid close attention to alien particularity. Consider Augustine's Christian reconstruals of Platonism and Aquinas's systematic expropriation of Aristotle. What riches might a serious evangelical engagement with particular alien teachings yield?

It does seem, though, that there is some resistance on the part of evangelical thinkers to this move. Adeney, for instance, approvingly notes the many commonalities that link Christian and Muslim practice, emphasizes the importance of empirical study of and response to the particulars of non-Christian forms of life, and observes that Islam contains many "patterns of wisdom, beauty, and caring." Yet she appears to draw the line at the thought that Christians might have things to learn from Muslims, things that they need to know. Revealingly, she says that she, as a Western theologian, must learn from Muslim-background Christians; she does not say that she must learn from Muslims. She does not explain the limitation, and there is nothing in what she does say that implies its need. Yong, too, while emphatic about the need for attention to particularity, does not commit himself as to the question of whether there really is any alien gold that Christians need for Christian purposes. The analyses offered by Grenz and Pillay also suggest a negative response to the question of the possibility of finding Egyptian gold. Grenz, for instance, advocates the assessment of particular alien forms of thought and practice by Christian criteria, something I endorse. But he appears to know in advance, for reasons he does not give, that engagement with the non-Christian will yield nothing new for the Christian.

6. See my "Seeking Egyptian Gold: A Fundamental Metaphor for the Christian Intellectual Life in a Religiously Diverse Age," *The Cresset* 63, no. 7 (2000): 5–16.

The point of these comments is to advocate to Christians, evangelical and otherwise, an open inclusivism on the question of alien truth. This question, to state it most abstractly, is the question of whether there are truths taught by non-Christians. I think that all the contributors to this volume (with the possible exception of Hexham) would answer this question in the affirmative. Indeed, it is difficult not to do so if faithfulness to the tradition and coherence are valued. But inclusivism on the question of alien truth comes in two varieties. A closed inclusivism acknowledges that there is alien truth and recognizes and embraces instances of it when they are found, but it denies that alien truths ever include truths not already known to Christians. An open inclusivism on alien truth does not include this denial; rather, it affirms the possibility of the existence of alien truth that Christians need to learn and then advocates empirical study of alien traditions in order to see whether the possibility is actual. I recommend open inclusivism to evangelicals for the reasons already given, and if it is not to be accepted, it would be good to know the reasons why.

Some moves in the direction I suggest are now being made, and the label "comparative theology" is used in some Catholic circles for them. The best example, perhaps, is found in the work of Frank Clooney. Brief comment on that work will show what I have in mind and will suggest what might turn out to be some fruitful avenues for evangelical thinkers. Clooney is a Jesuit who specializes in Hindu thought and practice. He has the linguistic skills (Sanskrit, Tamil) to engage the texts and living representatives of the tradition as any academic specialist would, but his interests in doing so are, in the beginning and at the end, Christian-theological. He wants, to put it briefly, to do Christian theology through and after a deep reading of the thought and practice of some very particular aliens.[7] He hopes (as Augustine and Aquinas also hoped) that Christian theology will be done better as a result. In my judgment, this is a properly and inevitably Christian hope and a properly and inevitably Christian response to one aspect of what an awareness of religious diversity requires. If Christian thought is anything at all, it is omnivorous: It wants to consume and transform everything, to baptize the world, to inscribe all thought into the margins of its scriptural commentaries. Seriously Christian attention to alien particularity is one aspect of this Christian omnivorousness.

7. Among Clooney's works in this line are *Theology after Vedanta: An Experiment in Comparative Theology* (Albany, N.Y.: State University of New York Press, 1993); and *Seeing through Texts: Doing Theology among the Srivaisnavas of South India* (Albany, N.Y.: State University of New York Press, 1996).

## What Is the Real Topic?

A concluding remark. Among the more interesting and puzzling features of the papers included in this volume is the extent to which they treat the questions raised by a theology of religions as if they were really questions of theological method. This is most striking in Hexham's paper: There we are told that awareness of religious diversity on the part of evangelicals is a major cause (perhaps *the* major cause) of the embrace of postmodernism by some of them; the body of the paper is then an extended diatribe against postmodernism. I suspect that the vast majority of those (evangelical and others) who have embraced postmodernism have done so on the basis of what they take to be good reasons internal to Christianity. Hexham does not, in any case, make clear why an awareness of religious diversity should contribute more to postmodernist leanings than awareness of other kinds of diversity. And while it is obviously correct to say that Christians should have confidence in the truth of what they claim, both in general and in the light of religious diversity, it is much less obvious that such confidence requires the particular philosophical views about truth and knowledge that Hexham advocates under the label of the "Christian Enlightenment Project." Captivity to modernity is no less captivity than captivity to postmodernity. But even if Hexham is correct in his empirical claims as to why some Christians are postmodernists, and correct, too, as to the necessity of hewing to Lockean Christianity (epistemologically speaking), his avoidance of the substantive questions involved in a theology of religions would still be impressive.

The same is true, though to a lesser degree, of the papers by Grenz, Pillay, and McDermott: They, too, use the topic of a theology of religions as an occasion to write an essay on theological method, an essay that never quite gets to a genuine engagement with the questions supposed to have occasioned it. This is a feature of evangelical thought about non-Christians that ought to stop. It is time to get down in the trenches and offer comment on and analysis of what non-Christians actually believe, teach, and recommend. Deferral by retreat to methodological analysis is always a comfort to scholars (it is what we do best), but when a theology of religions is the topic at hand, Christian thought cannot be satisfied with such a retreat.

# 8

# The Challenge of Interreligious Truth Telling

## RICHARD J. MOUW

In one sense, we evangelicals have always paid a great deal of attention to other religions. Our interreligious interests, though, have been shaped in large part by what we have appropriately labeled "a heart for the lost." In other words, our evangelical theology of religions has been dominated by soteriological and missiological categories. We have typically studied other religions with a focus on getting people to see that non-Christian belief systems cannot ultimately deliver on what they promise—that peace and security and holiness can be found only in the abundant life that comes from putting our trust in Christ as Savior and Lord.

We should be clear, however, that this theological focus has been an important evangelical strength. The study of religions is fraught with dangers, including spiritual ones. The investigation of a variety of religious perspectives requires us to explore themes that lie at the heart of our human condition, and it is easy for us—sinners that we are—to be fooled by counterfeits and misled by false promises. To explore such matters with a clear sense of the urgency of the evangelistic mandate is a helpful way to stay tethered to the truth as we go about studying alternative worldviews.

At the same time, though, an exclusive soteriological-missiological focus is itself attended by some important dangers. The most basic one is also spiritual in nature: the real possibility that we will bear false witness against our non-Christian neighbors. In evangelization contexts, we rightly want to get people to see the inadequacy of their present religious commitments. But such a desire can encourage us to try to portray those commitments in the worst possible light so that Christian belief and practice can clearly be seen as the better way. It is easy in such contexts to emphasize the negative aspects of the other perspective, or even to distort the positive elements of that perspective, so that things are portrayed as worse than they really are.

The situation is not improved much when evangelicals try to be more sympathetic in their assessments of other religions while continuing to make their case within soteriological categories. The result is that some people suggest that maybe many of the people who adhere to non-Christian worldviews are saved after all, or that they will at least get a second chance for salvation after they die. Those are not necessarily bad things for us to argue about, but the arguments do focus the discussion on the "salvific" status of other religions, which means that those of us who favor exclusivist formulations will be inclined to continue emphasizing what we see as the defects in other religions.

The essays in this volume, then, are an evangelical breath of fresh air. I found both the scope and the tone of the explorations here to be helpful. And, frankly, I am pleased by the differences in perspective that are displayed. We evangelicals need to have some energetic new arguments about these matters, and I hope these discussions signal the beginning of that kind of sustained discussion, not only among ourselves but also with representatives of other religious perspectives.

Amos Yong describes the general project nicely when he proposes that "the issue of the religions and the issue of the unevangelized should be kept separate for the purposes of doing theology of religions." It is unlikely, of course, that we can pull off a complete separation. Nor would it be a good thing if we succeeded in doing so. Yong himself recognizes this when he advises us to be careful not to say anything in our theology of religions that would inhibit our evangelization efforts. Certainly, one criterion for the adequacy of an evangelical theology of religions is whether our formulations comport well with our attempts to bring the gospel to those who have not yet accepted Christ. Nonetheless, it is a helpful exercise to attempt, temporarily at least—and especially because of our overemphasis in the other direction in the past—to bracket our overt interests in soteriology and missiology as we think about some broader topics in this area.

This bracketing will allow us to offer assessments that are not easy to make when we are concentrating primarily on salvific issues. When the main question is whether we have good reasons to believe that, say, a fully committed Buddhist—someone whose understanding of reality is spelled out in consistently Buddhist terms—can go to heaven, then many of us will have to answer in the negative. In this context, it is appropriate for evangelicals to say that Buddhism is a "false religion," in the sense that a person who wants to enter into a saving relationship with the one true God will not achieve that goal by following the Buddhist path.

But this is not the same as saying that there is no truth in Buddhism. If we can bracket the question as to whether Buddhists qua Buddhists can be saved, then we are free to evaluate this or that particular Buddhist teaching or practice in terms of whether it illuminates reality, and we may well find many good and true elements in the Buddhist worldview. Indeed, we might even find things in the Buddhist understanding of spiritual reality that can enrich—even by calling our attention to spiritual matters that we have not thought about clearly—our own Christian understanding of religious truth.

## The Role of Converts

As we engage in these interreligious explorations, one topic that deserves to be addressed explicitly is the role that evangelical converts from other religions will play in our attempts to wrestle honestly with questions posed in the study of those other religions. In the broader arena of interreligious dialogue and study, the testimonies of converts are often categorically dismissed. Some scholars have argued, for example, that the perspectives of converts are inevitably distorted because of the converts' need to justify their migration from one religion to another by making their previous commitments look bad. There is a point to this concern, although we must challenge the claim of inevitability, since some converts actually bring to the discussion the kinds of genuine insights that can come only from having experienced both sides of the interreligious divide. It is ironic that thinkers who talk much about the need to understand various religious perspectives "from the inside" are so dismissive of the experiences of people who have come to faith in Christ after years of sincere adherence to, say, Islamic teaching.

The complications here have affected me personally in my efforts to engage in dialogue with the Jewish community. Jewish believers in

Christ often worry that an interest in such dialogue on the part of people like me is itself a betrayal of their experience. Having been treated as outcasts and traitors by people within the Jewish community, they wonder about our motives when they see us engaged in friendly dialogue with people who despise them and refuse to converse with them about their spiritual transformation. While this should not dissuade us from engaging in the dialogue, it does mean that we cannot pursue those discussions without also expending much effort in reassuring these sisters and brothers in Christ that we do not mean to undercut their own witness. Indeed, our firm belief in the reality of genuine conversion has to be much on our minds as we go about our interreligious explorations. The stories of people who have experienced the inadequacy of the spiritual solutions offered by other religions and who have discovered the liberation that can be realized only at Calvary must be integral to our understanding of the larger religious environment, even as we attempt to listen carefully and empathetically to people who speak from within those other religious systems.

## The Point of Dialogue

If we are to gear up for some new evangelical explorations in this area, it is a good idea to pay attention to the basic *point* of the enterprise. Relativism runs rampant in contemporary culture, in both the "high" and the "low" versions, and it is important that we not encourage the dilettantish "samplings" of various worldviews.

I have already mentioned what I believe is a key motivation for evangelicals: the concern to be truth tellers about what our non-Christian neighbors believe. Our "spiritual warfare" strategies often feature a crusading approach, in which we feel justified in using any available weapon—including oversimplification and even demonization—that we think will be helpful in winning the battle against our non-Christian opponents. It might actually be good for evangelicals to set aside all of the warfare imagery for a while. But even if we do not, we should at least follow the relevant guidelines of "just war" theory as they apply to intellectual and spiritual skirmishes: For example, we should not be motivated by a desire simply to defeat other people, and we should employ tactics that are proportionate to the goals we are seeking to achieve.

Self-understanding is surely one of our key goals in interreligious discussion. Our explorations of other religious perspectives must be accompanied by the psalmist's prayer: "Search me, O God, and know my heart. . . . See if there is any offensive way in me" (Ps. 139:23–24 NIV). For one thing, we need to be clear about the harm we have done in the past to people of other faiths. The stories of our Christian dealings with Jews and Muslims, for example, include much about which we ought to be deeply ashamed. We cannot enter into dialogue with people from those religious groups as if we were victims of collective amnesia. We need to listen in humility to their grievances against us.

But to repeat a point made above, I am also convinced that we should be open to genuine lessons from other religious perspectives about the deepest issues of life. In one sense, of course, we cannot enter into these explorations with a completely open mind. Our commitment to Christ as the heaven-sent Savior is not something we bracket for the sake of truth seeking. But we can be open to new insights into the mysteries that are hidden in Christ.

The writers of the essays in this book are all explicitly trinitarian in their thinking, yet they each "spin" their trinitarian convictions in different ways. The important thing, though, is that the cosmic work of the Triune God is given its due here. We are reminded that the story of God's creating and redeeming purposes is not to be viewed simply as one of many tales that have been told about the human condition—it is the one true metanarrative. The Savior born in Bethlehem is also the divine Logos. The Spirit of the living God is at work in the broadest reaches of the cosmos.

The missionary movement of the past was, at its best, inspired by these universal themes. Missionary families ventured into what were for them uncharted regions, in the confidence that their Lord did indeed own the cattle on a thousand hills and that there was no human being whom they would encounter in any jungle clearing who was not created in the image and likeness of the Father. Our own interreligious explorations in this postmodern age must be guided by this same kind of confidence. Simone Weil's provocative comment about Christian truth seeking may be slightly overstated, but her point should not be lost on evangelicals as we engage in the serious study of other religions: "Christ likes us to prefer truth to him," she wrote, "because, before being Christ, he is truth. If one turns aside from him to go toward the truth, one will not go far before falling into his arms."[1]

## The Present Challenges

In his contribution to this volume, Irving Hexham expresses some worries that evangelical thinkers these days are a little too enamored with some of the irrationalist tendencies of much of postmodern

---

1. Simone Weil, *Waiting for God*, trans. Emma Craufurd (San Francisco: Harper & Row, 1973), 69.

thought. I share many of his concerns, but I must confess that I have not found much evidence in these chapters that these particular writers would resist Hexham's call "to return to our roots and affirm our faith in Christ, his church, and the truth of the gospel." To be sure, the views set forth in several of these essays are obviously influenced on significant matters by postmodern themes—for example, the importance of narrative, the influence of cultural context on our "packaging" of theological issues, and the insistence that the biblical writers themselves engaged in some cultural borrowing. But I do not see such emphases as a sign that we are slipping in our commitment to orthodoxy.

When I was a philosophy graduate student in the 1960s, I read Bishop Stephen Neill's book *Christian Faith and Other Faiths*. His advocacy for a dialogic approach to other religions had a deep impact on me, not just in my own understanding of how to deal with interreligious issues but more broadly in my sense of the proper patterns of philosophical and theological methodology. I have often returned to his discussion for a refresher course in the proper patterns of Christian empathy. This is one of the passages that is highlighted in my copy of Neill's book:

> The Christian must not be surprised if, between now and the end of this century, the work of Christian witness in India becomes more difficult than it has been for a century. He must be prepared to face the possibility that the greater part of his work must be from within Hinduism, in putting questions to the Hindu and helping him to understand himself better. But in doing so he will not be adapting himself to the Hindu ideal of what a missionary should be. . . . All the time he will be attempting to help the Hindu to see the radical unsatisfactoriness of all the answers that have been given to his questions, and so to point him to the One in Whom those questions can receive their all-sufficient answer, the Lord Jesus Christ.[2]

Neill's predictions were accurate. The task of Christian witness has indeed been difficult in recent decades. And things have not gotten any easier now that we have entered a new century—if anything, they seem to be more complicated than ever. But the assignment is still pretty much the same one that Bishop Neill prescribed. We must stand alongside people of other faiths (and those who claim to have no faith at all), taking their questions seriously and trying to assist them in understanding themselves better, so that we can point them to the One who has come to seek and to save those who are lost. And

2. Stephen Neill, *Christian Faith and Other Faiths* (New York: Oxford University Press, 1961), 98.

for some of us at least, the willingness to probe the depths of human hopes and fears, in all of their religious variety, can also mean that we will come to understand ourselves better, as people whose lives have been redeemed by the God who in these last days is pouring out his Spirit upon all flesh.

# 9

# Are There Disciples of Christ outside the Church?

## KEN R. GNANAKAN

The challenge of other religions is growing, and pertinent questions are being asked today even by Christians. Is Christianity truly unique? And if it is, what about followers of other religions? Are true adherents of other religions saved on the basis of their sincere beliefs? There is an urgent need for Christians to face squarely these challenges and boldly affirm our belief within the climate that prevails. At the same time, we may need to go beyond the narrow limits we have set for the outworking of God's grace.

The contributors to this volume have all tried sincerely, even boldly, to look at both sides of the challenge: one, from the perspective of our own claims and the attack on the uniqueness of Jesus Christ (for we believe we are the custodians of our faith), and the other, from the side of the religious quests of those who are not Christian. I am from a predominantly Hindu context, but I am also familiar with a growing Islamic influence. Viewed from my perspective, cultivated in part by my interactions with believers of these faiths, most of the treatments in this collection are fairly academic. That, perhaps, is to be expected, knowing that as the authors wrote, they were protected by volumes preserving the strong doctrines that have contributed to our Western evangelical heritage. Yet each addressed the growing pressure of pluralism, seeking to claim fresh ground, carefully justifying this as "biblical" lest he or she be branded a compromiser.

There is definitely biblical sanction for change in our rigid approach to other religions. While the people of God in the Old Testament handled plurality by distancing themselves from people of all other religions, early Christians were faced with a different context. They had to live alongside men and women of varying religious beliefs and had to work out their faith in God through Jesus within this rather hostile environment. But they would have remembered the way Jesus Christ lived and ministered in a world characterized by plurality. Jesus made positive references to the faith of men and women outside the Jewish community. There was little condemnation. In fact, we notice a commendation of some of the positive elements that he discerned amid the complexity of their traditions. Interestingly, most of his condemnation was aimed at men and women of the Jewish faith. How then do we handle plurality today? This is something the writers have helpfully addressed.

## Religion in Context

Amid the largely academic tone of the papers, Miriam Adeney helps us in addressing the very live Islamic context, particularly the popular one, through the eyes (and perhaps the heart) of her own experience. Her observations are no less convincing or objective merely because of this experiential starting point. Adeney states, "Religions are not merely doctrines. They are also lived." Thus, she writes about Zamboanga, not "disembodied Islam." Each religious context provides not only the ground for growth and cultivation but also hinders or opposes religious belief. This is true not only of Islam but also Hinduism and every other religion. One can make no sweeping generalized statements. Each context has given rise to a peculiar form of religion, consciously and unconsciously absorbing local elements. Each major religion displays denominational, geographical, and generational variety, as she rightly points out. The Hinduism I know in my particular part of South India is different from the one in Calcutta, and even more different from the kind in Fiji or Trinidad.

At the same time, however, the Hindu context is most conducive for the growth of various religious beliefs. India has received almost every religion into the labyrinth called Hinduism, and consequently, Hinduism is not one unified religion. The genius of the Indian mind has been its ability to absorb every belief, which is why this religion, if you can still call it one, has endured, allowing all elements within it to maintain their own distinctives. The belief in *sarva dharma sambhava* (all religions are equal) makes it possible for Christianity to survive alongside other religions, as long as it does not claim to be the best of all these religions. Frankly, therefore, is our responsibility that of proving our religion is the best?

The Hindu context has not only fostered but also provided some refreshing elements for indigenous Indian Christianity. And this Adeney also affirms, pointing out that we can learn from other religions, a thought most evangelicals hesitate to entertain. There is still a prevailing Barthian disdain for religions in most of us. What Adeney says, therefore, deserves to be underlined. "Religions contain patterns of wisdom, beauty, and caring, results of God's gift of creativity in his image. Therefore, I can learn from non-Christian religions." A positive step such as this in our approach to other religions will ensure significant strides as we seek to move closer to people of other faiths, a move that is much needed.

The challenge of religions in our world today demands an openness that will hold to essential Christian beliefs and at the same time be flexible with nonessential practices that help or hinder the outworking of these beliefs. I meet Christians who have told me that meditation is demonic, because for them meditation is associated with only the kind propagated by Maharishi Mahesh Yogi (of Transcendental Meditation). But what about the psalmist who spoke frequently about meditation? Have we not experienced the refreshing effects of even moments of quietness amid our cacophonous world? There are others who say that the practice of yoga is taboo for the Christian. But yoga has proven to be most effective in promoting health, and one wonders whether such well-being is evil.

Religion is an essential element of every culture, and people develop their religious beliefs and practices within their own cultures. Mistaken statements are made in general in relation to the Indian culture. Some tell me, "Don't get too absorbed with Indian culture as it is so closely intertwined with the Hindu religion." But then, is involvement in culture an option? Is not religion an integral part of culture? Moreover, while there may be religious elements in Indian culture, are there not equivalent elements in all cultures? Pagan practices have been absorbed into Western Christianity, which causes me to ask, What qualifies these elements as more conducive to Christianity than religious ones?

## Common Ground

Culture and religion are elements that we commonly share with all human beings. We see this clearly when we examine the creation accounts in the Bible. When we set out to study God's dealings with the world beginning with creation itself, we see revelation from the very start of God's activity with the world of human beings. A truly holistic perspective, a total horizon of God's revelation, must have some initial reference point, humanly speaking. Gerald McDermott demonstrates an openness, suggesting that "there is knowledge of the true God outside the Hebrew and Christian traditions." He cites Melchizedek, Abel, Enoch, Noah, Job, and Ruth, as well as New Testament instances in which Jesus praised the faith of pagans and urged Jews to learn from these pagan examples.

McDermott draws our attention to Paul at Athens and thus provides a good starting point for a theology of religions. Paul's attempts to establish a continuity between the gospel and the worship of the Athenians is probably the best place from which to build a case for a more positive attitude toward our non-Christian neighbors. Paul's attitude toward the universality of God's revelation in his Areopagus speech is paralleled in his teaching in the Epistle to the Romans. The one who claimed to be a "Jew to the Jew" and a "Gentile to the Gentile" could certainly demonstrate this adaptability when dealing with a situation such as the one he encountered in Athens.

It is a positive introduction: "I see that in every way you are very religious" (Acts 17:22 NIV). Paul had definitely observed several things that brought him to this conclusion, chief among them being the altar to "an unknown God." The continuity established was not merely a preacher's ploy. In fact, we should take a lesson for our proclamation today. Paul in no way differs from Jesus! Just as Jesus was able to commend the faith of the Gentile centurion, Paul was able to commend Athenian worship, even though it was to an unknown God.

Behind Paul's commendation is the fact that the Athenians possessed a sincere desire to worship the true God, even though they were surrounded by idols. This can be appreciated in India, where I meet many men and women, some who have moved away from idols and some who continue idolatrous practices, who truly desire to worship the true God. Although their desire is not adequate for salvation, the question that arises is whether one can build upon that foundation and lead these people to the truth.

Even amid the perversion that is externally apparent, there is a sincere search for the true God, a search that God himself may utilize for his glory. Just like the Greeks in the above passage, many Hindus search for the unknown beyond the known, the truth beyond the falsehood, the light beyond the darkness. The millions who went to the recently publicized *Kumbh Mela* worship event in Allahabad, India, the largest gathering of humans in an event in any one place, demonstrated the longing of humanity to come closer to God. Humans search in different ways and are never certain that their search will lead them to ultimate reality. Paul points out that this search has to be directed toward Jesus Christ, the one who is able to fulfill the longings of human beings and their sincere desire to know ultimate reality.

Our theology has often started from a "sin and redemption" framework, following Augustine, and consequently, a judgmental attitude has separated the "redeemed" from the "unredeemed," resulting in a gulf between Christians and people of other faiths. Christianity's attitude toward the world has also often been a negative one, distancing us from other people who are often described as "worldly." That is why Stanley Grenz's comments on community need to be explored even further. It is important for us to realize that we are meeting people, not merely confronting an abstract phantom called religion. We must strive for meaningful continuity with people of other religions rather than perpetuating questionable discontinuity.

The framework of creation leads ideally to the universality that the New Testament claims for the redemption of Christ, a universality noted by almost all the writers in this volume. One need not fear that starting from creation will allow for a universality that takes away from the distinctive Christian teaching of redemption. The Old Testament concept of election gives to this universality a particularity that keeps it from tending toward universalism. Election is an even more important theme than creation for the Jew, and therefore the Christian, for it is here that God begins to demonstrate his specific intentions for human beings.

## No Conflicts?

Does continuity rule out conflicts? Not at all! We need to distinguish carefully between a commonness as far as human beings are concerned and the differences between our religious beliefs. Fundamentally, there is a continuity on grounds of our humanness, a commonality on grounds of our being made in God's image, and this could be the key to a more positive understanding of community with people of other religions. If this commonness of being endowed with the image of God is accepted, then there is a common spiritual essence to all humankind, and this is evidenced in its quest to fulfill a longing that God himself has placed within each being. Seen this way, religion is a necessity for humans to be fully human. We would be naive to deny demonic activity in religion. However, even this does not negate the fact of a sincere longing within humankind to know the ultimate.

But the nagging question that concerns us is, Does this commonality lead us to a common faith, one that some would urge us to develop? Gerald Pillay correctly comments, "The commonalities among various religions cannot obscure irreducible differences." Some truth claims, he says, cannot be "too hastily ditched for the sake of a rational theology and harmonious religious coexistence." But why should harmonious coexistence lead to the surrendering of one's truth claims? Is there a lesson we can learn from Hinduism, which brings together groups of contrasting beliefs into one common community?

Conflicting truth claims are inevitable and must be handled with sensitivity. These irreconcilable claims have been cause for conflicts, only because they were made in arrogance as well as with ignorance, with little concern for the feelings of others. Colonial Christianity, like the American-style evangelism we continue to see today, provoked hearers. Some major Hindu reform movements arose out of reaction to the condemnation they received from Christians! Similarly, much of the reaction to the Christian message in India in recent times has arisen mainly as a consequence of callous comments and insensitive preaching. Fundamentalism gives rise to fundamentalism, and we are seeing the rise of a militant kind of Hinduism, foreign to the tolerant religion it has always been. There is a pressing need to develop our communication skills in tune with the compassionate Christ who healed rather than hurt, who agonized rather than antagonized, and in doing so drew masses to himself.

## Some Crucial Questions

The contributions to this volume are significant in addressing some crucial issues. There is some measure of truth in all religions. This truth is available to men and women due to the fact of their being made in the image of God, as well as the fact of God's revelation to all the world through his universal creative activity. However, and importantly, the point on which all contributors agree is that we cannot justify any grounds on which this truth can be salvific.

While I agree that all revelation and truth are not salvific, I hesitate to discard such a knowledge of God as having no value for salvation whatsoever. If it is truly God's truth, it must point to God, toward the ultimate salvation that he offers, otherwise there is little value in such an activity of God. There is sufficient testimony to the fact that those who have responded sincerely to the measure of truth they have seen have been led to an encounter with Jesus Christ, through whom they have discovered a relationship with God.

The writers all allow for an openness to recognize some meaning in the religious experiences of others, but they stop at the all-important question: Is there salvation in these religious experiences? Do religions lead their adherents to ultimate reality? Barth was categorical: Religion is rebellion! And all of the authors in this volume agree that there is no salvation outside Jesus Christ. Adeney comments, "As long as evangelicals remain fixated on the question of whether someone can be 'saved' through another religion, our theology will remain superficial. After all, who knows what God's Spirit does or does not do in human hearts?" I wish to give some attention to lucid insights in this regard from Lesslie Newbigin.

Newbigin, in grappling with this issue, looks first at the strictly exclusivist view that holds that all who do not accept Jesus as Lord and Savior are eternally lost. He states, "If it were true, then it would be not only permissible but obligatory to use any means available, all the modern techniques of brainwashing included, to rescue others from this appalling fate."[1] It is God alone who knows the heart of every person, he states, and so how are we to judge whether another person is saved? Some of us think it absolutely necessary to know who is saved and who is not and are then led into making the kind of judgments against which Scripture warns us.

Newbigin cautions against such declarations, which may have the effect of erecting unintended barriers in our communication of the gospel. He is concerned that we are bound to become judges of that which God alone knows. Newbigin's cautions are well taken, and we will need to avoid a glib and naive approach to "decisionism," an "easy believism" that has hindered rather than helped the evangelistic mission in recent decades. We seem to have taken up the business of selling salvation so cheaply that the question of one's eternity is settled by reference to a few external expressions of faith. Having made it so simple to grant people admission into the kingdom, we have not found it difficult to deny God's blessings to those outside those narrow terms.

Newbigin points to the tension between the two poles: "the amazing grace of God and the appalling sin of the world."[2] He refers to the "impossible position of knowing that one is—along with all others—at the same time the enemy of God and the beloved child of God. To live in this charged field of force is always at the same time supremely demanding and supremely affirming. But we are always tempted to slacken the tension by drawing away from one or other of the two poles."[3] Some may give to sin and rebellion such weight that the grace

---

1. Lesslie Newbigin, *The Gospel in a Pluralistic Society* (London: SPCK, 1989), 173.
2. Ibid.
3. Ibid., 175.

of God is minimized, or conversely, take for granted the grace of God, ignoring the gravity of sin. Newbigin comments, "We can opt for a solution which relies wholly on the universality and omnipotence of grace and move toward some form of universalism. Here the sharpness of the issue which God's action in Christ raises for every human soul is blunted."[4] This kind of an attitude, that everything will be all right for everybody in the end, does not take full account of sin.

But the other side of the tension is that God has made available his grace, which operates despite humanity's sin. Newbigin points out that "the Christian may be so conscious of the abyss of sin from which only the grace of God in Jesus Christ could rescue him that he is unwilling to believe that the same grace can operate in ways beyond his own experience and understanding."[5] Perhaps the limitations we have imposed on God need to be questioned. God's work, in order to be truly God's, must be beyond our comprehension. Is this what Paul, echoing Job, concedes: "How unsearchable his judgments, and his paths beyond tracing out!" (Rom. 11:33 NIV)?

We must humbly admit that we need to review the hard-line exclusivist position in the light of biblical implications, as well as the context in which we live. The questions we have asked need to be taken much further if we really want to consider the particularity of salvation through Jesus Christ alongside the universal availability of God's grace. The Bible provides some pointers, perhaps sometimes implicitly, and they need to be faithfully observed. We need to look critically at the entire scope of Scripture to explore the stand we need to take in relation to our present context. However, there are answers the Bible does not provide, and we must therefore be willing to accept that some questions are best left unanswered.

One thing that bothers me is the arrogant certainty most evangelicals seem to display in answering questions beyond our knowledge. I am relieved that I do not see too much of this in these contributions. We hear it so often: "Gandhi will go to hell because he did not acknowledge Jesus as Lord." Or, "Will the sincere Hindu be saved?" Even more often, "My husband, who just died, was a devout man but never made a public confession of Christ. Will he go to hell?" I have learned that it is best not to answer these questions, since such answers must be purely academic, even if orthodox.

In a similar vein, Newbigin responds to the question, What happens to the non-Christian after death? This is the wrong question, he responds, and as long as it remains the central question, we shall never

4. Ibid., 179.
5. Ibid., 176.

come to the truth. He offers three suggestions, briefly noted here. First, he says, "It is a question to which only God has the right to give an answer." Second, by concentrating on what happens to the soul after death we are dealing only with an abstraction. Third, "The question starts with the individual and his or her need . . . of ultimate happiness, and not with God and his glory."[6] I must add, life is complicated enough, and it is good to tackle some of the problems we know we have the answers for before getting into the unknown! I would spend more time with the woman asking about her husband than the academic concerned about Gandhi.

## Disciples?

Adeney's suggestion is that we enlarge the question, asking whether someone can become a full-fledged disciple of Jesus Christ while worshiping in another faith. I like the distinction, but I am forced to ask how we measure discipleship. I find the discussion on community introduced by Stanley Grenz helpful in providing a window. It adds the dimension of God establishing the human community, providing a biblical perspective, in fact a biblical justification, for God's universal activity. Grenz approaches it from the perspective of history, and that is to be commended. It is a universal community within all of creation, and that gives revelation its wider scope. This is still not the widest scope for God's community, of course, for Paul reminds us that God's sovereignty and redemptive significance extend to all creation.

Community is God with humankind. "From the creation of the heavens and the earth, with which the biblical drama begins, to the vision of the new earth, which forms the drama's climax, the plot of the biblical narrative is God at work creating community," says Grenz. The theme of the Bible is the establishment of community in the highest sense of the word—a redeemed people, living within a redeemed creation, enjoying the presence of the Triune God. Yet the central dimension of community as depicted throughout the biblical narrative, Grenz points out, is the quest for the presence of God among humans.

The universal story of God, Grenz affirms, is expansive, with saving intentions for all humankind (1 Tim. 2:3–4). The overarching context of creation gives a theocentric cast to the human reality. Despite the fall, "the Creator's purpose for humankind is not thereby annulled, for God remains resolute in his desire to bring the divine design, set forth in the beginning, to completion in the new creation." And if it is creation, it is universal. "God's saving purposes overflow the boundaries of any one

6. Ibid., 177.

people to encompass all. . . . After the flood, God enters into another covenant with all humankind through Noah (Gen. 9:1–17)," and with Abraham, God promises to bless "all peoples on earth" (Gen. 12:3).

More needs to be said about the wider community within which the Christian community must be located. Adeney's question needs to be answered with another question. Is the church the only place, the only community, in which discipleship takes place? Is discipleship not hindered in some churches? Is even Jesus' community wider than the church's community? Based on the perspective of God's community, we need to give the widest possible scope for this community and therefore accept possibilities of disciples in a wider sense. I know I am treading on dangerous ground, but I need to remind the reader that the Bible does allow for this. Perhaps rereading Jesus' parable of the sheep and the goats would be a good starting point.

## Our Challenge Today

The Indian Christian community faces an unprecedented attack from militant fundamentalist sections within the Hindu community. The tolerant Hindu is still in the majority, but it takes just a handful of militant Hindus to cause panic. Whether it was the dastardly burning to death of the Australian missionary Graham Staines and his two young sons, or the destroying of small churches in various parts of India, the media and political circles have widely publicized blatant blows against Christians. Some other pertinent questions being asked amid these attacks are: Will conversions continue? Will Christians continue to claim superiority for their religion? Isn't Christianity a Western religion? And if so, should not all Indian Christians convert back to Hinduism?

Setting ourselves within community should bring some changes, such as the decline of triumphalistic and aggressive language. There was a time when battlefield language was effective. Not today! While such language is certainly biblical, even biblical words had their own contexts. Interestingly, today such language is quite prevalent in the business world, rampant with fierce competition. But for the message of love, Jesus' message, it is counterproductive. The cross will continue to be an offense, but we do not need to make it offensive. And much more than an offense, is the cross not a sign of love, peace, forgiveness, and reconciliation? Do Christians not have a major role in bringing healing to the nations? Are Christians not the best agents of communal harmony? Rather than separating ourselves, we must integrate ourselves into a world of real people and make a Christlike impression in God's wider community.

# Afterword

## An Agenda for an Evangelical Theology of Religions

### JOHN G. STACKHOUSE, JR.

This volume succeeds if it prompts evangelical theologians to move ahead on a broad program of theological investigation of the phenomenon of world religions. The essays and responses in this book do not, of course, even raise every pertinent question, let alone answer them. Instead, they offer each author's particular contribution to the conversation at this point.

Systematic investigation of a theology of world religions will require more than idiosyncratic initiatives, however, no matter how worthy each may be. To assist in such investigation, then, it perhaps is worthwhile to consider a map of the issues that remain before us. No map is complete, of course, and every map can be improved upon. But some such map is necessary if we are to proceed with any sort of coherence. So, then, the agenda for an evangelical theology of religions that follows.

## Revelation

### General Revelation

Systematic theology typically divides the question of revelation into "general" and "special" categories. In the former of these, we need to ask several questions.

*What is it?* What is the nature of general revelation? Is general revelation embedded, as it were, in things themselves? Does one look at the heavens and immediately know, or perhaps properly, infer, that God exists and that he is powerful, creative, beautiful, and more? Is the revelation of God simply *there*, and human beings know it as we experience the world, unless we are corrupted by sin and thus are insensate?[1]

Does the Holy Spirit, instead, so move among and within human beings such that all have access to God's revelation—whether God's moral law, his ordering of the cosmos, his love for human beings, and so on?

Furthermore, what is the content of that revelation? Is it simply that God exists—and what then is meant by "God exists"? Is it that God is mighty and the maker of heaven and earth? Is it that God is all this and also the lover of our souls?

*How general is it?* Does everyone on earth have access to God's revelation? Do entire nations have less access than others, just as Gentiles had less access to special revelation than Israelites in the old covenant? What about individuals born with, or raised to have, important defects in their epistemic apparatus, whether mental, psychological, physical, or spiritual? Consider, that is, mentally handicapped persons, victims of sexual abuse, slaves, the blind, and those raised in horribly corrupt communities. How does the concept of general revelation need to be qualified, if at all, in the light of these realities?

*What is the point of it?* Some theologians have suggested that God gives us enough general revelation to condemn us but not enough to save us: We see the cliff of God's holiness, so to speak, but no rope to help us climb it. Others suggest that God's goodness and willingness to save are announced to all through the Holy Spirit. But is that true? And if so, what are God's intentions in working with and through that revelation?

### Special Revelation

Typically, again, systematic theology has pointed especially to the Bible and to Jesus as the key events of special revelation. These are revelations not generally available but specially available in just this document and just this person.

Special revelation, however, if it is defined simply as "revelation that is not generally available but made available on this occasion to this audience," takes in much more.

Prophecy, whether in the Old Testament, New Testament, or Christian church to the present, counts as special revelation. God speaks directly and specifically to a particular audience in such communication.

---

1. A standard evangelical treatment is Bruce A. Demarest, *General Revelation: Historical Views and Contemporary Issues* (Grand Rapids: Zondervan, 1982). Cf. Alvin Plantinga, *Warranted Christian Belief* (New York and Oxford: Oxford University Press, 2000), esp. part 3.

The Roman Catholic Church sees tradition as also a deposit of the Holy Spirit's special revelation. If Protestants disagree with that lofty estimation, what do we make instead of the history of doctrine, of liturgy, of Christian thought and life in general? Did God offer special revelation through the Nicene Creed, or the *solas* of the magisterial Reformation, or the piety of eighteenth-century revivals, or the rise of Pentecostalism?

What about the Holy Spirit's work of personal conviction of sin and offer of salvation through Christ? Is this special revelation? It certainly amounts to such for the individual involved. Some theologians might demur, pointing out that there is no new content being delivered that hasn't been delivered already through the Bible. But does this response overemphasize propositional revelation? And does it then offer a helpful alternative category for what seems to be indeed a new work of revelation by which God shows an individual spiritual truth he or she did not apprehend before?

What about ongoing personal guidance of Christians? Evangelicals particularly are inclined to celebrate God's direction in their lives and to testify to many occasions in which God moved them this way or that—whether as individuals or as groups. Does this count as special revelation? If it does, then perhaps we now recognize a quite broad category of special revelation by which the Holy Spirit reveals quite a lot of things to quite a lot of people, rather than restricting his activity to illuminating the Bible about the gospel of Jesus Christ—as some evangelical construals would have it. If this does not count as special revelation, however, then what is it?

Finally, what do we suppose is happening when a particular religion or philosophy emerges? What is the role of the Holy Spirit in the discoveries and resultant teachings of the Buddha, or Socrates, or Confucius? Early Christian apologists credited the Holy Spirit with inspiring the Socratic philosophers: Only the Holy Spirit could have enabled them to arrive at so many correct conclusions about God and the world, in the view of Justin Martyr, Athenagoras, and their colleagues.[2] So what about other religious and philosophical geniuses? And what about those who are not geniuses but who, nonetheless, have made their own smaller discoveries of truth, beauty, and goodness and offered them to others?

2. Avery Dulles, S.J., *A History of Apologetics* (New York: Corpus; Philadelphia: Westminster; and London: Hutchinson, 1971).

## Ingredients of Religions

God's activity in religions can be assumed at least insofar as any religion has any truth, goodness, or beauty in it. There is nothing virtuous in the universe that does not come as a gift of God, the fount of every blessing. How much more, however, is God involved in any particular religion?

An alternative to hypothesizing divine activity is, of course, to posit demonic distortion instead. Yes, a religion might include some good bits, but the religion itself might well be the construct of evil spiritual powers, intent on mischief rather than blessing. An evangelical theology of religions thus must wrestle with the question of just what Satan and company actually can do in this regard and might have done in the emergence of this or that religion.

God and the devil are not, to be sure, the only agents involved. Human beings appropriate the work of higher or lower spiritual powers and put our distinctive stamp upon it, for better and for worse. What, then, are the discernible human contributions to the career of Buddhism, or Baha'i, or Shinto? We Christians also should recognize, especially in this conversation, that our own religion bears the marks of all three types of agents: divine, devilish, and human. From this perspective we can more humbly and carefully examine other religions as well.

Furthermore, all students of religions recognize that religions evolve over time. Recognizing this fact gives rise to two more questions.

First, the question of origins: Where do the religions come from? What really happened to Gautama Buddha under the bo tree, or to Muhammad in that cave, or to Joseph Smith when he claimed he was visited by the angel Moroni, or to Jesus' body after his crucifixion? Can we investigate these matters historically? Does it matter if we do?

I have been struck by how scholars of religious studies tend to tiptoe around these matters, placing silent and invisible quotation marks around all such claims to supernatural origins as if to say, "Well, that's what the believers claim, and I'm not going to dispute that here." Surely, however, any thorough characterization of the very nature of Islam or Mormonism or Christianity (to name three religions that claim straightforward historicity for the supernatural careers of their founders) would require serious investigation of these narratives. Perhaps for Theravada Buddhism it doesn't matter whether Gautama Buddha actually received enlightenment under that tree or not: The point is the noble path he set out for his followers. To worry about the bo tree is to commit the genetic fallacy. Buddhism is true whether or not the story of its origin is true or not. But it obviously does matter to these other religions whether Muhammad was delusional, or Joseph Smith a charlatan, or Jesus just another failed "messiah."

Second, in considering the nature of religions, we need constantly to ask, Which religion do you mean? Religions change and divide and diversify over time. Theologies of religion must be informed by the historic complexity of actual religious traditions, not the convenient oversimplifications of stereotypes (such as "all Eastern thought is monistic" or "Christianity alone offers a religion of grace").

## Purpose of Religions

*Counterfeit/alternative to true religion?* Do other religions have what goodness, truth, and beauty they possess only as an enticement away from God's true way, whether the covenant with Israel or the new covenant in Christ? Are other religions allowed by God's providence the way in which other evils are allowed: to let our free will run its course, to demonstrate what we can get up to on our own (and especially with demonic encouragement), to provide alternatives to the true path so that no one can claim to be coerced into it by default?

*Restraint of evil and offering of (some) good?* Do other religions exist the way institutions exist (as per Romans 13), as divinely ordained structures that restrain evil and thereby offer at least some mitigated good? Are they mercies from God, at least the better ones, to supplant the even worse alternatives available through human and demonic rebellion and deceit?

It may be that other goods reside in other religions as well. Perhaps by their very (over)emphasis on this or that truth, they can remind Christians, as well as teach others, of truths that might be underplayed or even ignored in this or that tradition. Furthermore, it may be that God has actually revealed some things in other religious contexts that are not revealed in the Jewish and Christian traditions. (Perhaps he has done so in a way similar to his revelation of truth through science, history, and other fields beyond Christian religious resources.) Evangelical Christians thus can learn from other religions, as Gerald McDermott has argued, and not merely seek to teach them.[3]

*Propaedeutic of the gospel?* Do other religions offer "good dreams" of what actually came true in the life of Christ, as C. S. Lewis wondered?[4] Previous generations of missionaries have theorized that God provides other religions as foundations for the proclamation of the gospel. Does

3. Gerald R. McDermott, *Can Evangelicals Learn from World Religions? Jesus, Revelation, and Religious Traditions* (Downers Grove, Ill.: InterVarsity Press, 2000).

4. C. S. Lewis, *Mere Christianity* (1942; reprint, Glasgow: Fontana/Collins, 1955), 51.

God thus establish both points of contact and hunger for the truth among all people through both the blessings and inadequacies of their religions?

Along with this spectrum of options arises the question of how mutually exclusive these categories actually are. It might well be that a particular religion might serve two or even all three of these purposes under God's mysterious and beneficent providence.

It also remains to consider the purpose of all religions, in this case including Christianity rather than isolating it from the rest. The essays in this collection by Miriam Adeney and Stanley Grenz raise this point centrally, as Adeney points to discipleship and Grenz to community building—not merely "getting souls to heaven"—as key purposes of authentic religion. Thus, the theology of religions must interact with our theologies of conversion, sanctification, the church, and other key elements of the Christian religion.

## Basis of Salvation

### God's Work and Human Response

Perhaps salvation needs to be seen as God's work alone. Human beings are helpless to contribute to their own rescue, so God must save through his own love and power. Predestinarian orthodoxy, whether Protestant, Catholic, or Orthodox (although not as frequently or clearly articulated in the latter two traditions), claims just this dynamic. God is glorified in his doing all that needs to be done in saving an otherwise doomed humanity.

Ironically, however, a strong predestinarianism also constitutes the ground for universalism, the belief that all will be saved and hell will be empty, for God is all-good, God is all-powerful, and nothing successfully resists his will.

Much more common among Roman Catholic, Orthodox, Protestant, and, yes, evangelical Christians is the conviction that God's work is indeed foundational, but human beings have a role to play as well. God's grace comes first, brings the sinner to the moment of conversion, and sustains the Christian on the path to the New Jerusalem. Human beings, however, have the dignity and responsibility of deciding whether to cooperate with God or not, and without that cooperation, God allows his love for us to be frustrated.

Unorthodox theologies also find a home here. Process theology, for example, takes this dynamic for granted. And universalism can suggest that eventually all will find God so winsome that all will be saved, without exception.

### What Is "God's Work" and What Is "Human Response"?

*The definition and role of Christ.* Here in particular we can locate the question of who Christ is and what he has done. Since Christian faith rests upon Christ, and not "God in general," all Christian theology worthy of the name rests foundationally on the person and work of Christ. A theology of religions, therefore, must set this out both thoroughly (so as not to claim too little for Christ, as in "moral example," "spiritual guide," and so on) and carefully (so as not to claim too much, as in "God's only revelation of himself," "the only teacher of truth"). Theologies that claim too little for Christ will then find it easier to see other religions as adequate alternatives to Christianity. Theologies that claim too much will find it difficult to appreciate and account for the virtues evident in those other faiths, let alone understand how they can serve the divine plan in any way.

It is in this context that the term *exclusivism* perhaps is best deployed to denote the conviction that there is one and only one basis upon which human beings come to their highest good. In Christian terms, exclusivism would denote the belief that the work of Christ is the one and only means by which salvation comes to humanity. *Pluralism,* by this account, would say that Christ's work does matter (more or less), but it provides merely one basis among others upon which we can enjoy fulfillment.

*The definition and role of faith.* Christian commitment can be characterized along generic religious lines. It involves three broad elements: the affective (what and whom one loves and hates, esteems and despises), the cognitive (what one believes), and the practical (what one does). What, then, does "saving faith" comprise? What does "mature faith" comprise?

Here is one location in which to consider the hard cases of infants, the mentally handicapped or deranged, and the emotionally or otherwise psychologically crippled. What is needful in their cases when it comes to faith? Can others have faith on their behalf (as in Catholic baptismal services)? Does God use "middle knowledge" to know what they would have done had they not been disadvantaged? Does God create such people for his own mysterious purposes and thus treat them differently from those created with normal opportunity to exercise faith?

Clearly, these questions matter also when considering people in other religions and cultures and what their standing is before God; what their needs are to which Christians properly can minister; and what gifts, if any, they might bring to us in exchange.

## Revelation and Salvation: "Means"

### "Epistemological" versus "Ontological"

A traditional Christian understanding of salvation says that all who are saved are saved only on the basis of their understanding and accepting the gospel of Jesus Christ. Critics of this position sometimes respond with a distinction between a human being's epistemological condition and her ontological condition vis-à-vis Christ.

She might, that is, not know the factual content of the story of Jesus of Nazareth. But she has responded to God with proper faith—that is, faith proper to her circumstances, benighted as they are without knowledge of the gospel—and thus is ontologically saved by Christ's work. Thus, she is epistemologically not a "Christian," but she is ontologically a "believer," and thus saved by God's work in Christ just as anyone else is.[5]

This distinction might be clear as far as it goes. But it may not go far enough, as proponents of the distinction themselves often recognize, for this "believer" still needs to be believing *something* about *someone* (who is God) in order for the fundamental direction of her faith to be properly oriented and fruitful. An epistemologically (or "cognitively") empty faith is inconceivable. Those who wish to defend this distinction, therefore, have an agenda item before them: What *is* the necessary content of saving faith?

In the light of this point, perhaps the so-called hard cases of infants and the mentally or psychologically incapacitated simply don't apply to this question because such people are in fact incapable of faith. If so, they thus must fall under some other dimension of God's economy, and it is better for a theology of religions (and of salvation, of course) to bracket them out rather than try to find some way to fit them in.

### Four Options

*Evangelism/"restrictivism."* This view asserts that only by the explicit preaching and reception of the gospel can someone come to saving faith. Whatever else God might do for the unevangelized is mysterious at best and ominous at worst. What is clear is that "faith comes by hearing, and hearing by the word of God" (Rom. 10:17 NKJV).

This position breaks out into at least three versions distinguished by the chronological question of just when someone might hear the gospel and thus have the opportunity to respond in faith. Most widespread of

---

5. This distinction emerged in contemporary evangelical discussion out of the following books: Clark H. Pinnock, *A Wideness in God's Mercy: The Finality of Jesus Christ in a World of Religions* (Grand Rapids: Zondervan, 1992); and John Sanders, *No Other Name: An Investigation into the Destiny of the Unevangelized* (Grand Rapids: Eerdmans, 1992).

these versions is that of evangelism *before death:* The gospel is preached by Christians to their neighbors, and only those neighbors who respond to this proclamation have the opportunity to repent and be saved.

A second version of this emphasis on evangelism suggests that those who do not have the opportunity to hear the gospel in the normal course of their lives will have it declared to them directly by the Holy Spirit *at death.* No one will be left bereft of the gospel message, that is, as he or she faces judgment in the world to come.

A third version also ensures that no one can accuse God of withholding the gospel from him or her. It affirms that *after death* each person receives the opportunity to hear and respond to the gospel that was not available in life.

This group is sometimes termed "exclusivists" because of their emphasis both on the unique and necessary work of Christ and on the necessity of preaching and responding to the gospel message, thus excluding all other options—at least as far as we know. (Again, God might have mercies to bestow on others outside this economy of salvation, but we have few clues as to what these mercies might be.) But "exclusivism" is best reserved for belief in just one basis for salvation. "Restrictivists" would then be those who believe that salvation is restricted to those who hear and respond in faith to the gospel message.[6]

*Inclusivism.* This term then applies to those who believe there is one basis upon which human beings reach religious fulfillment, but there are several means available by which people may access the benefits of that one basis.

In orthodox Christian terms, inclusivists share with restrictivists the exclusivistic belief in the central and necessary place of Christ's work on behalf of humanity. Orthodox inclusivists, then, are those who believe that God applies the salvific benefits of the work of Christ to those who have not heard the gospel but who, nonetheless, are granted the gift of saving faith as they respond to what light of the Holy Spirit they have been granted. (Thus, the question of revelation resurfaces here quite significantly.)

It is worth noting in passing, however, that there are at least two unorthodox versions of Christian inclusivism available as well. The first is the pattern set out by Wilfred Cantwell Smith, John Hick, and other os-

---

6. I am therefore suggesting a scheme somewhat different from the one influentially outlined by John Sanders in *No Other Name.* For evangelical statements of restrictivism, see Ronald H. Nash, *Is Jesus the Only Savior?* (Grand Rapids: Zondervan, 1994); and Harold A. Netland, *Dissonant Voices: Religious Pluralism and the Question of Truth* (Grand Rapids: Eerdmans, 1991).

tensible "pluralists." These theorists suggest that there are multiple paths to human fulfillment, many of them having nothing to do with Jesus Christ, explicitly or implicitly. In Hick's formulation, one can be rightly oriented toward the Ultimately Real with or without the assistance of Jesus. Such a view, however, rests (as orthodoxy does) on the fundamental conviction that there is only one basis upon which people can reach their *summum bonum*. What Smith, Hick, and their ilk say is that this basis is *not* the person and work of Jesus Christ. They suggest instead that it is the revelation of God abroad in the world, the correct response to which is "other-mindedness," charity, and moral rectitude. There are not really multiple paths but multiple versions of the same path to the same end.[7]

So, too, does mysticism offer multiple versions of the same path to the same end: union with the divine. Whether the Christian mysticism of Meister Eckhart or the Society of Friends, or the non-Christian mysticism of Sufi Muslims or bhakti Hindus, mysticism around the world has the same basic ethos and trajectory, which are expressed in multiple forms.

*Pluralism.* This view is actually quite rare: the idea that there really are distinctly different and independent religious paths. This view doesn't require one to endorse any and every religious option. Perhaps some are truly shams, or inadequate in some respect, or simply evil. It is difficult, however, to suggest what pluralism really means in detail. It's not even clear that this is a coherent concept. What sort of universe would it be in which Buddhists, Jains, Hegelians, Daoists, and Maoris all pursued such different paths, each of them real and valid on its own terms? What sort of God or Ultimate Principle would be behind all of these in order for them to be efficacious? Yet this is what espousal of true pluralism of religious "means" would entail.

## Results, Destinies, "Ends"

In the Christian range of options, there seem to be only three general scenarios.

*Heaven and hell.* First, there is the traditional pair of heaven (or, as many would suggest, is a more accurate view, the New Jerusalem) and hell. Roman Catholicism adds to this view by positing purgatory as a way station for Christians on their journey to heaven, but this is merely a modification of the basic Christian scheme.

7. John Hick, *An Interpretation of Religion* (London: Macmillan; and New Haven: Yale University Press, 1989); and idem, *A Christian Theology of Religions: The Rainbow of Faiths* (Louisville: Westminster John Knox Press, 1995).

Orthodox Christians of all sorts do debate, however, the nature of hell. Is it a condition or even a place of eternal, conscious torment of the damned? Christian tradition weighs in heavily on this side.

Does it denote instead a termination of the rebellious human life as God honors the human decision to resist him forever, and thus to take leave of the very basis of one's own existence? (This latter view is sometimes referred to as "annihilationism," an unhappy term that suggests that God destroys an otherwise existing person, rather than recognizing the biblical teaching that nothing exists at all, moment by moment, without God's express will and power. Thus, no one is annihilated: Some, instead, choose to be utterly without God and therefore utterly without the basis of their own being.)[8]

Some have wondered, within orthodox bounds, whether hell is shut once forever, or if human beings are there only by choice, in a place of shadows, from which some might emerge by God's grace as repentant.[9] This would make hell an eternal punishment for some and a purgatory for others. (Few theologians, however, have advocated any such construal of the afterlife.)

*Multiple ends.* Only in this generation have orthodox theologians suggested that perhaps, in God's mysterious and gracious providence, the world's great religions (and perhaps some of the minor ones) really do deliver what they promise. That is, perhaps faithful Christians do go to heaven, but faithful Muslims find themselves in an Islamic paradise, faithful Vaishnava Hindus dwell in company with Krishna, devoted Buddhists enjoy nirvana, Native Americans go to a happy hunting or fishing ground, and so on. These alternative religious ends are not, from the Christian point of view, nearly as blessed as the Christian beatitude of fellowship with the Triune God and Christ's church in the New Jerusalem. But they are granted by God as intermediate ends, which people have chosen and properly pursued, and from which some, perhaps, will yet move onward to the celestial city.[10]

This radical suggestion is still too new to have received sustained attention by the theological community, and it remains the one true pluralism of religious ends on offer.

*Heaven for all/universalism.* The belief that all roads ultimately lead to the one end of universal beatitude actually can be located in all of

8. Edward William Fudge and Robert A. Peterson, *Two Views of Hell: A Biblical and Theological Dialogue* (Downers Grove, Ill.: InterVarsity Press, 2000).

9. So C. S. Lewis's popular story of *The Great Divorce*—a parable that Lewis himself might not have meant at all literally and metaphysically (1946; reprint, London: HarperCollins, 1997).

10. S. Mark Heim, *The Depth of the Riches: A Trinitarian Theology of Religious Ends* (Grand Rapids: Eerdmans, 2001).

the options under "means." In restrictivist terms, that is, perhaps everyone will hear the gospel, whether during life, at the point of death, or after death, and each will respond in faith. Perhaps, instead, the work of Christ will be applied to everyone, regardless of his or her current religious outlook, as everyone eventually is brought under the influence of the Holy Spirit. Perhaps, third, God is pleased to accept the religious strivings of all humankind and welcome everyone home at the end of the cosmic day.

## Mission

What, then, is the Christian mission in regard to religions? Looking inward, first, requires the Christian theologian to recognize afresh what a "mixed field" is the church itself and its religion. Part of the Christian mission to religions, therefore, is the purification and strengthening of the Christian religion. Furthermore, if there are resources beyond the church in other religions that can help in this project—as some in this volume have suggested there are—then Christians will do well to discern and appropriate them, with thanksgiving.

Looking outward, second, requires the Christian theologian to appreciate that differing answers to the questions posed in the previous categories will make a significant difference in certain aspects of Christian mission. If other religions are simply demonic counterfeits, for example, then one engages in dialogue with their devotees only to find avenues for Christian proclamation and persuasion. But taking seriously the natures of other religions can prompt the Christian to think hard about just why those people would possibly believe and practice *that*. It may be that people are Buddhists or Hindus or Jews because, among other things, they really prefer that construal of the cosmos to the Christian one. It may be that they really don't want what Christians offer. And sensitive Christian mission will take that possibility more carefully into account beyond the reflexive writing-off of all resistance as just rebellion against God. Perhaps, that is, there is something interesting and worthwhile to consider in other religions' diffidence toward the Christian message and way—a diffidence, again, that might not always simply have to do with resistance to Jesus but just resistance to *us* and our religion.

One should not, however, exaggerate the differences between this or that theology of religions and this or that missionary outlook. Any evangelical—indeed, any orthodox Christian—theology or mission that does not name Jesus as Lord is unworthy of the name "Christian." Any theology or mission that does not "love your neighbor as you love yourself" is offering a truncated and therefore heretical gospel. Upon these two convictions hang all theology and mission.

I return, then, to the theoretical issue once more to raise one more practical point: To what extent does the Christian faith come as replacement, as fulfillment, as corrective, or as complement to another religion? Answering that question requires not only a general theology of religions but also adequate knowledge of the particular religion in question. And that sort of knowledge is in especially short supply among evangelicals, who (to put it gently) have not encouraged their bright young people to devote themselves to the serious study of other faiths.

For the evangelical theology of religions to advance, therefore, will require not only attention to the actual definition and phenomenon of "religion," as Paul Griffiths points out. It will require sustained engagement with actual religions in an academic, as well as missionary, mode. Short of that, our theologizing will remain at best abstract and at worst simply mistaken.

## Not a Conclusion

There may well be refinements, even wholesale changes, that need to be applied to this attempt to map the way forward for an evangelical theology of religions. What is quite clear, however, is that evangelical theology cannot remain stuck on the very particular question of "the destiny of the unevangelized" when so much else is at stake in the theology of religions.[11]

Indeed, a thoroughgoing program of investigation will entail opening up most of the rest of the theological curriculum: Trinity, Christology, revelation, salvation, providence, anthropology, ecclesiology, mission, theological method—in fact, it is difficult to name a branch of systematic theology not affected by such consideration.

Evangelicals have confronted the world's religions for centuries as missionaries, with some difficulties and even disasters, yes, but also with great gain for the kingdom. Perhaps it is time now for evangelical theologians—not just individuals, here and there, but the community of theologians—to take our turn.

11. John Sanders, ed., *What about Those Who Have Never Heard? Three Views on the Destiny of the Unevangelized* (Downers Grove, Ill.: InterVarsity Press, 1995).

# Subject Index

# Scripture Index